"A rare gem. One of the only magical self-help books that is beautiful, moral and wise. Marion's methods of working have greatly influenced my life."

Margot Adler
author of *Drawing Down the Moon*

"...many congratulations on an absolutely delightful book, written — unlike most things of this kind — with real humour and insight."

Colin Wilson
author of *The Occult, Mysteries, The Outsider, The War Against Sleep*, etc.

"Clearly written with wit and intelligence, this guide to self-transformation through occult knowledge is long overdue....will strike a responsive chord in many contemporary seekers."

Elizabeth Pepper
in *The Witches' Almanac*

"...I wanted to read it as soon as possible. Aside from finding a vast amount of fascinating information, I found myself feeling as if I were in a state of deep meditation. I experienced powerful feelings of hope — feelings that did not require that I blind myself to the problems of the world but did provide me with a strengthening of belief that they could be overcome."

Merlin Stone
author of *When God Was A Woman* and *Ancient Mirrors of Womanhood*

"Marion Weinstein's book is amazingly practical, helpful, knowledgeable, sensible and easy to understand. Reading it makes you aware of powers you probably never knew you had, and what's more it tells you precisely how to use them."

Dan Greenburg
author of *How to Be a Jewish Mother, Something's There, Scoring, Love Kills*, etc.

"All occult work is the very essence of creativity; it is the deepest expression of the self. To believe and to trust in the Invisible World and one's own potential mastery of Unseen Forces, to trust in and use the as-yet-unknown parts of the *self* — this is what occult work is traditionally all about. Fortunately, the occult tradition provides positive reinforcement, in modern psychological terms. It heightens self-esteem, it encourages belief and trust, it *works*.

"I hope that by the time you finish the book, you will have experienced the magic fully enough to know what it feels like. That's what *Positive Magic: Occult Self-Help* is all about, sharing the experience...."

Luna.

Positive Magic

Occult Self-Help

by Marion Weinstein

Revised Edition
Foreword by Colin Wilson

Phoenix Publishing Inc.
P.O. Box 10, Custer, Washington, U.S.A. 98240

Also by the author: *Earth Magic, A Dianic Book of Shadows*
Phoenix Publishing, Custer, WA. 1980.

Selections from *The I Ching or Book of Changes*. The Richard Wilhelm translation
rendered into English by Cary F. Baynes. Bollingen Series XIX. Copyright 1950,© 1967 by
Princeton University Press.© renewed 1977 by Princeton University Press. Reprinted by
permission.
Lyrics from *"Everything's Coming Up Roses"* © 1959 & 1961 Norbeth Productions Inc.
and Stephen Sondheim, Williamson Music Inc. & Stratford Music Corp. Owners of
publication and allied rights throughout the world. Used by permission of Chappell Music
Canada Ltd.
Lyrics from *"Where Or When"* ©1937 by Chappell & Co. Inc. Copyright renewed. Used
by permission of Chappell Music Canada Ltd.
Lyrics from *"They All Laughed"* © 1937 by Gershwin Publishing Corp. Copyright
renewed. Chappell & Co. Inc. sole selling agent. Used by permission of Chappell Music
Canada Ltd.
Lyrics from *"On the Sunny Side of the Street"*©MCMXXX by Shapiro, Bernstein & Co.,
Inc. Copyright renewed. Used by permission.
Lyrics from *"When You Wish Upon a Star"* by Ned Washington; music by Leigh Harline.
Copyright © 1940 by Bourne Co. International copyright secured. Copyright renewed. All
rights reserved. Used by permission.

PHOENIX PUBLISHING INC.
P.O. Box 10
Custer. Washington. U.S.A. 98240

published simultaneously in Canada by
PHOENIX PUBLISHING INC.
10202 - 152nd Street
Surrey. B.C. V3R 6N7

ISBN: 0 919345-00-X

Printed in the U.S.A.

For my mother

Cataloguing in Publication Data

Weinstein, Marion.
Positive magic

Originally published: New York : Pocket
Books, 1979
Bibliography: p.
Includes index.
ISBN 0-919345-00-X

1. Occult sciences. 2. Success. I. Title
BF1411.W44 1981 131 C81-091339-9

Acknowledgements

The author wishes to thank those whose talents and help contributed to this book:
- Ronnie Carson — a veritable living muse — for encouragement, inspiration, and editing of the manuscript from its earliest stages.
- Leslie Austin, for special editing help, also astrological input and psychic clarification.
- Pat Millman, for putting the final manuscript into form.
- Cynthia Davidson, for proofreading and meaningful feedback.
- My sister, Bette Weinstein, for proofing and advice.
- Linda Perry, for sharing the completion.
- All the members of my coven, whose magic and blessings are part of the work.
- My listeners, for sending so much positive energy through the airwaves — and for asking so many questions.
- WBAI-FM, for widening the circle.
- My friends and loved ones in the Invisible Realm, who provided insights and information.
- And my familiar, Muffin, who stayed with me through it all.
- Cameron Nuttall is the first astrologer who introduced me to the information of the Aquarian Age; his knowledge provided a foundation for much of the "Time" section in Chapter II.
- The Church of Religious Science was the first place I studied metaphysics. Although the work of this book does not represent that organization's teachings, my studies there helped to sow the seeds for some of the ideas in Chapter VIII.
- A succinct idea from Witch Devlin helped me to clarify the "monotheism/polytheism" statements in Chapter IV.
- Mel Brooks, Robert Klein, and the Rev. John Scudder gave kind permission for me to quote them directly.
- Thanks also, to: David Cohen, Norma Jean Darden, Annemarie Geckeler, Ellen Goldman, Pat Golbitz, Richard Rabkin, Jed Mattes, Toby Nemiroff, and Jane Rotrosen.
- Special thanks to all the people whose belief in Positive Magic directly participated in the printing and publication of my work.
- And very special thanks to my parents — who made it possible for me to devote the years of linear time which were necessary for me to research and write this book.

And for preparing the Second Edition — in addition to those mentioned above, many of whom helped all over again, much gratitude to the following people:
- Wayne Booher, for revisions in Chapter V.
- Doug Brown and his circle of friends, for publishing.
- Suzy Greengras, for help with the graphics.
- Nina Kimché for typing and proofing.
- Mary E. Smith, for proofing and clarifying.
- Barbara Stacy, for editing.

- Merlin Stone, for inspiration and advice.
- Elizabeth Pepper, for graphics and magic.
- Sylvia Weinstein, for editing.
- Colin Wilson, for the foreword.
- All the people who worked magic to get *Positive Magic* back in print.

Front cover photograph by Jay Krajic (© Jay Krajic 1987)

Contents

PART I
BASIC OCCULT INFORMATION

Foreword

What is a witch? One of the best explanations I have ever heard occurs in a letter written to me by Marion Weinstein: She is describing how, as a child of ten or eleven, she noticed "how things seemed to be able to just 'work out' sometimes when I managed a certain attitude towards a problem, a sort of all-encompassing belief which seemed to take on a life of its own and shape my own life thereby. ....I wondered how I could control this process." This is something everyone has noticed — that at certain times, we seem to fall into "the right mood," and suddenly everything we do comes out right. The sceptic in us insists that this is mere chance, or that there is a more practical explanation.

Let me explain that I myself started out as a total sceptic, convinced that all this fashionable stuff about magic and witchcraft was self-deception, invented by people who are bored with the dullness of modern urban life. Researching a commissioned book on the occult gradually convinced me that the evidence for "psychical phenomena" such as ghosts, poltergeists, precognition, telepathy is as powerful as the evidence for neutrons or quasars. Yet I still remained basically sceptical, and in a chapter on witchcraft, completely dismiss the idea that the North Berwick witches, executed in 1591 for raising a storm that had almost sunk the king's ship, could have been genuinely guilty. Yet in that same chapter, I have cited an account by a friend of mine — Negley Farson — of how he saw African witchdoctors conjure rain out of a clear sky, which I found quite acceptable. It was only after going much further into this whole matter that it struck me that I was being illogical in assuming that all European witches who died at the stake or on the gallows were "innocent."

Not, I should emphasise, that most witches *are* likely to cast malevolent spells. I would guess that a "bad witch" is just about as rare as a doctor who uses his medical skill to murder his patients. In that sense, the mediaeval idea of a witch — as evil old crone in league with the devil — *was* absurd. Most witches then — as now — were people born with some odd power of healing, "second sight," divination or weather-control: In short, what we would now call a "psychic." If Professor Margaret Murray is correct (and I personally find her arguments convincing), "organised" witches were simply members of the old pagan fertility cult, the world's oldest religion, whose goddess was the moon. (I have discussed the subject at some length in my book *Mysteries*.). No doubt some witches *did* use their powers to do harm to people they disliked; but I find it difficult to accept that, in such cases, they called upon "powers of darkness."

In saying that witches were what we would now call "psychics," I am in danger of creating a false impression. No doubt it is true that many witches were psychic and vice versa; but I think it would be a mistake to confuse the two. A psychic is a person who happens to be born with unusual *sensitivity* to what goes on in other people's minds. I like to cite the example of a Dutch house-painter called Pieter Van der Hurk, who fell off a ladder and cracked his skull; when he woke up in hospital, he discovered — to his astonishment — that he could read other people's minds. Shaking hands with someone, he would instantly "know" all kinds of intimate things about him. But this insight was by no means an unmixed blessing. Van der Hurk found that his mind was like a radio set picking up half a dozen different stations at the same time. It made him quite incapable of concentrating on any ordinary work. He might have starved to death if someone had not suggested that he use his curious powers as a mind-reader on the stage. As Peter Hurkos, he went on to become famous as a psychic or "paragnost."

Most psychics and mediums could tell a similar story. The majority were born with these unusual powers. No doubt we all possess them. However, it is far more useful, from the point of view of survival, to be able to concentrate on your everyday job. Our remote ancestors probably possessed far greater "psychic" powers than we do. We have deliberately *suppressed* them. In other words, I believe that we possess some odd power of which we were unaware. When the poet Robert Graves once commented to me that many young men use a form of "unconscious sorcery" to attract girls (and no doubt the reverse is also true) I instantly knew just what he meant.

And this, I think, is what Marion Weinstein is talking about when she says that she could influence events by inducing in herself a certain "attitude" towards them.

But how can such "powers" be explained? Here I can only offer my own theory, with the admission that it may be quite irrelevant. During the second half of the 19th century, when men like Darwin, Oken and Pasteur turned biology into an exact science, there was a general agreement that living beings are highly complicated machines. Darwin seemed to have demonstrated that evolution itself is a purely mechanical process. The idea of a "living soul" became superfluous. Yet towards the turn of the century, a number of biologists began to doubt whether life is purely a "mechanism." They called themselves "vitalists", because the French philosopher Henry Bergson spoke of the *élan vital*, or vital spark, that drives the evolutionary process. One of the most famous was Hans Driesch, who devoted a classic work, *The Science and Philosophy of Organism*, to arguing in favour of the basic "autonomy of life" — that is to say, to the view that although life has to use mechanical processes to express itself, it stands above such mechanisms — just as the driver of a car 'stands above' the car. A man from Mars, who studied our freeways through some enormous telescope, might well end by believing that cars are some form of beetle, which migrates in and and out of cities according to certain natural laws. We know they are driven by individuals who *choose* where they want to go.

Driesch's views were finally rejected by his fellow scientists, who said, in effect: we have often seen a driver outside his car, but we have never seen "life" outside of matter...

Besides, while you and I have no doubt that we have a certain degree of free-will, we also acknowledge that it is rather limited. As far as everyday life is concerned, the major limitation is force of habit. Have you ever played that game where someone fires questions at you, and you are not allowed to say Yes or No, or to nod or shake your head? It is incredibly difficult not to do these things, because we do them so *automatically*.

And this, I think, could well be the answer to why our "powers" are apparently so limited. They are *counterbalanced* by the automatic part of us — what you might call "the robot". The more tired you feel, the more your reactions are governed by the robot. On the other hand, in certain moments of happiness or excitement — or even anger — the balance alters. Your "powers" are no longer tied hand-and-foot by habit and mechanicalness. But of course, in 99 cases out of a hundred, we fail to realise this because we do not attempt to *use* them.

Marion Weinstein tells me that she always had this odd intuition that she had unknown powers that could be "used", and that she tried very hard to learn how this could be done. As a small child, she had a strong desire to help people. (I can understand this; as a child, I used to feel wracked with misery at the sight of a blind man or a boy in ragged clothes, and would daydream for hours of being a kind of magician who could dispense universal happiness). When she went to high school, she began reading books on witchcraft, magic and fairy-lore. At the age of 15, she decided to do a term paper on Mother Goose, and researched it in the New York Public Library. She discovered that the original Mother Goose was Charlemagne's mother in law, known as "la reine pedauque" (or the "web-foot queen"), because she had a club foot (or goose foot, as they called it). Her research into the goose foot queen "seemed to open doors into an earlier time, a time when witches were real." From then on, research was a passion.

On the practical level, Marion's interest was in the theatre; she wanted to be an actress. But she found her attempts to make a theatrical career disappointing and frustrating; she was thrown back on her interest in witchcraft and magic, and studied Margaret Murray, Gerald Gardner (the man whose *Witchcraft Today* was responsible for the modern witchcraft revival) and Jung. She was also fascinated by the Jewish Kabbala — although, as a woman, she was excluded from practical participation in this branch of study. Jung led her on to the *I Ching*, and this in turn to the Tarot pack. And so, step by step, she was drawn into the world of mysticism and *the occult* — that is, into a knowledge-system that predates modern science by at least twenty five thousand years.

In 1969 she made a trial broadcast for a New York radio station and found she enjoyed it. As she steadily became more successful, it must have been a temptation to allow the public personality to take precedence over the magical studies — a temptation she successfully resisted, as this book shows. For although Marion Weinstein is a "populariser," she remains primarily a serious student of the occult.

My own first impression of *Positive Magic* was that it was another of those "do-it-yourself" books aimed at the paperback market. That impression was dispelled within the first ten pages. She may be determined to communicate to the widest possible audience; but she knows what she is talking about. She may have something of the flamboyance of the actress; but underneath that is the seriousness of a scholar. I expected to find much in it that would strike me as superficial; I ended by respecting her as someone who is willing to try very hard indeed to avoid superficiality. This is as good and sound an introduction to the field of occultism as I have ever come across.

And why *should* any level-head, sensible person pay the slightest attention to all this stuff about astrology, divination, karma, magic and witchcraft; surely it is only a sign of frivolity or silly credulity?

Oddly enough, I have no objection whatever to people who take such a view; they strike me as infinitely preferable to the idiots who swallow everything from *Napoleon's Book of Fate* to the daily horoscope column in the newspapers. But then, it seems to me that any open-minded person recognises that feeling that there are hidden *patterns* behind the world of everyday experience - that things are "working out," or going persistently and disastrously wrong. (Statistically, you would expect your good luck and bad luck to be thoroughly mixed-up). Most of us have noted coincidences occur - the way, for example, that we often seem to stumble across an important book just at the moment when we most need it. I have always noticed that when I am mentally healthy, the "good" coincidences occur, or things seem to go smoothly right.

How do I distinguish between this kind of meaningful coincidence — which Jung calls "synchronicity" — and the "ordinary" kind? As it happens, I can here be quite specific, and cite two examples that have occurred within the past twenty four hours. Here is the first. Wishing to check on something in Auerbach's book *Mimesis,* I take the book off the shelf, and also notice Jacques Barzun's *House of Intellect,* which I haven't looked at in years. So I take both books to bed with me. Glancing down the table of contents in Auerbach, I see the essays of Montaigne. Then I open *The House of Intellect,* and read the first two chapters, during the course of which I find a reference to Montaigne, and to the fact that he originated the phrase "the human condition."

I am sitting watching a television programme about road accidents, and one of the experts who gives his opinion is called Dr. Mayer Hillman. It strikes me that I have seen that name within the past hour or so, and I pick up the *Times,* which is by my chair. In fact, the correspondence page has a letter, signed by Mayer Hillman and by a lady, on the subject of cuts in British Rail services.

Now oddly enough, I do not count the first coincidence as especially meaningful. Auerbach and Barzun are both literary critics with a European background, so although I note the coincidence with interest — I shall never now forget that Montaigne invented the phrase "the human condition" — it nevertheless strikes me as quite within the realm of ordinary coincidence to find them both referring to the same phrase. But the second is odder. I have never come across Dr. Hillman's name before, and probably never shall again. I do not usually read the Times correspondence column with much attention — on five days out of six I do not read it at all — and I certainly do not usually notice the signature on letters about British Rail that I happen to glance at casually. There is no obvious connection between road accidents due to alcohol and cuts on British Rail. This is a million-to-one coincidence, while the Barzun is only, say, a thousand to one...

And why count either as "meaningful?" What *is* their meaning? Well, before I stopped writing for the day, at five o'clock yesterday, I had written the sentence about things going smoothly when I am mentally healthy. I was hoping to find a good example of synchronicity to offer, and decided that I would have to make do with one I had already used elsewhere. Then, as if in answer to my "request," I am presented with two excellent examples during the next twelve hours, before I return to my typewriter at ten this morning...

Absurd: Yes, if you like. But Jung came to accept such coincidences as important, and I am inclined to follow him. In *The Nature of the Physical World,* Eddington remarks that, where "ultimate meaning" is concerned, the universe seems to be inscrutable, and he cites those lines from *Alice Through the Looking Glass:*

But I was thinking of a plan
To dye one's whiskers green,
Then always use so large a fan
That they could not be seen.

If the universe has green whiskers — or a sense of underlying meaning — says Eddington, it covers them up so carefully that the scientist can never hope to discover them. Modern writers from Dreiser and Hemingway to Sartre and Camus have emphasised this sense of chaotic meaningless that seems to characterise everyday experience. Jung feels that "coincidences" like this are just one of many indications that the universe it not quite as chaotically absurd as it looks.

It seems to me that there is a whole world of difference between this kind of observation — anyone who wishes to follow it further should look into Marion Weinstein's chapter on the *I Ching,* or into Jung's autobiography *Memories, Dreams, Reflections* — and the kind of credulity that scientists rightly dismiss as a mild form of idiocy. And in every subject associated with "the occult" (which only means "hidden) — astrology, healing, divination, precognition — it is possible to find a "way into it" that appeals to common sense rather than to pure credulity. For example, although it sounds quite absurd to believe that the position of the planets at your moment of birth can influence your character or destiny, the researches of Michel Gauquelin have convinced a number of hard-headed scientists — including the psychologist Hans Eysenck — that something of the sort *does* occur. (Gauquelin's statistical researches showed, for example, that there is a tendency for sportsmen to be born "under Mars" and scientists and doctors "under Saturn.") Elaborate tests into precognition — the gift of foreseeing the future — have been conducted in laboratories, and the results are impressive.

Serious and convincing discussions of these matters can be found in a number of excellent books — such as John Randall's *Parapsychology and the Nature of Life* and Benjamin Wolman's massive compilation *A Handbook of Parapsychology.* But these are never going to reach the general public; their approach is too technical. Marion Weinstein sees herself as a "medium," whose self-appointed task is to reach ordinary readers and listeners, and offer them the basic facts about the occult tradition in a form that is neither insultingly oversimplified nor cheaply exploitive. In a note to me, she writes: "Things are much easier for me now. My work is 'in', which I find ironic. If I hadn't gone through such a lonely and trying period seeking out the work, and then putting myself on the line publicly along with my deepest beliefs, I might trust them both less." She adds: "Witchcraft is my religion, my philosophy, my way of life. For most of my life — *this* life — I have had little or no reinforcement from the outside, but now I have lots of company in my work. Knowing what I now know about reincarnation, I believe I have been a witch in many other lifetimes. Nothing I have learned in the last twenty years of research has ever suprised me: It was simply a process of *remembering*." You may or may not reject such a startling notion; but it is difficult to reject the air of *lived* conviction that permeates the whole book.

Colin Wilson

Cornwall, England
December 1980

Introduction to Second Edition

Here is some information I'd like to share with you: This book represents my major work of this lifetime up until now. It was originally published by Simon & Schuster Pocket Books in May, 1978, as a paperback original in mass market format — in other words, a tiny cog in a giant corporate publishing wheel. Thousands of copies were scattered throughout airport, drugstores, supermarkets and even bookstores. Some of the people who read it became my friends; this was a joyous side-effect for me.

Just one year after it emerged so fully, *Positive Magic* suddenly disappeared: sold out, out of stock, out of print. I set out to have it published again, but this seemed impossible. I was told repeatedly, "The occult fad is over." I felt impelled to live fully by the very principles the book taught others. I worked magic to get it republished by the perfect publisher. My friends joined in....countless readers of the book joined in. Over a year passed, and nothing appeared to be happening. Did I get discouraged? I certainly did. The most difficult part about working magic, and sustaining one's belief in it, is dealing with that apparent time lapse which sometimes occurs when nothing seems to be happening. But that is precisely the time when everything is actually happening — in the Invisible World. This is the lesson the second edition taught me: *There is no time lapse.* In sequential time perception, the work of positive magic is often invisible before it becomes visible.

How appropriate that my new publishers are named Phoenix — that fabulous bird of legend (or reality) which seems to be finished, dead, gone, reduced to a pile of ashes, when suddenly it emerges again, healthy and whole and ready to fly. I am so happy with this second edition. I had a chance to rewrite, revise, re-edit and redesign, Some of my new friends helped this time (and the old ones helped too). We put love and care into this edition. When I handed the final manuscript, my editor commented that it had the longest list of acknowledgements he'd ever seen. Actually, the list could have been even longer! I don't know all the names of the people who worked positive magic for this book to emerge again. I want you to know that there was a time when this all seemed impossible, even to me (the key word here is *seemed*) but you see, the magic worked. May it work for you.

Marion Weinstein

Atlantic Beach
April 19, 1981

Introduction
NOTES FROM A CITY WITCH

They all laughed at Christopher Columbus
When he said the world was round:
They all laughed when Edison recorded sound.

They all laughed at Wilbur and his brother
When they said that man could fly;
They told Marconi
Wireless was a phoney —
It's the same old cry!...

— Ira Gershwin[1]

A few years ago I could not have written this book and expected it to be read by the general public. A few hundred years ago, I could not have written this book and expected to live.

Today, many sensible people are experimenting with self-help techniques far more weird than any I have written about. And scientists are exploring telepathy, telekinesis, precognitive dreams, the "nonrational" parts of the brain — psychic phenomena of all kinds. Witches and occultists have studied, understood, and used effectively these very phenomena for centuries. These methods have always proved most practical when applied to self-help, self-realization, and self-understanding. Of course, occult and magical work extends into unusual and specialized areas. But this kind of work also is used, and always has been used, *in daily life.*

Times change. The test of any self-help philosophy or technique is: Will it apply to me? In my own life? Now? It's one thing to use magic for helping the crops to grow and to keep away the evil spirits of the village.

But what about the needs of a more urban and introspective culture? I believe that the work of magic *translates* very well. It has a built-in ability to change with the people and with the times, never losing its essence. Many cultures other than our own know this, and in most areas of our planet magic is alive and well. It is part of the folk heritage. Today in the West, we might equate magic with superstition, and search far afield for meaningful ways to deal with the unknown. But let's not overlook the rich tradition which exists right in our own backyard.

Bad press to the contrary, the traditional role of witch in olden times was that of a village helper. The witch supplied herbs and remedies, psychic protection and various specialized means of dealing with all that seemed frightening, dark and unknown. The occult and witchcraft philosophies still have many remedies for us which translate effectively to suit modern needs. Today we are a global village, and we live in a do-it-yourself culture. So today, being a village helper means showing you how to do it yourself, whomever and wherever you are.

I am referring, of course, to positive magic, or magic for good. A lot of people may still believe that magic is used mainly for harm. Many people suspected that the telephone was the devil's work — at first, anyway. Then there may be people who think the whole idea of magic is preposterous. Let's bear in mind that a lot of people laughed at the first airplanes too — see above lyric.

Even if you are already a witch or occultist, or otherwise believe in magic, it may be a new idea for you to apply such work in practical everyday ways. But isn't that how it all began anyway, — as a functioning part of everyday life?

If you're new to the occult, this book may provide a new vantage point, perhaps a different way of looking at life. Part One establishes the occult vantage point: the philosophy and the background out of which the work develops. Part Two explains the actual techniques.

All the material is based on my own research in both the oral and written traditions, as well as my personal experiences. It also includes the experiences of my friends and the listening audience of my radio shows on WBAI. There is not a single technique included in this book which I haven't used and benefitted from. Whenever possible, sources and supplementary reading notes have been provided. I am not giving away any traditional secrets, by the way. All the information in this book can be verified. I have simply put the available material together in one place, and suggested some new personal applications for the work to keep up with changing times and changing needs.

You don't have to be a witch to benefit from this work. In fact, please don't even *try* to do the work if it doesn't feel right to you. I'm not making any promises nor saying that this book has all the answers. Nor am I giving any guarantees that your life will fall right into place immediately. It might take a couple of days. But seriously, folks, it has always seemed a shame to me that *everyone* didn't have access to the information that is in this book. I want as many people as possible to have the information and to be able to try it if they want to. As my old friend the *I Ching* puts it:

> A magnaninous, liberal-minded man should not regard what he possesses as his exclusive, personal property, but should place it at the disposal of the ruler or of the people at large. In so doing, he takes the right attitude towards his possession, which as private property can never endure.[2]

There is an ancient occult tradition of drawing a magic circle and inviting all the participants — those people who are present to work the magic — to step inside. The purpose of this book is to draw that circle once again, and to invite you in.

SOME DEFINITIONS:

"Occult" literally means "hidden," "not revealed," "secret," "abstruse," "mysterious," etc. When you uncover it, reveal it, strip away the mystery and the abstruesness, what do you have? *Magic.*

But *"magic"* is more difficult to define. For one thing, the word also popularly means *"prestidigitation"*: sleight of hand such as card tricks, pulling rabbits out of hats, etc. Such acts are simulations of occult magic: They look like magic, but they are tricks. Usually. Sometimes the borderline can get extremely thin. The point is, this book is *not* about tricks. It's about that other, more ancient kind of magic — *transformation.*

Technically, when you reveal something which is hidden, then it's not hidden anymore. So one might say that by the very process of explaining occult work and making it accessible, it is no longer literally "occult." But I like the word and it's been around a long time, so for purposes of facility I will be using the words "magic" and "occult" side by side and even interchangeably in this book.

To get back to the word "magic" — another reason that it's so hard to define is that a lot of the definition comes by way of experience. I hope that by the time you finish this book, you will have experienced magic fully enough to know what it feels like. That's what *Positive Magic: Occult Self-Help* is all about, sharing the experience.

---

[1]"They All Laughed," Gershwin Publishing Corp., 1937

[2]The *I Ching,* or *Book of Changes,* Wilhelm/Baynes translation, Bollingen Series, Princeton University Press, Princeton, N.J. 1970. Hexagram 14, "Possession in Great Measure," nine in the third place, p. 61. The *I Ching* is not by definition Western in origin. But since the excellent Wilhelm/Baynes translation came out, it is eminently accessible to the West, so I am including it in this book. For more about the *I Ching,* see Chapter VII.

BASIC
OCCULT
INFORMATION

Chapter I

MAGIC, A WORLD UNTO ITSELF

Magic and Self-Help, an Ancient Tradition

The roots of magic go back thousands of years, predating Christianity, Judaism, and recorded history. The Eleusynian Mysteries, the Egyptian Mystery schools, and the occult culture of Atlantis all derive from these same roots. Magical traditions grew right along with monotheism: the Jewish Caballah, Christian Gnosticism, the Christian Qaballah and ceremonial magic societies, alchemists, and astrologers. And in all of these magical studies (which are still with us today) one unifying theme emerges: the development of the self. This is both the *goal* and the *starting point* of all the work. The basic idea is: Get your life in order first. Get your entire life in harmony — mentally, emotionally, physically, spiritually and psychically. Only then will you be able to embark truly on the great work. And what is the ultimate purpose of the work? To fulfill the self on an even higher level. To transform, uplift, and so fully develop the self that the whole Universe may benefit thereby.

If you get involved deeply enough in any valid magic or occult study, you will find a treasure of self-help techniques. Why hasn't everyone known about these techniques? Why hasn't everyone tried them?

Magic hasn't exactly been required reading in the education of most Westerners. It's a field which has been obscured by the biased "history" of the medieval Inquisitors, who sought to stamp magic out of our culture. Their work has been all too effective — until recently. I found that I really had to work hard to uncover positive magic. I had to plow through a swamp of superstitions, misinformation, dangerous misuse (such as so-called "black" magic), exploitation, and general nonsense in order to get to the good material. And I learned a lot along the way, such as:

Magic vs. Fantasy

To a lot of people, a magical experience means a trip to Disneyland or perhaps an early Disney cartoon such as "Sleeping Beauty," "Cinderella," or "Pinocchio." But where did Walt Disney get his material? From fairy tales; fairy tales derived from old folk legends. These stories depict a familiar theme — the fairy godmother, or the good fairy. Someone who can grant a wish. There are countless other stories, which you may remember, involving magical helpers — benevolent elves, wizards, or perhaps a good witch (my favorite). These are all *the theme of the magical helper.* Sometimes the magical being was disguised as an ordinary person, often poor. Some deserving mortal is usually depicted as being in dire need, when into the mortal's life swoops the magical helper who grants a wish (or three wishes, three being a traditional number in magic). Poof! The mortal's life is transformed. A frog turns into a prince, pebbles turn into jewels, and a week's work is performed overnight!

Sometimes the fortunate recipients of this magic don't know what to do with their bounty. In one funny story which has many variations, a man and his wife quarrel over their wishes:

MAN: I wish your nose would fall of your face!
WOMAN: I wish your nose would fall off *your* face!
(Exit noses)
WOMAN: Wait a minute, I wish our noses were both back on our faces!

The noses were replaced. And the wishes, alas, had been used up.

Sometimes, however, the wishes were used well, and the mortals wished for sensible things. Things such as enough to eat, enough money to live comfortably, love, etc. Things we still might want in our loves today. And then when the wishes came true, the people lived happily ever after. I believe these legends were based on fact. Everybody thought all the Greek myths were based on fact. Everybody thought all the Greek myths were just that — myth — until Schleimann discovered the ruins of Troy. In addition, many people who thought that the ancient legends about angels and "fiery chariots" were also myths reconsidered their beliefs when Von Daniken popularized the theory of ancient astronauts.

Here is my theory about the wish-fulfillment legends: In the West as well as in the East, isolated cultures and subcultures have always followed ancient mystic traditions. Members of such communities usually kept quietly to themselves. Witches and Druids are good

4

examples, but there are legends of other "lost," hidden, insular groups possessing "strange powers." It is entirely possible that such mystics ventured forth from time to time, took a liking to some simple person who was sincere or in need, and tried to help that person. Such adepts would have *seemed* like magical beings, and the help would have *seemed* to the uninitiated like some unearthly, impossible, accomplishment. But to the adept — the person from the more advanced culture — it was all in a day's work.

In popular usage, "adept" means "expert." In occult work, "adept" means "magical worker" or "mage."

The legends come down to us from the viewpoint of the simple person upon whom the magical favor has been bestowed. Of course, the stories consequently became distorted, embroidered, exaggerated — as any oral folk history changes when it is perpetuated by generations who do not understand what they are perpetuating. So by the time that the legends get to us, they are fodder for Disney's mill — fanciful tales, *fantasy*. That is, if we continue to perceive them from the point of view of the nonadept.

But if we approach these legends from the point of view of learned mystic tradition, new realms of possibilities open. It is all a question of shifting the frame of reference. For example, there are cultures in the South Pacific which worship World War II U.S. Army shirts.[1] These are relics of magical beings who once came down from the skies in a blaze of light, riding strange large birds. The worshippers still construct radio antenna-like artifacts out of twigs and leaves. The artifacts are meant to look like the magical devices which the unearthly creatures used to get messages in a mysterious language; messages which came as voices crackling out of the very air! From the frame of reference of these Pacific "cargo cults," a couple of ordinary Army pilots in the 1940s seemed like wizards, indeed, the stuff that legends are made of. But from the frame of reference of modern aviation, a pilot is just a man doing his job — nothing to worship and nothing to carry on about. It's all in the point of view, the frame of reference.

Here is another magical legend, *The Story of the Frog Prince:*

Once there was a lonely young woman who wished most of all for a handsome prince to come into her life and marry her. One day, a tired and hungry old woman came to her door, and the girl was generous enough to share her humble meal with the old woman. "Thank you, my child," said the old woman, "for being so kind to me. Make any wish you like and it shall be granted." The younger woman wished with all her might that her pet frog might turn into a handsome prince. She went into the yard and kissed her pet frog. And lo and behold, he turned into a handsome prince who

5

proposed marriage forthwith.

That's from the point of view of the unitiated. Switch the frame of reference. Here's the old woman's version:

The other day when I was gathering herbs to make some medieval antibiotics, I walked a little farther than I had planned and found myself far from our village. I was tired and hungry, so I sent a telepathic message out into the area. The message stated, "For a perfect exchange of services which will benefit everyone, I am seeking food and drink in a friendly, safe atmosphere." My telepathic message was picked up subconsciously by a receptive young peasant girl nearby. I followed her vibrations and came to her house, where with no questions asked she shared her food with me most generously. To complete our exchange of services, I asked her what she wanted in exchange. Since she understood nothing about psychic phenomena, the most effective way I could explain to her how to concentrate her psychic energies was to suggest that she make a wish. She wished strongly for what she wanted and needed most — *love*. In her case, it was a reciprocal love relationship with a suitable young man. I immediately sent out a telepathic call for the appropriate young man, with similar needs and desires, to contact her. That is, the young girl's own *energy* actually sent out the call, and I simply helped her to direct that energy by our traditional telepathic methods. She insisted on performing some personal superstitious ceremony indigenous to her culture; she actually picked up a frog and kissed it! When the young man appeared (it was a local merchant's son, I believe, quite handsomely dressed), the frog jumped away in fear. After that, nothing could convince the girl that the frog hadn't actually been transformed into a prince.

This is a typical example of transcendence over the everyday world, *by traditional occult methods.* These methods have been used by occultists for centuries. You can use them, too. The only difference is that in the past the helpful adepts performed the deeds *for* the ordinary mortals, for the people doing the wishing. In our case, the people doing the wishing can perform the deeds *for themselves.*

There are traditions all over the world which are based on these methods. There always have been. People who practice these traditions are the mystic élite — shamans, "witch" doctors, sorcerers — call them what you will. Those who approach life in this way know, as part of their deeply rooted heritage, that wish-fulfillment is not fantasy; it is *work.* Such people are free to do this work because their belief-systems have totally bypassed a certain limiting idea.

The "Too-Good-To-Be-True" Syndrome

Peculiarly symptomatic of the modern West, this idea can permeate our thinking so deeply that sometimes we may not even know it is operative. I think this syndrome is a primary reason for many people's staunch disbelief in occult phenomena (i.e., *positive* occult phenomena) such as spirit contact with loved ones, life after death, telepathy, and, yes, wish-fulfillment. Anything which suggests that an Unseen World is not only *there*, but that it can be *helpful*, seems literally too good to be true. The human spirit longs for this invisible beneficence, but dares not trust it. Because to many, this seems dangerously like putting one's trust — even one's deepest hopes — into thin air.

If one dares not trust in something, one dares not attempt to work with it. This is not limited to belief (and consequent exploration) in occult phenomena. A familiar principle in psychology, manifest in the formation of self-defeat patterns, is that *hope creates anxiety*.[2]

These patterns are particularly common in embarking on any creative act. The rewards of creativity are potentially so great that the devastation of failure is equally as great. Many may refuse to expose the self to the possibility of such a failure. The assumption that it is "safer" not to attempt something at all is a protective mechanism.

> To embark upon the uncharted seas of selfhood, to reach out creatively to the potentials of life, and to select of these as our own reason permits requires that one be able to bear the anxieties intrinsic to a creative approach...we find that a creative approach to life — be it in the arts, sciences, or any other life context — can evolve only when there is sufficient esteem for the self.[3]

How does this statement apply to occult work? All occult work is the very essence of creativity; occult work is the deepest expression of the self. To believe and to trust in the Invisible World, and one's own potential mastery of Unseen forces, to trust in and use the as-yet-unknown parts of the self — this is what occult work is traditionally all about. The adept would be frozen, grounded, drawn to a halt, if he/she did not "dare" to embark on a path which promised so much. Fortunately, the occult tradition provides positive reinforcement, in modern psychological terms. The tradition heightens self-esteem, encouraging belief and trust, and the tradition works when it is followed from the point of view of the adept. The tradition does not work from the point of view of the frightened, awed, or childlike disbeliever who dares not risk the anxiety of potential disappointment.

7

The Adept's Point of View

In cultures other than our own, in traditions where occult work was respected, the atmosphere of the society at large provided encouragement for the adept before he/she even began the path of magic. From earliest childhood, people who were born into such cultures have had certain advantages over many of us. We must take the leap and seek our reinforcement within the work itself. But as I said, occult work provides this nourishment for us. By the very nature of the work itself, a beneficial personal cycle is set in motion.

How to begin?

The adept knows that magic is work. And it is a specific kind of work. It is not work in the Horatio Alger sense; it is not like putting your nose to the grindstone. The work of magic is natural.

I can give you some analogies. Working magic is like using a natural talent, in this case a talent which we all have. If you can sing, dance, play an instrument, play ball, paint, write, build model airplanes, cook, whatever — you know that you have to *practice*. Well, you practice magic, too. Like in the old joke — you practice it until you get it right.[4] For us to shift over to the adept's attitude, we have to plow through our own psyches to find an niche which allows that *anything is possible*, and *nothing is too good to be true*. For some of us, these ideas may require quite a leap of credulity. But we are fortunate today to find that modern psychology has helped to pave the way.

The Two Sides of the Brain

There is a most helpful idea in *The Psychology of Consciousness*[5] by Robert Ornstein which applies to occult and magical work. According to Ornstein the brain has two sides, the "rational" and the "relational." Both have distinctly different modes of perception. Some activities and ideas are better dealt with by the "rational" side of the brain. Our culture has reinforced the use of this side of the brain. In fact, up until quite recently the "rational" was practically the only side of the brain which a person needed to use in order to survive in our culture. So much has the "rational" been emphasized that it has been a revolutionary idea to consider that the other side — the "relational" — exists at all! As you've probably guessed, occult work, magical work, is definitely relational. And what Ornstein has done so effectively is build a bridge between both sides of the brain. By explaining the very concept of the two sides of the brain, and by describing the "relational" side in *rational* terms, he has built a bridge. So even a person who is used to dealing mainly —

8

let's even say only — with the "rational" side of the brain need not be limited. Such a person can now walk over that bridge into the "relational." Which is where the work of magic is done.

The Work of Magic

The work of magic involves transformation, and the first transformation is the shift of perception. And once we establish that anything is possible, then the world as we know it can be flexible. Witches say that the World of Form (that which we perceive with our five senses) is not a limitation, and we are not in bondage to it.[6] The sorcerer Don Juan puts it this way: "The world we look at every day is only a description."[7] And I say, *the World of Form is more flexible than we may think*. And for self-help applications, the World of Form may include relationships, jobs, health, personal finances, etc. With the applied use of magic, these forms are no longer limitations because they become flexible. You will see, step by step, how the techniques of positive magic use this idea of flexibility to change our lives for the better.

You may then employ the "rational" side of your brain, as well as the "intuitive" side to deal with the techniques of magic. It is necessary to understand *fully* how and why everything works before you attempt any of the actual work itself. So you may find that the two sides of your brain take turns. At first, you may need the "relational" even to accept the idea of working magic and to comprehend its validity. But once you actually begin to do the work, you may need to employ the "rational" side of your brain to study each technique. Because if you don't understand what you are doing, the work could be ineffectual or even dangerous. But this is true when dealing with any potential power source, isn't it? from electricity to nuclear power to steam. Magic is a source of enormous power. But you don't have to worry, as there are sufficient specific warnings presented here against the dangers in magic — in fact, a whole chapter (Chapter III, "The Ten-Foot-Pole Department"). For now, just remember that it is necessary to understand everything *before* you try it.

For centuries, many people have feared magic — and rightly so — because they didn't understand how it worked. To the uninitiated, magic may appear frightening because it involves the use of Unseen forces. Once these factors become known quantities, they are no more frightening than "seen" forces. (In fact, the work of magic involves many ways of seeing Unseen forces and knowing them.) The uninitiated fears the unknown, and superstition is a primitive response to the unknown. It's a way of placating and dealing with that which is sensed but not understood. However here the motivation is fear. Magic

9

is also a response to the unknown, but is not a primitive response; it is informed and information-seeking. The motivation for working magic — unlike superstition — is not fear; it is the desire to understand.

And the better you understand magic, the more it works. This is part of the personal reinforcement process. The more it works, the deeper goes your belief and trust, which encourages you to understand magic better and to use it more effectively. Magic for self-help is an accelerating process.

The work of magic also requires a strong sense of responsibility towards the self, towards the work, and towards others — in magic, these are all one and the same. The commitment strengthens the self. Now, this is where magic departs from many other self-help philosophies: YOU CANNOT USE MAGIC TO HELP YOURSELF IF IT HARMS ANOTHER. The adept understands that we are all cosmically linked, and that harm to another comes back and harms the self. This understanding requires a transcendence, a letting-go of certain cultural limitations. One of these is the old "winners/losers" philosophy: in order for one person to become happy, another must suffer. To work magic, we must let go of this idea. In any self-help philosophy, it is often necessary to let go of old and limiting ideas. In this regard, magic is no different from contemporary self-help techniques: We must let go of that which has limited our fulfillment in the past. However, in other self-help philosophies, we may then simply allow ourselves to be guided by a new outer set of rules. In magic, we must seek the rules within ourselves.

In magic, we let go of old limiting ideas, and are then faced with infinite new possibilities. *Anything is possible!* And all the material in this book is merely a beginning, a suggested compendium of possibilties that are open to you. When you come right down to it, nobody can tell you what is "right" for you. So how will you know?

In other words, how will you know what to wish for?

This may be more difficult than it sounds, because we often wish for things out of a limited past state. Once we get into the adept's working place, and we see how unlimited our lives can become, we may have difficulty at first in knowing what it is we really *do* want. Remember the couple in the story who wished for each other's noses to fall off their faces? They were making their wishes out of old, limited feelings, so they made extremely limited wishes. The couple did not know what the goal is of magic, of wish-fulfillment.

This goal is different for everyone, so no one else can tell you what is right for you. And yet it is the same for every one in this regard: Anything which truly fulfills the self is the goal of magic. And remember, it is also the starting point. What fulfills the self? Only you will know for yourself. But because self-fulfillment is so integrally built into the work, magic provides many clues for you to find your own deepest fulfillment. These clues are already deep inside you, according to occult belief. They are present as your *Inner Bell.*

You do not have to be involved in magic in order to know your Inner Bell, but magic can help you to find it.

The Inner Bell

This is my term for the inner sense of truth, the inner reality, the inner knowing which exists deep within all of us. We may not be aware of it. But some people have a very strong awareness of the Inner Bell. And in those people who followed their deepest beliefs — no matter what anyone else said — we may find some dramatic precedents.

They all laughed at Christopher Columbus
When he said the world was round...

I think that when Columbus set out across the uncharted ocean, he was listening to the sound of his Inner Bell. He simply *knew* something was out there. True, he was in for a few surprises specifically about what continent happened to be there. But he was sure that the world was not flat. And this inner conviction was stronger for him than the entire scientific-philosophic-geographic belief of his day. (Among the more enlightened people at that time, the world was considered merely flat; for the many less informed, it was believed to be the back of a giant turtle).

Once the Inner Bell is located it must be heard, and truth is perceived from within — no matter how anyone else is defining reality at the time. Most great inventors, explorers (inner and outer), scientists, innovators of every sort, have heard, respected and listened to their own Inner Bells. For example, Maria Mayer, the American physicist who won the Nobel Prize in 1963, discovered that the atomic nucleus consists of concentric shells. She discovered this "in an intuitive flash of insight..." sparked by a colleague's chance remark. And, furthermore, she unabashedly labeled the arrangement of protons and neutrons which came to her in that flash, "Magic Numbers"![8] The French mathematician Poincaré and the nineteenth century German chemist Kekulé "owed important scientific discoveries" (as they themselves admit) to sudden pictorial" 'revelations' from the unconscious." And Descartes had a similar flash of intuition which revealed to him the "order of all sciences."[9]

The Inner Bell sounds, and new truth is revealed about the Universe. Often — particularly in science and in technological inventions — the

11

new truth seems to contradict older "known" truths existing in the culture. Old truths such as "the world is flat" or "it'll never get off the ground" or "get a horse!" etc. But then the new truth turns out to be more valid than the older truths, and civilization shifts.

> They all laughed at Fulton and his steamboat
> Hershey and his chocolate bar
> Ford and his Lizzie
> Kept the laughers busy
> That's how people are...

And of course the Inner Bell is also that flash of inspiration behind great art — poetry, painting, prose, and religious or philosophical thought. Not all of us may aspire to great works, but all of us could benefit from locating our own Inner Bell, from being able to hear its seemingly elusive ring above the din of daily "reality." The Inner Bell can also reveal truths about ourselves. It is akin to intuition, but it is a heightened sense of inner truth which goes beyond intuition.

The Inner Bell is what "told" certain people to cancel their reservations aboard the Titanic. The same process gave Levi Strauss the idea for pants made of denim — canvas left over from the covered wagons. Rodgers and Hammerstein had an idea for a new type of musical, called "Oklahoma!" which nobody wanted to produce. A daring record producer named John Hammond had a series of "hunches" to record a series of unknown singers over the years: Bessie Smith, Billie Holiday, and Bob Dylan, to name just a few. James Cagney saw a street-corner character in New York who walked and talked in a certain style; it suddenly occurred to him to impersonate that particular character in his films.

Many of these flashes are life-saving, in effect. The mother who has a sudden "feeling" to peek in on a sleeping child, and finds the child suddenly ill or in danger. Many popular examples exist of people who followed sudden hunches and were able to save other persons just in the nick of time. Most of us have had some specific experience — or know someone who has had such an experience — of following some compelling inner prompting with dramatic results.

Every technique in the work of magic for self-help is designed to develop the Inner Bell. This will be particularly graphic in the work of divination. These techniques are ancient, tried and true, used by centuries of adepts. Such techniques have lurked beneath the surface of our "rational" culture and have always been available to those on an inner quest. The sound of one's Inner bell need not be an isolated, once-in-a-lifetime experience. The work of positive magic helps to develop the Inner Bell as a consistent aid to daily living.

Magic and Society

It may be difficult for us to envision a society in which the "relational" aspects of the brain were emphasized as a matter of course. But there was a time on this planet (a mere few thousands of years ago) when religion, theater, art, philosophy and science were all considered to be part of one thing: magic. In "primitive," premonotheistic times, magic permeated all of life. Later, in the West, each field of endeavor branched off and developed by itself. In such specialization, vast strides were made in each field, but some valuable aspects of each field were also left behind. These positive aspects are worth reviewing. For example:

Astrology developed into astronomy, whereby great advances were made with improved telescopes and complex math. The ignorance and superstition of medieval astrology were left behind. But also left behind was any acknowledgement of the *causal* relationship between life on this planet and energy forces from other bodies in our solar system.

When Western monotheism replaced paganism, several positive ideas were discarded: the relationship between humankind and the rest of nature; the acknowledgment of personal usage of the Universal Power; much information about the Unseen World — including spirit contact, the validity and value of reincarnation and personal karma. The idea of the importance of women was also discarded. And by "importance," I am not referring to a state of matriarchy; I am referring to the cosmic validity of the female aspect of Deity, the balance of female and male. Specifically, this inequality has manifested in centuries of unbalanced (patriarchal) spiritual leadership. Whatever happened to the priestesses?

In theater, when the functional aspect of ritual was replaced by pure entertainment, the proscenium went up and audience participation went down. A vast area of dynamic and effective group ritual was consequently left behind. Theater used to be a participatory area for both performers and audience.

Notice that in each of these highly developed and specialized fields a curious reversal is currently taking place. Audience participation and ritual aspects are returning in the theater. Astronomers are acknowledging the moon's influence on mental health and exploring the possibility of other planetary influences on human life. In religion, women are making their voices heard and are beginning to take positions of leadership. So what was once discarded is now being reclaimed.

Investigators in laboratories all over this planet are pursuing ideas which used to be considered part of the domain of magic. They call their studies "parapsychology" and "psychic phenomena." In my opinion, most of our feelings of reverence and awe have been transferred from God over to Science. When scientists say that the occult is valid, then people believe that it's valid. This is a most positive trend, but I would like to point out a catch in such reasoning: We really don't need anyone to say that magic is valid. The validity of magic is ultimately not measurable by the authority-oriented ("rational") part of our minds or of our culture. This work is more appropriately ascertained by the "relational." In other words, we do not need anyone else to decree that magic is OK. Only our own Inner Bells can ultimately decide this for us, each of us for ourselves. But it's important to remember — that when you say that magic is valid *as long as it remains a part of something else* (e.g. science), this is basically a denial of its validity.

A new cultural phenomenon exists in the West. Sincere occultists, students of magic, "neo-pagans," and various revival versions of the Celtic witchcraft religion are beginning to emerge. These groups are attempting to explore the possibilities of magic and the occult on both personal and social levels. But unfortunately many of them are still trying to "pass": In describing themselves, they may use phrases such as "folkloric parapsychologists," "new religious movements," "occult technologists." In explaining their work, they often say, "Our work is just like..." (science, religion, anything else). But I think the whole point is that magic is not just like anything else. And we don't have to say that it is. There are political implications here. Every minority group has learned that when anyone tries to "pass" as something or somebody else, then the energy and the significance of that minority is syphoned off into tokenism. Lack of credibility is a subtle form of repression. Such repression is subtly effective because you hardly notice it — especially when it applies to *you.*

I am not really criticizing these new occultists, neo-pagans, neo-witches, spiritual seekers, and magicians of all kinds. They are part of an important cultural movement, and before such people came along the work of the magician or witch was a lonely business.

Of course magic also *is* just like a myriad of other things and cannot be disassociated from them. In fact, it's part of our language: the magic of music, of painting, of poetry. But this is true only up to a point.

And after that point is where the work begins.

[1]*The New York Times*, Apr. 19, 1970, "On a Pacific Island, They Wait for the G.I. Who Became God."

[2]Samuel J. Warner, Ph.D., *Self-Realization and Self-Defeat*, Grove Press, Inc. New York, 1966, Chapter IX, "Significance and the Creative Approach."

[3]Ibid., pp. 168-169.

[4]The Old Joke: At a concert, the soprano was singing her aria from *Aida*. When she finished, there was thunderous applause, and then a loud call for "encore," "encore!" She held up her hand, stepped forward, and announced, "Thank you. And now for my next song, I will perform..." She couldn't finish her statement. A man stood up in the balcony raving, *"Encore, encore!"* The soprano had to deal with this graciously. "Thank you, sir," she said, "but now I would like to go on with the program." The man bent down and shook his finger at her: "Sing *Aida* again!" he yelled. "And *keep* singing it! Until you get it right!"

[5]Viking Press, New York, 1973.

[6]Justine Glass refers to this concept throughout *Witchcraft, The Sixth Sense*, Wilshire Book Company, California, 1970, as a primary goal of operative witch magic.

[7]Carlos Castaneda, *Journey to Istlan: The Lessons of Don Juan*, Pocket Books, New York, 1974, p. 256.

[8]Carl G. Jung, ed., *Man and His Symbols*, A Windfall Book, Doubleday and Co., Inc., Garden City, New York, 1964, p. 307.

[9]Ibid., p. 38.

Chapter II

LOCATION IN TIME AND SPACE

TIME: The Cusp
SPACE: The Earth Plane

Establishing a "Fix" in Time and Space

Our first shift of perception on the road to positive magic led us to the idea that *anything is possible*. Our next shift of perception will lead us to redefining our ideas of time and space — and our location in both.

Let us now investigate the occult definitions of time and space, concentrating specifically on those concepts which apply to the individual and are most practical for the use of magic as self-help.

From the adept's point of view, time and space are linked. In fact, time and space are virtually identical in the occult — one might say that all time and all space coexist inextricably.

The work we are about to do can *transcend* time and space, move through it. For example, we may use magic to see into the future — so time is no longer a barrier; or we may use our magic to retrieve a lost object — so space is not a barrier either. This book cannot show you how to transcend time and space, but it will show you how to transcend your limited *perceptions* of time and space. Time and space are not limited; our perceptions of these concepts are somewhat limited because of our limited experience in human form.

How do we transcend our perceptions? We may use the analogy of the nearsighted person. If a nearsighted person were to remove his/her glasses, that person would not be able to see something which was really there but far away. With the glasses back on, what had seemed invisible just a moment before would become visible. Does this mean that nothing was there when the person was not wearing glasses? No, the distant view was there, just waiting to be seen. So it is with the occult concept of time — the future is already there, just waiting to be seen. So it is with the occult concept of space — other realities are also already there, waiting to be seen. Some magicians and occultists have a natural gift, an extended vision, it would seem, from the very start. Others must find ways of putting on their new glasses. But all adepts know that what they think they may not be able to see — in time and in space — is already there. All time and all space, already there, all at once; there for the seeing, there for the using.

> ALL TIME IS NOW,
> ALL SPACE IS HERE[1]

So goes the traditional occult statement, which is the essence of this chapter in a nutshell.

> The modern disciples of Einstein recognize nothing
> but an eternal present, which is also what the
> ancient mystics believed.[2]

TIME: The Cusp
"All Time Is Now"

Future, present, past, are all together, but usually we do not experience time in this way. Instead we have chosen to experience time as a sequence of minutes, hours, days, etc. This is a direct result of our life choices: to live on this planet, to live in this galaxy. Our subconscious minds, our souls, have made these choices,[3] to live within certain obvious measurements. This planet has days and nights, seasons and years. It revolves in a certain way, a certain number of revolutions, on a certain tilt, in space. The point is that these measurements — minutes, hours, days, weeks, months, years, centuries — *are not the only measurements for time.* There are cultures on other parts of our planet which calculate their months differently. The Chinese demarcate different years than we Westerners. Jews number the years differently than Christians, some places have longer days and some longer nights. So even on our own planet, specific measurements vary.

But let's not dispense with these measurements! We need them because we are in our physical bodies, living on a certain part of this planet, and our time measurements serve obvious practical functions. But now let's add an important occult measurement system: *astrological demarcations.*

Astrological Ages

When I first began talking about the occult on radio, not very many people knew that the year is divided into the twelve signs of the zodiac, and that everybody living on Earth is born under a certain Sun sign. Now everybody seems to know this; it's cocktail party talk. "What sign are you?" is no longer a question heard only from astrologers. I predict that another important system, once known only to astrologers, will also be popular knowledge soon: *Astrological Ages.* Quite simply, this means that our entire planet passes through all twelve of the zodiac signs also. In an astrological year, each zodiac sign period lasts approximately one month. But when the entire planet passes through its astrological cycle, each zodiac sign period lasts approximately *2,000 years.* Each of these is an Astrological Age. A basic knowledge of Astrological Ages is of enormous importance in occult work. Whereas astrologers know that using only the twelve signs of the zodiac — the Sun signs — is far too general a technique for analyzing individual people, nonetheless, Sun sign generalities do have their place. And this most dramatically applies to analyzing an Astrological Age.

Why analyze an Astrological Age? Occultists do this in order to deepen their understanding of the social, cultural, and metaphysical atmosphere in which we are living; the astrological inheritance of our time; and the choices available for the planet. Because in the occult time is not neutral. This may seem like a strange idea to those of us who accept the hours of the day, the days of the week, as empty canvases, so to speak, waiting to be filled in. In the occult, those hours, those days, weeks, months, are not empty. These time measurements all contain their own significant meanings: specific planetary aspects, metaphysical vibrations, colors, even musical notes. These attributes and others are taken into consideration when precise occult work is done.

These subtle and complex time attributes do not affect us significantly in basic occult work for self-help — but the specific attributes of the Astrological Ages do affect all of us. They affect the entire planet. The astrological influences during each Age permeate the entire culture, influence mass consciousness, and touch deeply upon the lives of every being in existence during that Age. This is not to discount our own personal astrological inheritance — our own individual sun signs or our own natal charts. But the influences of the Age are of a broader social nature. They help us to understand the time we live in, and to deal with it in occult terms.

Much talk (and song) in the air around us heralded "The Age Of Aquarius." And our planet, Earth, is indeed just about entering the

Astrological Age of Aquarius, which will last approximately 2,000 years. We are now in the transition period — the Cusp — between the two Ages. The past 2,000-year Age of Pisces is just about over. If you know a bit about the sequence of astrological signs during the course of the year, you will note that Pisces is supposed to come after Aquarius, not before. But the sequence of Astrological Ages appears to move backwards because of the *precession of the equinoxes.*[4]

Cusps

A Cusp is the transitional time period during which the sun passes from one sign of the zodiac into the next. During the course of a year, each Cusp period lasts approximately one day. For Astrological Ages, of course, the Cusp period is much longer; it lasts for approximately thirty years.[5]

At this point, *all* demarcations of Astrological Ages are only approximate. Our popular calendar was changed in 1582 C.E., and prior to that the literacy level was low and few precise records were kept. So we simply can't know for sure exactly when the Piscean Age began, not to mention the remote Ages which came before it long over 2,000 years ago.

But it really doesn't matter if the Astrological Age demarcations are a bit hazy. It is said that a Cusp *casts its shadow ahead.* The Aquarian influence was felt in our culture perhaps as early as the end of the Victorian period, during the burst of "spiritualism" and the first influx of Eastern religions into the West. Now that the Age is drawing close, these movements are more widespread and more integrated into our entire cultural atmosphere. So if any astrologer claims to know exactly when the Aquarian Age began, please take such information with a grain of salt. Identifying the precise moment of change-over is not significant. What is significant is to take careful note of the gradual, shifting changes — the trends — as we live through the Cusp period.

A Cusp period is a dramatic, exciting and important time in which to live. The transition from one Age to the next is felt by everyone. The air is literally crackling with change.

The time of the Cusp influences the ensuing 2,000-year cycle. For example, the last Cusp — Aries/Pisces — was at the beginning of Christianity. this was 2,000 years ago, give or take some years. Jesus is said to have lived during that traditional Cusp period of thirty-three years, and Christianity has been the dominant cultural influence on our planet during the past 2,000 years. You may point out that this is true only in the West. But the West has dominated our planet during this time period, for better or for worse. Since Christianity dominated Western culture, so Christianity dominated the planet — and

Christianity began during the last Cusp.

During a Cusp period, the astrological influences of both Ages are felt: the one that is coming up, and the one that is passing. People are confronted by choices between the old and the new.

> The old order changeth, Yielding place to new;
> And God fulfills Himself in many ways;
> Lest one good custom should corrupt the world.
> —Alfred, Lord Tennyson[6]

Now, the Cusp choices recently have been between Piscean Age themes and Aquarian Age themes. Many of us have been struggling with these choices in our own lives during recent years. There were also choices within the Piscean Age, and there will be choices within the Aquarian Age coming up. Here is a breakdown of some of the dominant themes of the Piscean Age, Aquarian Age, and current Cusp. Note the choices!

Pisces was a time of duality.[7] The sign of Pisces, the fish, illustrates this: One fish is going one way, the other fish is going the other way. The duality in religious beliefs during Pisces posited that spirit had to be either *inside* or *outside*. The mass choice was that God was "outside," essentially an externalized, individualized, higher Deity. Jesus emerged as an authority figure. (Jesus may not have intended this, but Christianity evolved according to the choices made during the Age which followed him). The outer-Deity concept also led to an outer-authority-oriented religion, which led to the tradition of mediators between God and the people in most Western religious structures. Another aspect of the duality theme was the concept of good vs. evil, God vs. the Devil.

"Following orders" was a Piscean Age trait. Rulers were outer authority figures. Government was essentially outside the people. Kings, queens, priests, cardinals, dukes, and other rulers were higher; the peasants were lower. The institutions of feudalism, monarchy, hierarchy, and government bureaucracy were all Piscean; so were the concepts of allegiance, regimentation, nationalism and patriotism.

Duality also applied to man and woman, literally considered two different species. Man was higher, woman was lower. Thus patriarchy was perpetuated in the Piscean Age, and God was unquestionable male. There was duality also within male/female relationships; "sacred" vs. "profane" love. Spirituality was higher, sexuality lower. Hence chastity, chivalry, asceticism, celibacy, and sexual repression — all Piscean.

Now a look at the Aquarian — and current Cusp — counterparts of the above themes.

The dominant attributes of Aquarius are equality and the oneness of all life. Duality is not an Aquarian issue. Neither is the concept of higher vs. lower, winner vs. loser, inner vs. outer. There are no polarities.

This can be seen in the Aquarian view of sex. The unisex concept popularized during the 1960s was an Aquarian phenomenon — men and women dressing alike, looking alike, acting alike. The Gay Movement, the Women's Movement, transsexualism, the open recognition of bisexuality as well as homosexuality are Aquarian. In the Aquarian Age, male will no longer be superior and neither will female. There will be an equality and a oneness between the sexes. In male/female relationships, sexuality is no longer considered "lower" than spirituality. Love includes sex, instead of being seen in contrast to sex. The acceptance of Masters and Johnson techniques, legalized abortion, sex education, sex therapy, widespread birth control, the so-called sexual revolution, and the idea of sex-as-healthy — these are all Aquarian.

But now we come to the overlap, or Cusp, area. Sexual exploitation, "dirty movies," etc., show that sex is out in the open yet still considered prurient. This is a Piscean *attitude* toward an Aquarian *idea*.

In the Cusp, the Piscean trait of following orders is exiting, having peaked in World War II Nazism and declined during Vietnam and Watergate. Nationalism is rapidly becoming archaic. Loyalty is no longer due to an outer authority — such as the army, government, church, or ruler — but to one's own conscience. In Aquarius, we will be governed by our own inner authority.

People literally governing themselves will demonstrate the Aquarian ideal of government, but this hasn't happened quite yet. Democracy, socialism, and communism are self-government in theory, but they are still dominated by totalitarian practices, bureaucracy and authority figures. They are Cusp, because the *idea* is Aquarian, but the *form* is still Piscean.

The organic or "quiet" revolution is Aquarian, the change from within as opposed to social revolution of a violent nature, which is Cusp.[8]

Communes are Aquarian. Communes run by one or several people as little dictatorships (such as Manson's "family") are Cusp — Aquarian *ideas* in a Piscean *form*.

The Aquarian God concept is all-inclusive, existing literally in every cell, every bit of matter, every living thing. God is neither exclusively inside nor outside, male nor female, nor necessarily manifest in any human image. There is also no need for a devil figure to blame for human misdeeds, because the Aquarian mentality is very much concerned with personal responsibility. Aquarian religious themes won't include proselytizing, conversion, hierarchy, heresy, persecution, or "holy war" (all Piscean). Aquarian religious adepts will serve new functions, because people will no longer require the intercession of clergy or saints to reach God. People will be able to reach God directly because God is within everyone.

Meditation is Aquarian. But any rigid, structured or commercial organizations dispensing meditation — and/or other spiritual techniques — are Cusp. This includes the so-called human potential movement. "Enlightenment" for a *fee*, delineated according to a given set of rules, is an Aquarian *idea* in Piscean *form*.[9] East-West blends of religions, gurus, messiahs, religious cults, are all Cusp — because they embody Aquarian religious ideas within a Piscean structure of following the leader. Nuns wearing street clothes, women rabbis, married priests, gay churches — Aquarian innovations grafted onto Piscean religious forms — are also Cusp.

It was Piscean to see a duality between the *practical* and the *mystical*. In the Piscean Age, you could either be a man of God (such as a holy mystic in a hair shirt, living on a mountain top), or you could be a practical man of action (warrior, king, knight — and later, businessman, scientist). If you were a woman, these choices were not open to you. You could be either a good woman (celibate nun or holy wife/mother) or harlot (rich courtesan or poor whore).

Now in the Cusp, the practical and the mystical are beginning to merge. Science as a Piscean institution categorically denied the existence of occult phenomena. The Cusp science of parapsychology works with occult phenomena. In this new field, as in most other Cusp pursuits, male/female roles are becoming irrelevant. The emotional transference of old religious feelings to newer idealogies, such as psychiatry, is Cusp. "Wayout" psychiatric and psychological techniques are also Cusp.

Exploitation of the planet is an idea which grew out of Piscean dualities — man as separate from God, separate from the rest of the Universe. The Aquarian counterpart is ecology: save the planet and revere nature because we are all inextricably linked to our environment. A Cusp phenomenon occurs when oil, coal, or other (Piscean) energy companies, which are still exploiting natural resources, use advertising campaigns to "pass" as ecologically sound (Aquarian) ventures.

Pisces is a water sign; boat travel was the main Piscean Age means of exploration. Aquarius is an air sign. Airplanes, rocket ships, and satellites are all Aquarian ways to explore space.

Getting high on liquids is Piscean. Getting high on "air" (marijuana) is Aquarian.

23

The major form of mass communication during the Piscean Age was the printing press, first owned by government and church, and then by big business. Communication through air is Aquarian: television, radio, telephone. But these forms will remain Cusp as long as they are owned by institutions. *Psychic* communication is Aquarian: ESP techniques such as telepathy, spirit contact, etc. No one can own these phenomena or regulate them. Now, in the Cusp, they are just beginning to be explored and accepted. Interplanetary and interspecies communication are also Aquarian.

Man-as-center-of-the-Universe is a Piscean belief. Racism is a related Piscean belief. Equal-opportunity legislation, integration, minority liberation and anti-defamation groups are all Cusp. By the Aquarian Age, racism, nationalism, and sexism doubtless will no longer be significant issues as the prerequisite feelings of duality will be gone from the culture.

During the Cusp, we may find ourselves grappling with the themes of the past Age vs. the themes of the new Age: the old ways vs. the new. *This is deceptive.* Ultimately there is no real choice between old and new, because as Tennyson told us, the old order is destined to yield place to new.

Another Cusp problem may be a doomsday feeling. Sometimes it may appear that the world is going to come to an end, and we hear talk of holocausts and other dire predictions. (Hollywood disaster movies depicting destruction by fire, flood, or the Devil are outlets for the doomsday fear and are harmless — unless they are taken seriously). Such doomsday thought is a primitive fear reaction and it is important not to yield to it. The feeling seems to surface during every Cusp, and is a misunderstanding of the turning point. The *world* is not coming to an end; the Piscean Age is!

Science fiction predictions of nightmare cultures of the future, such as George Orwell's *1984*, are expressions of the doomsday fear. So are fears of the government taking over, big business taking over, communism taking over, and so on. Any prediction of a rigid authoritarian takeover is a Piscean projection. The exiting Age sometimes projects its own demise as seen in its own most negative terms. It is best not to give in to Cusp fears, worries, or end-of-the-world jitters. Negative predictions can put forth negative vibrations into the atmosphere. It is far more productive to look ahead optimistically, and plan for the coming Age.

We can afford to be optimistic about Aquarius! It has long been heralded in occult lore as a Golden Age for the planet. And in assessing the Piscean Age, there is no reason to say that it was all negative. We must acknowledge the positive accomplishments of the passing Age so that we can build on them in the next Age. We can then clearly turn our attention to new themes and choices, bearing in mind that every individual choice, in each person's life, influences the culture of the Age.

A major theme of Aquarius is that *God is within.* The goal in the Age of Aquarius will be *how to bring this idea into meaningful reality.* The choices will involve innovative ways of helping everyone to be happy and fulfilled, making sure that no one is hungry and no one is poor. And this is to be realized not according to some authority's ideas, but in response to the real basic needs of everyone.

Other relevant choices will be:

- What is true spirituality and what is illusion?
- How can we use our new personal freedom responsibly?
- How can we conserve and utilize the resources and energy of our own planet in creative and life-affirming ways?
- What are the safest and most responsible ways to explore space?
- What are the values of mind-expanding techniques — and what are the dangers and self-indulgences?

Most areas of our culture will undergo significant change, and in each area we will be confronted with Aquarian choices. For example, new art forms will emerge and be important. These will make use of light and shadow, the art forms of literal illusion. We have already begun to use television, film and photography techniques in art forms. These will be extended into new techniques, including holograms and the use of three dimensions. The challenge will be to use light and shadow in meaningful and creative ways rather than opting for mere deception and empty escapism.

We will be entering new realms of exploration in space and in time. What space is there to explore?

> There is no question that there is an unseen
> world. The problem is, how far is it from midtown
> and how late is it open?

Woody Allen[10]

SPACE: The Earth Plane
"All Space Is Here"

All space includes:

- outer space (other planets, galaxies, etc.)
- inner space (within our own minds, within our body cells)
- coexisting space (coexisting planes of existence, such as

alternate universes)
- the Earth Plane

According to occult definition, this last — the Earth Plane — is where we are now. In the ancient Hebrew mystic tradition of the Caballah, the Earth Plane is called *Malkuth* (מַלְכוּת·). This is where form manifests.

What we can readily perceive with our five senses — mainly what we can see and touch — is called the *World of Form*. This includes the rooms we live in, the furniture, the cups of coffee, and other physical objects. Those areas which we cannot readily perceive in this way are called the *Invisible Realm*, also known as the *Unseen World*, the *Invisible World* or the *Unseen Realm*.

But if "all space is here," why do we not perceive it all? Why does the Earth Plane (the world of Form) seem like such a convincing and total reality?

Choice again. We have chosen to live in physical bodies, to be human, to be *individualizations* of spiritual essence, to live on the planet Earth in the World of Form. These choices define our perceptions, and our perceptions define our environments. An important attribute of the Earth Plane is that here ideas manifest into form. You can touch forms and you can see them — as you can touch and see this page. We perceive forms readily, and we accept their existence. And so we might stop there and think that forms are all that exist.

But it is important to transcend this belief. We are starting to do so already! We know that there is more to life than what we can immediately perceive with our senses, because we have begun to explore space that our culture didn't know existed a hundred years ago. We are doing this with microscopes, with telescopes, and with photography (specifically Kirlian photography of the aura). And there will be many more ways of exploring space, ways we can deal with easily, which do not require us to "wig out" suddenly into other dimensions.

This exploration will be facilitated for us personally, in our own lives, if we simply acknowledge that:
- we are here by choice...
- we may choose to go beyond our immediate perceptions of where we are...
- *man is not the center of the Universe.* (Just ask any woman)
It is equally limiting to think that the human race on this planet is the center of the Universe! We are not living in the only neighborhood in the Universe. Nor is our particular locale, the Earth Plane, the center of all the action, either. Instead, let us acknowledge that just as with time,

26

we have chosen to perceive where we are as a starting point. And it's not a bad starting point: we do not have to dispense with it! We can go on from here.

When Castaneda's Don Juan says, "The world we see around us is a description," who is the describer? We are. All we need to do now is to say that we have created the world we see around us *by choosing to perceive it in this way.* Then we can choose to extend our boundaries.

The World of Form includes only the space within our immediate perception — the earth, the sky, the trees, the water. The Unseen Realm includes all space other than our immediate perception recognizes: places where ghosts, auras, and microscopic organisms are; the outer galaxies; the astral planes we may someday travel; the alternate universes we may someday investigate; and our own minds, where our own thoughts and ideas are. These are all in the Unseen Realm.

Astral Planes and Coexisting Dimensions

The Unseen Realm, as we have said, contains various areas of space: inner space, outer space, and coexisting space. These areas cannot be visualized in the familiar geographical sense. In fact, they all coexist because *all space is here,* so these areas coexist along with the World of Form. For example, outer space coexists as a broad backdrop with our own immediate environment, the planet Earth. Inner (microscopic) space coexists with our own larger, more visible spatial realities: the invisible atoms in a chair coexist with the whole chair which is visible to the naked eye. And the inner space of our minds and ideas coexists with the tangible forms of our lives. All space exists together in many ways.

In the occult, when we talk about "coexisting space" we are usually referring specifically to coexisting *planes,* or dimensions, also known as "astral planes." I believe that these are the same dimensions which science refers to as "alternate universes." Here reside spirits, ghosts, invisible beings, and thought forms. Here also are the human auras and astral bodies, invisible counterparts of the physical human bodies. "Astral travel" or "astral projection" are catch-all phrases for ways of traveling in these dimensions.

In the Piscean Age, specifically during the nineteenth century, students of the occult began a concerted effort to explore the astral planes. At that time there was a trend to work entirely in the Invisible World, and much astral travel was being attempted — and perhaps being accomplished — in certain occult circles.

Astral travel is not recommended in this book. Most people are not

27

consciously aware of their astral bodies, and their physical and astral selves remain united. To separate them and send the astral self off into other dimensions is a *very* specialized area of occult work, fraught with danger and requiring careful training and supervision which are impossible to impart in a book. Also, it is easy to fall into illusory experiences which are not astral travel, but mental fantasies. However, there are specialized cases of people who do have a natural gift for safe, spontaneous astral travel, usually during sleep.

The focus of astral study in the nineteenth century attempted to measure and delineate the astral planes in rigid linear terms. However, such an approach is not appropriate for invisible areas, because it limits the Invisible Realm to perceptions which commonly define the Earth Plane. Books exist which still describe the Invisible Realm as a series of specified, stratified astral planes. Some even give directions for traveling on them just like road maps: on the "higher" planes you may encounter the angels and higher spirit entities; on the "lower" planes you may encounter the in-between spiritual beings. This is a (Piscean) hierarchal, élitist view of invisible entities, and it is also a simplistic linear view of nonlinear space. Let's not lapse into this Piscean Age pitfall.

When the early European explorers set out to cross the oceans, they were convinced they'd bump into India on the other side. The explorers did not expect the American continent, they were suprised to find it, and some of them even insisted that this was indeed India, and called the inhabitants "Indians." It took a while for these explorers to allow the true nature of their discovery to reveal itself. And so it is with the astral planes. We cannot explore them with preconceived notions of what they are, how they are constructed, and who lives on them. We must let the true nature of our discoveries reveal itself to us organically.

I lean towards the occult view that planes are different stages of psychic awareness. Science posits that these dimensions may be composed of different rates of vibrations of energy. The extent of one's perception defines the extent of one's capacity to voyage into this realm of space. As we get into the Aquarian Age, it seems an inevitable consequence of exploring new realms of space that new areas of communication will become more common. This will probably include more widespread spirit-human contact and interspecies contact, not only between humans and other life-forms on our own planet, but also between humans and other life-forms from other planets.

To the Piscean Age mentality, such possibilities seem fanciful or ridiculous; to the Aquarian, they are a challenge to be met. And in the Cusp — well, the communication has already begun.

Coexisting Space: Spirit Entities

Spirits are living beings composed entirely of invisible essence. Our own invisible essences are enclosed in physical form (our bodies). Spirits have visible form only when they choose to project recognizable forms as images, and we choose to perceive such images. Some spirits were in human form in other lifetimes, and some will be again. Some were never human, and some never will be. It is all a matter of their own personal choice. Rarely, some entities manifesting as "spirits" may also be aspects of the self, in another time/space dimension.

All spirits exist in the Unseen Realm. Some spirits do reside on the astral planes, and these we may encounter only in advanced occult work and astral travel. By choice, others come closer to the World of Form; these may coexist in the same room with us, ready to be perceived if we choose to become aware of their presence. Spirits are also capable of contacting us telepathically, just as other living people are, if both parties are openly receptive to such communication.

Unfortunately, contact between the Worlds has not yet been sustained on a consistently meaningful or even credible level. The modes of communication available to spirits and humans so far have been either spontaneous (hauntings), primitively-contrived (ouija boards), or subject to the elusive variables of pure mind-contact (mediums and séances). Much confusion has arisen over ghosts and hauntings. Most commonly a spirit will appear as a ghost — quite visibly, and sometimes affecting sounds or odors — reenacting some traumatic event suffered in the same location. Usually such a ghost is a neurotic entity, not even aware that it is "dead." Simple exorcisms are most effective when they inform the spirit that it is no longer locked into physical form and that the spirit is actually free to leave the Earth Plane and move on to a more appropriate place.

Ouija boards are akin to primitive telephone lines between the World of Form and the Invisible Realm. In the hands of sensitive, discriminating people (and spirits), positive contacts can often be established. I look forward to the day when the same scientific skill applied to long-distance talking on this plane is applied to spirit-human conversation.

One of the most popular "serious" methods of spirit-human contact is through a sensitive person who acts as a medium, or primary contact. A spirit guide may often talk "through" such a receptive person. The medium may or may not go into a trance state. The Cusp trend seems to be in the direction of mediumistic contacts. A spirit guide may actually become part of a family or community of friends, and this is in my opinion a potentially positive and mind-expanding experience.[11]

Since all spirit contact is particularly susceptible to the pitfall of illusion, it is important to be aware of the limitations. Many people seem automatically to assume that spirits are all-knowing because they happen to be invisible. Such an assumption overlooks the main advantage spirits do have to offer us: they have *the vantage point of the Invisible World*. Obviously spirits are not locked into viewing reality solely in terms of form, so they can help us to achieve an overview of our own existence as essences. Spirits can help us to be less rigid, less limited, less locked into the World of Form, and more aware of the flexibility of our lives. Also they often have clear memories of many lifetimes of accumulated knowledge. But this does not mean that *all* spirits are categorically wiser than we are, nor necessarily authorities on whatever subject they decide to talk about, nor that they can regularly predict the future — all common misconceptions. Unfortunately the spirit world can be as full of mischief-makers and self-styled authorities as this world. Ouija boards can contact crank spirits, just as we may have human crank phone callers. Such spirits may spell out ridiculous messages, make threats, or claim to be Napoleon.

Spirit guides working through mediums are usually more reliable if the contact is a proven working relationship over a reasonable period of time, preferable several years. But the medium who plays host or hostess to just any spirit who happens to drop in may find a most unsavory guest can enter. *It is also important to be discriminating in spirit contact*; this cannot be emphasized enough. In a crowded city it's unwise to leave the front door open night and day to whomever decides to wander in. And so it is with our doorways to the Invisible World. Often the most delightful guests are the most polite and the least imposing — while the rowdies, social outcasts and unbalanced entities are the most eager to talk and intrude. This is the reason that so many séances seem to be fakes, offering famous departed people spouting nonsense. Often the mediums aren't fakes — the spirits are! They can pose as anyone if the humans are eager to be duped. This is saddest when spirits pose as departed loved ones, and most laughable when spirits who have no idea what they're talking about pose as a glamorous authorities.

Just as an irresponsible spirit can pretend to be all-knowing, so can he or she also take advantage of human ignorance, fear and superstitition, and may even enjoy frightening people. Remember that being invisible does not mean one has any special powers, and spirits are not necessarily more dangerous company than humans — no more and no less. There is no built-in reason to fear them, and you can always terminate the contact from your end. You never have any obligation to sustain contact if you don't like it. Simply state clearly and firmly that you wish to end the communication, just as you would close the door on an unwelcome visitor or hang up the phone on an unwelcome caller. It takes two to communicate, and if you refuse to continue, the spirit has no choice but to leave.

I do not mean to indicate that spirit-human relationships are necessarily troublesome. They can be unique and enriching experiences for both parties.

It is important to realize that sometimes when people think that they see or hear a spirit, they are actually encountering their own imagination, an illusion. So if you're not sure what is really happening, or if you don't like what is going on — or if you don't like the idea of communicating with a spirit — best to drop it for now.

Outer-Space Entities

All of the above advice goes for contacts with space entities too. Many people are running around saying that they've seen space people, talked to them, gotten on board their ships — or even that they *are* space people. And a lot of these people are making up such stories. Illusion, again. But some space contacts are genuine, in my opinion.

I have an image of natives standing on the shores of the Americas, ready to venerate the European explorers who had different color skins, strange clothing, and ships. Well, the next explorers who come to our shores may have different color skins, strange clothing, and different kinds of ships. But this does not mean that we have to venerate them, nor do whatever they say — nor that they are necessarily superior to us Earthlings in any way. Such visitors just happen to have the ships that got them here. Some of them may be spiritually more advanced, some of them may not be. There is no categorical reason to fear them; they will just be different, that is all.

The more we know about other dimensions of time and space, and the more we learn about their inhabitants, the more we will be able to put our own lives into perspective with the rest of the Universe. Witches and other positive magicians place equal value on both worlds

— the World of Form and the Unseen Realm. The traditional stance from which to work magic in witchcraft is called "Between the Worlds."

Thus magic works backward and forward in time and across space. Magic knows no boundaries. It is a powerful process, and we must approach it with wisdom, discretion, and a keen sense of responsibility. Any power source can be misused, and magic is no exception. Like electricity or nuclear power — magic is neutral energy and can be used in either constructive or destructive ways.

Let us now, at the very beginning of the work, take note of which ways are destructive and best avoided, ways to watch out for and never to touch — not even with a ten-foot-pole!

[1]As succinctly stated by psychic Rev. John Scudder.

[2]Jacques Bergier and Louis Pauwels, *The Morning of the Magicians,* Avon Books, New York, 1968, p. 46.

[3]More about life choices under "Karma," Chapter V.

[4]See Dal Lee's *Dictionary of Astrology,* Paperback Library, New York, 1968, p. 85, or any good astrology text for a precise definition of the precession of the equinoxes.

[5]Some astrologers say thirty-three years and some say three hundred years; opinions vary.

[6]Alfred, Lord Tennyson, *Idylls of the King,* "The Passing of Arthur," lines 408-410.

[7]I want to emphasize that I am referring to the *Piscean Age* in this chapter, not the Sun sign of Pisces nor people whose birth sign is Pisces.

[8]Excellently delineated in Charles A. Reich's *The Greening of America,* Random House Bantam Books, New York, 1970. This book gives an accurate description of many Aquarian and Cusp phenomena even though it may not have been written by an astrologer.

[9]See Chapter III of this book for more about these Cusp phenomena, noting possible dangers.

[10]Woody Allen, *Without Feathers,* Warner Books, New York, 1975, p. 11.

[11]An excellent example of this may be found in the "Seth books," by Jane Roberts. For advanced work on a more personal level see the author's *Spirit Contact*, instructions for witches in *Earth Magic, A Dianic Book of Shadows,* Earth Magic Productions, New York, 1980, p. 42.

Chapter III

THE TEN-FOOT POLE DEPARTMENT

NEGATIVE MAGIC: The Pitfalls, Pratfalls, and Dangers in Both Traditional and Modern Forms.

> ...a compromise with evil is not possible;
> evil must under all circumstances be openly
> discredited.
> —The *I Ching*, Hexagram 43, Book One

What Is Negative Magic?

There are two kinds of magic. This is such an important basic point that I wish I could write it in flashing neon lights, letters that jump out of the page, perhaps use animated film. But this is a book. So THERE ARE TWO KINDS OF MAGIC, two kinds of occult work, two kinds of workers. Here is where the worker stands up in the appropriate category for labelling and classification. The matter is simple, but for centuries too many people have missed the point. In the old Western movies, there were the Good Guys and the Bad Guys, clearly defined. And so it is in magic. The only difference is that in the old Westerns, the Good Guys wanted to be good and the Bad Guys were bad by choice. In magic this hasn't always been the case. People have often done the "wrong" kind of work unwittingly; they are often unaware of the power, the results, the feedback and the fallout of their endeavors.

Perhaps the two kinds of magic, good and bad, sound too subjective? "Good" meaning good for whom? And "bad" meaning "bad for you, but maybe good for me?" Fortunately, the two types of magic are not subjective and not subject to the individual interpretation. The types are as clear cut and differentiated as day and night.

THERE IS POSITIVE MAGIC AND THERE IS NEGATIVE MAGIC.

If the work harms even one person or being, then it is negative magic. Manipulation — which does not respect free will — is a form of harm. Compromise, sacrifice — even self-sacrifice — can also be forms of harm. However, positive ("good") magic is for the good of all and helps everyone. Positive magic may seem rare or difficult if one doesn't know about the Universal Principles (see p. 210), specifically about nonmanipulation and respecting equal Power in every living being. Positive magic is a matter of technique and playing by the rules. Good intentions are not enough. If you know you are setting out to harm someone, to do some dire deed, of course that would make the negative nature of your work much clearer. But even when we are dealing with "minor" manipulations — trespassing and denial of personal power — these too must get classified as negative magic.

In the past, these two kinds of magic were traditionally labelled white magic (positive) and black magic (negative). Today these terms seem to have fallen into disuse. However when dealing with medieval manuscripts and early occult lore, we may still read "white" magic as positive and "black" magic as negative.

Another outdated definition refers to positive magic as "the right-hand path" and negative magic as "the left-hand path." I once used these terms on the air (just once!) and a listener who was left-handed called me up and had no trouble convincing me to dispense with them. But again, it is important to note these archaic terms because they still abound in traditional magic and occult literature.

Today we say simply *positive* and *negative* work. And needless to say, the kind of work I recommend unequivocally is positive work. However two major points have long complicated the picture:

1. Positive work has been misunderstood to be negative work.
2. Negative work has masqueraded as positive work.

It is weird that most of the misunderstanding and fear about *all* magic spring from these two confused issues. Because of their importance, let us examine each of these.

• *Positive work has been misunderstood to be negative work* because *all* magic — both positive and negative — has been secret, hidden, and generally inaccessible to the public. All magic works in the same way, using the Unseen Realm. Many ceremonies and rituals may look similar, even though they are directed for entirely different purposes.

For example, imagine a village in which two groups dressed almost alike, acted almost alike, and held ceremonies on the same traditionally (magically) powerful night. One group was working to curse someone, while the other was working to heal someone. If you were a villager, you might not know necessarily which group was which. You might assume that both had set out to do harm — especially if the curse happened to take effect.

But what if the healing magic also happened to take effect? All too often it might go unnoticed, because positive magic such as healing often takes effect in a natural-looking gradual manner. This is one of its attributes, as positive magic works in harmony with the forces of nature. But negative magic — which works against the life-affirming flow of nature — sometimes appears to work more quickly and dramatically.

Returning to our hypothetical village, the day after both ceremonies had taken place an ill person might slowly and steadily return to health — but a previously healthy person might suddenly and mysteriously die.

Which group "did" which?

As we shall see, the results of positive magic may appear to the uninitiated as an accidental stroke of luck. Also traditionally no one claims "credit" for positive work. It is most often done anonymously. The positive magicians and witches usually directed their work to benefit the community at large: psychic healing of the sick, blessing of the crops, protective spells for pregnant women and newborn babies, fertility magic, etc. By contrast, negative magicians usually directed their efforts at one specific "enemy" — some person or small group who had incurred the negative workers' wrath. Such work included blighting of crops, cursing or killing a person or a family, desecration of graves, ritual murder, and other evil practices.

Both groups worked in secret and at night, so it was only natural for the average villager to wonder if there were really two different groups. Anyone who wasn't a churchgoing Christian was a suspected magician, and therefore considered a follower of the devil. When all magic was secret, how could a person be sure? Why was all magic secret?

Let's go back a few thousand years. In premonotheistic times, the work of magic was more open; it had an acknowledged and important role in the community. Even though the work itself was not practised by everyone, the facts about it were widely available. Positive and negative work were more clearly defined. Workers were specialized, and most people knew the difference. It's true that the specific methods were cloaked in secrecy, because magic is specialized knowledge and dangerous in the hands of the uninitiated. To practice magic of any kind, to use the Unseen Realm effectively, one had to be well trained, able to read and write, and willing to devote a great deal of time to the art. But although not everyone was able actually to do it, most people knew whom to turn to and for what purposes.

But later, in the Middle Ages, all magic — both positive and negative — went underground. This was the result of the massive political and religious takeover of pagan Europe by the governmental arm of the medieval Church (which is not to be confused with the spiritual body of the Catholic Church). At this time, all magic was denounced as evil, and anyone suspected of practicing magic received the death penalty. This heavy repression, and the heightened secrecy which followed, caused immeasurable confusion. All magic became secret. Wherever evidence of magic did surface, negative magic attracted the most attention.

Since the Middle Ages, negative magic has continued to get more publicity, create more hoopla, and inspire more fear. Most people came to believe that there really is no other kind. Thus positive work has been misunderstood to be negative work.

• Negative work has masqueraded as positive work. Negative "specialists" have been known intentionally to camouflage their work as positive magic in order to dupe unsuspecting people into participating. Such practitioners do this because they require extra human energies to keep their work going. Since the very nature of negative work is manipulative, these people do not hesitate to take advantage of others by lying and/or disguising the facts involved. It is not in the "best" interests of such people to inform others that there is a choice, and that the negative path is not the only one. It is also not in their "best" interests to tell the other participants about the negative feedback and karmic pain which will follow. Negative feedback is automatically built into such magic.

These results follow because all magic works in the same way — in the Invisible Realm and by cause and effect. If you work by sending out a positive cause, all the effects which come back to you will be positive. Not only will the direct results of your work be positive, but the side effects and other manifestations will be of a positive nature also. But if you work by sending out a negative cause (cursing, killing, manipulating, or whatever), all the effects will be of a negative nature! This includes the side effects on yourself.

Direct results of all magical work are carefully planned, and they often work exactly as planned — for good or for ill. But the side effects which come back in other areas of the magicians life are not necessarily controllable. A positive magician enjoys these delightful little surprises ("gifts from the Cosmos," as we sometimes call them). These may manifest in myriad ways. This is why positive magicians seem continually to be blessed with health and general good luck. But negative workers set off a chain of unpleasant events in their own lives by this same process. These unpleasant events are equally surprising and unpredictable. The negative specialist knows this, expects this, and still chooses to continue with negative work. This is the meaning of the symbolic gesture of "selling one's soul to the devil." To compound the penalties, negative magicians also believe in reincarnation, so they are aware that the negative feedback may stretch for lifetimes into their future. This is what I mean by reaping *karmic dues*.

It seems to be a mystery how a person could knowingly choose such a life. The most common theory is that negative specialists believe that they are balancing out polarities of Light and Dark forces for the planet, in a perverse sort of self-sacrifice. I believe this is a Piscean Age misunderstanding about the nature of polarity, which will be cleared up in the light of the Aquarian Age. Another theory is that negative specialists are so involved with ego (in its most negative, limiting sense) that they actually believe that they can escape their karmic dues!

To the uninformed, negative work may seem quicker and more dramatic — in the short run. Positive magic may seem to work more slowly; but in the long run, it is ultimately more effective and also sets off a positive chain of events in the magician's life. So if you are going to get involved in magic, *please be aware that you have a choice.*

The Invisible World is the traditional domain of magic. When magic was officially extracted from the culture, certain unfulfilled needs remained in people's psyches. Alternate support systems including religion, psychiatry, philosophy, and science do not always seem to have all the solutions. Thus there are moments when otherwise "rational" people may turn to magic — yes, even people who claim they don't believe in it. This usually happens during emotional times — times of fear, crisis, desperation, specifically times of a diminished feeling of the self and of personal power. During such crisis periods, the outer world and its mysterious events seem overwhelming. When people have been in such straits, often negative magic has seemed to be the most readily available or the only available kind.

On the surface, negative magic may also appear to be an ideal outlet for such feelings of vulnerabilty because it appeals to the superficial self — the ego, or sense of self-esteem. When a person feels so low as to experience no sense of personal power, negative magic offers an alignment with an (allegedly) enormous source of power: demonic power. Negative magic promises more power than any human being could possible have. Upon closer investigation, you can see how this is just the flip side of diminished power, i.e., "no" power = "all" powerful. Both extremes amount to the same thing. Negative magic reinforces the feelings of powerlessness by acknowledging a need for added power from an outside force. Psychologically, this is a superficial solution; in occult terms, it is a dangerous one.

Positive magic works on a deeper level. Instead of tapping power from an outside source, positive magic works for an awareness and an affirmation of the true inner power of the self. It does not function specifically at the ego level. Positive magic goes beyond to the development of the deepest inner self: the soul, the part that is involved with — *and part of* — the God and Goddess. This kind of magic does not promise exorbitant power because it does not acknowledge the need for such overcompensation in the first place.

At the time of this writing, there is still far too much negative magic (masquerading as positive) widely available to the public. Manipulative spells, charms, curses, recipes and formulas can readily be found in books or purchased in stores. These cheap and "easy" solutions are purveyed by people who may or may not know what they are doing. At worst, such techniques are dangerous hoaxes perpetrated upon unsuspecting people in genuine need. At best, these techniques are misrepresentations of a far more helpful kind of magical work. In any case, the possibility of severe negative fallout still applies.

Here is . an all-too-common example: the typical old case of unrequited love.

Negative magic (manipulative) most often recommends a love spell to bring one's lover back against his/her will. Even more specifically, the love spell may "make" the loved one call on the phone, "make" the loved one yield to a sexual impulse, and so on. The technique is based on *forcing* the loved one to respond. *Positive magic* (non-manipulative) readjusts one's focus away from the loved one and back on the self and the self's needs, specifically the *essence* of those needs. The recommended method for this would be a self-blessing to bring true love into one's life. *No names are used* and no specific person is drawn; true fulfillment in love is the goal. (For further information about working love magic, see Chapter VIII).

Oddly enough, nonbelievers may be particularly susceptible to negative "pop"-occult solutions because such people are usually least likely to apply their investigative faculties to occult research. A person whose belief in magic is sporadic or halfhearted may turn to it only under severe emotional stress, and then drop it for more "rational" ways of dealing with problems. Can negative magic still work — and still be dangerous — even if you don't "really" believe in it? Yes, if emotions and intellect are separated to the point where you might try something you don't believe in but emotionally need. If you rationalize this emotional belief and claim you are doing the magic for the "psychological" benefit of trying something different just for fun, negative magic can still work. And be dangerous!

Emotions plus intellect are needed to direct the work of magic effectively and discriminatingly. Traditionally, adepts have always been the literate ones, the scholars. Magic was considered beyond the grasp of most people simply because they could not read and write. It is ironic that in these more literate times, many intelligent people put aside their critical talents to deal with the realm of magic purely emotionally. Such an approach differs little from the superstitious attitude of a medieval peasant.

If you are going to use magic, I suggest that you do as much research and investigation as you possibly can. Use every part of your brain. Let this book be the beginning of your study, not the end of it! And in any case, if there's even the outside chance that you may try a magical technique (even if you're not sure whether you "believe" in it), be aware that THERE ARE TWO KINDS OF MAGIC. And you always have a choice.

The Traditional Dangers of Negative Magic

A study of negative magic reveals a ritualized compendium of what Jung calls the "shadow" side of human nature. According to Jung's theory, the shadow is that part of every person which embodies negativity, inferiority, primitivism, and uncontrolled emotionalism. Mental and emotional stability is achieved only to the extent that an individual is able to recognize his/her shadow and to integrate it into the rest of the personality. When the shadow is not acknowledged, it may "take over" and the person lapses into serious mental illness — or, more usually, the shadow-attributes are unconsciously projected outside the self, onto others.

In the Middle Ages, an entire culture embraced a simplistic religious doctrine which categorically denied the existence of the shadow within people's natures. In fact, the culture denied the existence of any negativity within God's scheme. As a result, a tremendous need inevitably arose for people to project their cumulative shadows somewhere. A need also rose for a sort of "repository" for the countless cases of (what today would be recognized as) mental disturbance, for those people whose shadows had indeed taken over the rest of their psyches. The field of negative magic fulfilled both of these social/psychological needs. Here we may see an organization of all the baser *unacknowledged* aspects of the human psyche: anger, fear, greed, lust, hate.

The forerunner of all organized negative magic in the West began with Satanism. Who is Satan (alias Satanas, Sathan, Lucifer, the Devil)? He is the Antichrist. He stands for the opposite of Christianity. Jung explains the concept this way:

41

If we see the traditional figure of Christ as a parallel to the psychic manifestation of the self, then the Antichrist would correspond to the shadow of the self, namely the dark half of the human totality, which ought not to be judged too optimistically.... In the empirical self, light and shadow form a paradoxical unity. In the Christian concept, on the other hand, the archetype is hopelessly split into two irreconcilable halves, leading ultimately to a meta-physical dualism — the final separation of the kingdom of heaven from the fiery world of the damned.... Psychologically, the case is clear, since the dogmatic figure of Christ is so sublime and spotless that everything else turns dark beside it. It is, in fact, so one-sidedly perfect that it demands a psychic complement to restore the balance.[1]

All the negative human feelings and ideas which are anathema to Christianity fall under Satan's dominion.

The character of Satan was "invented" in the fourteenth century to answer a cultural need: If God were all good and all pure, then another force had to be all bad and all debased. For the simplistic, authority-oriented Piscean Age mentality, a strong figurehead was needed to explain — in fact, to be responsible for — all the pain and suffering in the world. And so Satan emerged as the embodiment of all evil.

Satan is a Western Piscean Age phenomenon. In earlier pagan times, including Greek, Roman and Egyptian, the gods were neither all good nor all bad. They were glorified human and/or animalistic personalities with special powers and recognizable failings. Osiris, the main pagan god of the underworld, was both admirable and vulnerable; the underworld over which he presided was not a bad, judgmental place. In fact, before the Piscean Age there was no "hell" and no "purgatory," no "heaven," no paradise. There were mythical places where departed souls were said to reside, and there were the heavenly abodes of the gods. But since there was no hell, there was no Lord Of Hell. And since there was no one good external God, there was no one bad external Anti-God.

In early Judaism and Christianity, no important devil figure existed either; there was no need for one. The God figure, whether called Jehovah or Christ was believed to encompass all aspects of humanity.[2] But in the Middle Ages, the "word" of God became interpreted strictly and turned into rules. As a result, much of human experience was forbidden and considered sinful. The power of Church and king, in the people's minds, was synonymous with God's wrath and permeated them with fear. Any concept of personal freedom was virtually

42

unknown. A strong psychological need arose for people to project all those natural emotions which they dared not express in any healthy way nor even acknowledge within themselves: sexual desire, anger, frustration, political dissidence, aggression, etc. God was not responsible for these feelings any more than He was responsible for the incredible suffering resulting from the feudal system. The people needed a figure upon which to project all their own emotions and fears.

The government/Church needed a scapegoat to blame for the people's agony. In the fourteenth century, when the suffering in Europe was at its peak, the Crusaders returned from the East with stories of a belief in the forces of light pitted against the forces of darkness. The Crusaders told about Persian deities of darkness, manlike in form and wearing horns. The target was clear: the pre-Christian Horned God was still popular among witches and other pagans in Europe. He had developed out of the traditional image of Pan, the male element in nature, the Goat-foot God with horns. The Horned God has always been known as a robust, life-affirming folk deity; nothing in His tradition resembled the forces of evil. The worst that could be said about the Horned God was the He derived from an early fertility tradition and favored open sex. Of course, to the medieval Church such beliefs were anathema. Also, the physical characteristics of this deity seemed to resemble the Persian devil-type figures. But most important, the religion of the Horned God was still popular among the common folk of Europe. In some places, this God's influence surpassed any belief in Christ.

The pagans also worshipped a female nature deity — the Earth Mother or Goddess. But in the conversion to Christianity, it was an easy transition to worship the Virgin Mary and/or various female saints for the same feminine aspects which the Goddess represented. Such female religious figures represent motherhood, protection, and all the attributes of nurturing concern for human nature. No need existed to depose the Goddess, but there was a need to depose the Horned God. Any strong male deity in patriarchal times was a distinctly threatening power-figure to the Church. Thus a concordance of events and ideas led to the official labelling of the Horned God as the Devil, or Satan.

So Satan was a medieval phenomenon. The Horned God had existed for thousands of years before the Middle Ages, but the idea of the Devil, or Satan, had not.

No evidence can be found in either the Old or the New Testament of any character answering this description. What we do find are several Biblical references to fallen angels or perhaps kings named Satan and Lucifer. That the Satan mentioned in the Book of Job, the Lucifer in Isaiah, and the Satan in the Gospel of St. Luke could be one and the same being was a purely medieval interpretation. To modern scholars, these names appear to refer to several different characters. In no Biblical allusion do Satan or Lucifer possess any particular power or position as the ultimate anti-God.

Lucifer translates literally as "shining one" or "light giver"; Satan translates as "adversary." Modern Biblical translations reveal that Lucifer is actually a reference by Isaiah to a mortal king, probably Nebuchadnezzar, and that Satan (Ha-Satan) in the Old Testament actually refers to the office of adversary. This was not necessarily always a negative office, but a military appointment. The word "Satan" took on a more negative meaning in the New Testament. Jesus rebuked Peter by calling him "Satan" (Luke 4:8), and Satan is given two main titles: "prince of this world" (John 16:11) and "prince of the power of the air" (Ephesians 2:2). But this is as negative as it gets in the Bible! No evidence exists of any connection between the references, and there are no allusions to vast negative power.[3]

On the whole, Satan and Lucifer appear in the Bible as unpleasant minor characters, fallen from a higher state and trying to tempt righteous men. There is no Lord of Hell, no Arch-Fiend, no embodiment of evil, no all-encompassing Devil. However within the traditions of Pagan, Judaic and early Christian belief evil spirits, imps, demons and assorted "devils" were recognized. These represented a hodgepodge of noncanonical superstitions and legends, and no one particular figure was in charge of all of those troublesome beings. And finally, the physical definition of Satan as having horns, cleft feet, and a pointed tail, appears nowhere in the Old or New Testaments. The character of Satan results from a compilation of semiliterate medieval dogma.

The worship of Satan became officially recognized early in the fourteenth century when the governmental arm of the Church officially defined Satanism and labelled all dissenters from Christianity as members of this new religion. Such dissenters included witches, Druids, Jews, gypsies, sorcerers (including astrologers), and all pagans. In brief, any belief which was not Christian was considered the worship of Satan.

This worship was said to include every area of human activity which the Church condemned, a vast array of "sins" from the most harmless to the most fanciful to the most grisly. Satanism included everything from fortune-telling to folk medicine, from pagan prayers to fertility magic, from nonmarital sex to cursing, from "consorting" with demons to murder.

Satan was acknowledged as a powerful deity, comparable to Christ in strength, and *personally responsible* for every aspect of human suffering on this planet. It was therefore "justifiable" to declare open war on Satan, and to imprison, torture and kill anyone allegedly involved in his worship. Any non-Christian belief became dangerous to pursue, or even to appear to pursue. (At this time many aged and eccentric people were accused of Satanism). Actually to convert to this new form of anti-Christianity, actually to become a Satanist seemed to be outrageously dangerous. *And yet many people began to do so!* Such people are not to be confused with the persecuted religious minorities mentioned above. I am referring to the thousands of medieval men and women who flocked to the new Church of Satan — by choice. The modern mind has difficulty in fully comprehending the reality which the concept of Satan held for medieval people, and for the intensity of emotion surrounding his image. Let us review some of the reasons for this phenomenon.

The Lure Of Satanism (c. 1300-1600)

When Church and government were one and the same, a disgruntled populace could not defy one without repudiating the other — God ruled the kings who ruled men. The people were literally enslaved by the feudal system. In their desperation people reasoned that by overthrowing the one at the top (the God) that the king might go next — and then some of the intolerable suffering might be alleviated. But in this most oppressive time, outright revolution was impossible; it would mean certain death. However, religious revolution — especially if secret and undiscovered — was somewhat less risky and might be equally effective, because Satan was seen as a power figure. To the tortured minds of suffering peasants, Satan even may have seemed like a sort of perverse savior. He was clearly an *alternative* to the existing God, and he seemed to be winning anyway. Everything that went wrong, the authorities claimed to be the work of Satan: the plague, starvation, poverty, disease, death, crop failure. In an odd way, it seemed that life might be *safer* on Satan's side (not unlike the reasoning behind some people turning to Nazism during World War II, when Hitler seemed to be winning).

The peasants needed an authority somehow to condone forbidden activities they could not bear to give up: folk magic, superstitious rituals, dancing in the fields, old pagan festivals, and sex. They believed what they had been told — that these practices were Satanism — so now their folk practices had an offical label. If such a cultural inheritance was the work of the devil, then it seemed better to side with the devil than to give up all that had been the very substance of their lives for generations. And many of the peasants clearly did not understand any real distinction between the new devil and their beloved Horned God.

As the word "witch" became politically synonymous with "devil worshipper," some people became convinced that they must then indeed be witches. These were the new "witches of the devil"; self-proclaimed witches according to the new Satanic definition. They differed from the Satanists in that the witches retained many of their own folk beliefs mingled with their acceptance of the devil. And the witches differed from the true pagan — (pre-Christian) witches of the Old Religion in almost every basic belief and practice. (The ancient witchcraft tradition, as we shall see in the next chapter, has nothing to do with Satan).

Not only peasants turned to Satan. Members of the nobility also converted because they too needed an authority figure to approve many of the forbidden activities in which they engaged. Their Piscean Age temperament required a structured *raison d'étre* for their political intrigues and kinky sex.

Satanism had (and still has) a clear, simple definition: it is the *antithesis* of Christianity — specifically Christianity in its medieval (early Catholic) doctrine. For example:

• In Catholicism, the Lord's Prayer is said in Latin; the modern version is said in English. In Satanism, the Lord's Prayer is said in Latin — backwards. The modern version is said in English — backwards.
• Medieval Christian services were led by priests. Satanic services were led by defrocked or excommunicated priests.
• In Christianity, the cross is displayed upright. In Satanism, the cross is displayed upside down.
• The Satanic Mass ("Black Mass") is the Catholic Mass delivered backwards, with the name of Satan substituted for God or Christ. The Satanic Mass also includes wherever possible desecrations of ritual holy objects such as the wafer.
• In Christianity, nonmarital sex was considered a sin. In Satanism, all sex was and still is considered not only permissible, but celebratory. (This is still one of Satanism's main lures: a religion which *requires sex!*)

Out of such practices developed:

• *The Satanic Altar* consists of a naked woman lying down with various anti-Christian statements and/or symbols painted in blood on her body. In medieval terms, this was the perfect desecration of the Christian altar because nakedness was considered a sin and women inherently sinful because of the lust they aroused in men.
• *Satanists ceremonially repudiate Christ and dedicate (or "sell") their souls to Satan.* Christians dedicate their souls to Christ.

And so on. The Satanic dogma proceeds technically and specifically.

Every Christian tenet that can be dealt with in this way was turned into its opposite by Satanists. Ironically Satanism — that unholy tradition of licentiousness — is structured quite rigidly. It is literally an authority-oriented religion. But Satanism had its more grisly side. The practice became a breeding ground for every demented aspect of perversion. Many expressions of Satanic worship included ritual sacrifice and torture — the spilling of blood, both animal and human. Such practices are not to be confused with devotional animal sacrifice still observed by some cultures today. The Satanic animal sacrifice included torture, and was often specifically aimed at harming the animal as a symbol of harming someone at a distance.

Satanism included sexual orgies in which not all the participants were voluntary, nor did they always survive. Satanic practice advocated the desecration of Christian holy objects, graves, and buildings; fecal matter, blood and corpses were some traditional agents of desecration. And the "magical" work done in the name of Satan involved murder, cursing, and manipulation of the human soul, as well as alleged manipulation of various nonhuman entities.

Today Satanism exists in diluted form. In our culture no need exists comparable to the extreme conditions in the Middle Ages which laid the groundwork for Satanism. Modern Satanists present their tradition as a jolly, permissive religion in which all sex is open and honest and self-expression is the main goal. Some see Satanism as an exciting foray into a magical tradition. I suspect that few of these people fully comprehend the dangerous karma attached to the roots of Satanic practises. Thus the idea of Satan was created as a political maneuver and perpetuated by people who turned to his worship, given further power by the millions who recognized and feared his existence, and given more energy and power by the widespread persecution carried out "against" him. The millions of burnings, tortures, murders, and brutalities which were committed out of fear of Satan actually began his official work on this planet. So to go back to our original question: Who is Satan? We may answer in the occultists' terms: *Satan is a thought-form.*

This means that Satan is an idea — specifically an idea in the form of a character — which originates in people's *thoughts* and takes on "reality" from the intense belief, energy, and emotion which generations pour into it. As the thought-form originally derives power from human thought, so its power may dissipate when such an idea is no longer credible. A thought-form dissolves when people no longer give it power. In fact, for people who do not believe in Satan, he simply does not exist! The idea of Satan, and the fear of his existence, is an enslaving concept because he is a *negative* thought-form, and "his" energy came from a projection of negative energy.

47

In the Aquarian Age, the need for belief in Satan will no longer exist, and this thought-form is already well on its way toward dissolution. In psychological terms, as more people accept responsibility for *every* aspect of human life — including integrating the negative or "shadow" side of our natures into our conscious awareness — the Satanic archetype automatically disappears.

Meanwhile, in occult work, as long as negative magic is still being practiced on this planet, it is important to acknowledge such practice and wise to categorically avoid it. The dangers of negative magic would be simpler to deal with if Satanism in its specific traditional form were the only kind around. But unfortunately various offshoots have appeared and taken more subtle forms than Satanism; these have been widespread in our culture. These practices link mainly to two traditions: *demonology* and *"black" ceremonial or ritual magic*. Let's make clear again that "black" here is used in its traditional occult meaning as negative magic. This usage has nothing to do with the magical practices of black people, many of which are unequivocally positive and directly linked to ancient African religions. This is a discussion of Western traditions.

Ritual and ceremonial magic takes two forms. Because these two forms have so often been confused, let's examine the positive form first.

Positive ("White") Ceremonial And Ritual Magic

There are three main branches of this occult work:

1.   Pagan work, which dates back to the Eleusynian mysteries, and may involve Egyptian, Greek, Roman or Celtic deities.
2.   Jewish work, which connects directly to the Caballah, drawing heavily on the Talmud and other sacred works in Hebrew.
3.   Christian work, also based on the Caballah, but intermingling that with spiritual precepts of Christianity, often including the Gnostic tradition dating back to the time of Jesus.

There are many combinations and blends of these three branches of ceremonial work. Most of them have in common the complex use of ritual and the heavy emphasis on scholarship and dedication. The work includes a study and application of astrology, numerology, metaphysics, and often alchemy. There is a strong emphasis on the power of words and the structure of alphabetical and numerological combinations. Some sects are more cerebral, devoted specifically to study and research. Others get more involved in invocation, calling up beneficent forces of nature, positive thought-forms, and heavenly beings such as angels, usually to help in the work. The rituals themselves are often quite elaborate. They involve fasting, rites of purification, special robes and garments, consecrated tools, incense, specially constructed altars and pillars, and specifically drawn circles, pentagrams, and other diagrams. The emphasis on scholarship and gradual development often manifests in initiation rites and the earning of symbolic degrees along the paths of knowledge.

Usually people work in groups, with a strict emphasis on privacy and secrecy. Often the newly initiated members of such an organization cannot participate in — or even know about — the more advanced work until they have put in the appropriate amount of study and earned their advanced degrees. In the nineteenth century, a number of secret societies, mystery schools, and occult fraternitities revealed themselves to the public eye, specifically in England. These groups were often direct outgrowths of the medieval ceremonial orders. Some of the better-known groups which emerged at this time include the Secret Order of the Golden Dawn, the Rosicrucians, the Freemasons and the Theosophists. The names of famous scholars and literary figures have been linked with these orders. In time, splinter groups branched off and some groups ceased to exist. Others relaxed their regulations and eventually lapsed into purely social organizations or even deteriorated into negative ritual practices.

However, some positive ceremonial and ritual groups still function. Their work blends in harmony with the life-forces of the Universe and harms no one. The work strives for such spiritual and lofty goals as self-knowledge, universal oneness, karmic research, and cultural enlightenment. *But these groups traditionally have been difficult to join — or even to locate.* And the intense study and dedication integral to their work demands a deep and unusual commitment on the part of the members. Few books are readily available, and these few provide only the most superficial and vague aspects of the work. Behind all this secrecy and theory prevails that the power of the work may not be dissipated or misused. Members of these groups believe that people karmically suited to find the true work will do so in the old tradition of "when the student is ready, the teacher will be revealed."

Negative ("Black") Ceremonial and Ritual Magic

Negative ceremonies and rituals often bear a surface resemblance to the positive ones. Negative practices also include a predilection for cermonial robes, incense, ritual tools, altars, and similar diagrams such as circles and even pentagrams. The instructions may be in their original complex medieval forms, and they may be pseudo scholarly in appearance and mood.

49

There may be religious-sounding phrases, often a smattering of Hebrew, Greek, Latin, and even some ancient "unknown" languages. Ceremonies may include alleged references to the Caballah, alphabetical and numerological combinations, astrology, alchemy, or other occult practices. But the positive ritualists' emphasis on scholarship is usually conspicuously absent. In fact, many negative magicians do not understand fully the processes of their work. Some even do not comprehend the meaning of the *words* they use — especially the words derived from other languages. Negative workers may misspell or mispronounce the words, not even knowing which language is which. This is one possible explanation for the "unknown" ancient languages, which may simply be distortions.

Not all negative ritual makes use of the technically complex. The versions one may find most easily — in books or magazine articles — are usually watered-down, haphazard combinations of "magical" words and gestures, folk superstition, and plain old cursing of one's enemies. Virtually all negative magic in the West grew out of Satanism, although many groups do not allude directly to the devil himself.

The use of demons in negative magic is unmistakable. Negative rituals and ceremonies are devoted essentially to evoking demons, imps, fallen angels and spirits, and forcing them to do one's bidding. This important phenomenon bears a closer look.

I have said earlier that positive ceremonial work often involves *invocation*, the calling up of positive entities from the Invisible Realm and inviting them to aid in the positive work. Technically invocation contacts an entity which is spiritually equal to or superior to the magician. So categorically such an entity cannot be commanded to do anything for a human being. The magician can only state the request for help and the invocation usually includes verbal proof of the magician's sincerity, purity, and spiritual intent. Such a ritual is sometimes called "High Magic."[4]

On the other hand, *evocation* ("Low Magic") involves contacting an entity spiritually and often mentally lower than human, and getting it to join in the work — whether the entity wants to or not. The rituals include coercing, manipulating, threatening, and generally forcing the entity to obey. Why would anyone want or need the help of a lower entity? Again we can refer to the whole psychology of negative magic and the magician's feeling of diminished power. The idea is that many entities — even those of a lower order — have special powers derived from the Invisible World which supposedly help a magician. And surely for any magical work designed to do harm, nothing and no one other than a lower being would participate. Such practice also appeals to human ego, as the magician must ultimately prove to be smarter, more cunning, and perversely more powerful to compel the negative entity to join the work or even to appear in the first place. And perhaps the magician who escapes from such a ritual *alive* feels a sense of triumph, because this is extremely dangerous work.

Vast confusion surrounds this work. Some versions of the work have become intertwined with an assortment of regional folk beliefs and folk magical practices, such as sympathetic magic.[5] Negative rituals may often erroneously be labelled "witchcraft" practices (see next chapter).

Unlike Satanism, "black" magic is not a specific religion. The term refers to disorganized, catch-all practices for various superstitious beliefs and semi-literate ritual. The roots of "black" magic are found in a combination of medieval propaganda and legends. It does not necessarily require the full-time commitment of Satanism. "Black" magic may be resorted to at many levels, from joining a specific organization to occasionally working a simple ritualistic "spell" in private.

It is important to understand that negative ritual magic is based upon the medieval tradition of *demonology*. This is the foundation; if no demons existed to boss around, no "school" of magic devoted entirely to dealing with them would need to exist. Today the word "demon" may be understood only vaguely. The word derives from the ancient Latin and Greek *daemon*, or *daimon*, meaning both "spirit" and "genius." It is popularly considered synonymous with any troublesome invisible being — the traditional idea of so-called "evil spirit." But in the Middle Ages, the definition of demons was considered a serious matter and was extremely specific. An entire field of study evolved to recognize demons and assign them identities.

Demonology

Again, the modern mind has difficulty in comprehending the *literal* importance granted to personifying the forces of evil. Demonology is based on the concept of Satanism with demons as Satan's workers. The concept considered Satan too important to deign carrying out all his work personally, specifically as it manifested among the peasants and serfs. Also, witchhunters feared Satan greatly and didn't want to confront him personally every time they burned or tortured a suspect. In addition the Piscean mentality needed a hierarchy in each important area of human expression: in government, a hierarchy of rulers, nobles, and structured lower classes of peasants; in the Church, a hierarchy of higher clerics, middle, and down to lowly monks and nuns; in the view of heaven, God and a hierarchy of angels and saints. Consequently, it seemed that in hell, there would also have to be a hierarchy.

The medieval mind viewed hell as a well-organized place, with Satan in charge of a huge staff of official demons. Each demon had charge of some specific type of sin or human transgression. The work of demonology, the classification of demons, was a branch of clerical study and a highly respected medieval science. Demonology seems to have been based mainly on the fevered imaginations of ascetic witchhunters, because instigating sexual acts remained one of the recurrent themes among Satan's staff of helpers. Sexual acts in dreams or in imagined circumstances were also taken quite literally; if no one was visible when a Christian had a sexual thought, then some demon was believed to have been involved — invisibly, of course.

We may see demonology as a *deductive* "science." When torturing an accused "witch" or "sorcerer," all the demonologist had to know was what sin the victim had committed (or thought about), and then the demonologist would know which demon was responsible. Of course, the sins often existed entirely in the minds of the witch-hunters. Under torture, millions of peasants confessed to specific demonic acts and repeated the names of any demons with which the victims were accused of dealing. These confessions were considered evidence for the demons' existence. The official categories for demons branched off into subcategories: fallen angels, evil spirits, imps. and elementals (spirits of the forces of nature). The work of the demonologists was confusing, complex, and subject to the most serious debates. The debates raged around such issues as: Did a fallen angel automatically turn into a demon? Or did a fallen angel simply act like a demon, but belong in a separate category? Over issues such as this, various schools of thought and expertise arose.

Two books were considered the most reliable sources of information about demons in the Middle Ages: *The Book of Enoch*, a compilation of pseudo-Biblical legends purporting to be about angels, including many details about fallen angels and how they "fell" (mainly by having sexual relations with human women); *The Goetia, or Lesser Key of Solomon*, also allegedly based on the Bible. Neither of these books had anything to do with the Bible. The Goetia is the main *grimoire* (book of "black" magic), and most traditional *grimoires* derive from this one. It recounts a popular medieval legend: that King Solomon employed demons for all sorts of work — from construction of his temple, to household chores, to exercising power over people and vanquishing his enemies. This book names and describes seventy-two basic fallen angels, and explains how each rules over large numbers of evil spirits and demons.

Here is the important point: At first, the field of demonology was instituted as a way for the Church officially to define — and relentlessly root out — all that was considered evil, nasty, and "godless." But as time went by and the demons became neatly classified, they began to seem controllable. Thus the *Goetia* delineates and advocates specific magical instructions for evoking Solomon's original demons and using them *for one's own ends.* After all, the name of Solomon had such a nice, Biblical-sounding ring that many people rationalized that they were working a "higher" sort of magic; when actually they were touching upon the negative path. The *Goetia* is still believed to be a primary source for ritual magic! And some occult circles still consider the *Book of Enoch* "accurate." (Actually the *Book of Enoch* has some *allegorical* value, as noted in Jung's "Answer to Job.")

I am amazed that these two remnants of medieval literature are still taken seriously. But many people seem to think that just because an occult book is old, the information in it is somehow valid. This belief hardly seems justifiable in the case of medieval works, since contemporary religious dogma so distorted research. I have carefully traced the development of negative magic up to this point, so that you can see exactly how all that is popularly known today as "black" magic came about. It has become so accessible, so misunderstood, and so widespread throughout our Western culture — in books, films, and the media — that it has given all of magic a bad name.

"Gray" Magic

The term "gray" magic evolved for magic which classified as neither white or nor black. Minor revenge would be considered a type of gray magic. By now, I hope you view gray magic as a contradiction in terms. It must be considered negative by our witch's definitions, and is best avoided.

Aleister Crowley: Any student of the occult — or shopper in an

53

occult bookstore — may encounter the work of (or references to) this controversial magician. Crowley lived at the turn of the last century and popularized the spelling of "magick." A self-styled ceremonial magician, Crowley delved deeply into sexual magical practices and drugs, had a devoted band of initiates and followers, wrote poetry, and enjoyed bizarre publicity. Crowley arouses controversy in the world of magic because he is so difficult to define: negative or positive? He had the title "Great Beast" printed on his calling cards, and several of the people closest to him suffered breakdowns and suicides. Yet no specific evidence seems to exist that he ever directly harmed anyone. Crowley seems to have considered himself a "white" magician, a scholar, a pagan, and a cabalist. He may seem an interesting figure to some, but my own personal Inner Bell tells me to avoid his teachings with a ten-foot-pole.

In general, the line between positive and negative work can be thin — but not too thin to be drawn clearly: ANY FORM OF MAGIC — RITUAL, CEREMONIAL, OR OTHERWISE — WHICH MANIPULATES OR HARMS ANY BEING, INCLUDING INVISIBLE BEINGS, IS UNEQUIVOCALLY NEGATIVE WORK. No matter what books or authorities you encounter in your studies, this definition should make everything clear as a bell.

Practices To Avoid:

1. Ritual renunciation of your own religion as a prerequisite to the magical work. Most popularly, this can take the form of reciting a traditional meaningful prayer *backwards*.
2. Desecration of any traditional holy object: a cross, Star of David, pentagram, etc. Such desecration could involve spitting on the object, trampling on it, otherwise befouling it, or simply *turning it upside down*.
3. Making *deals;* promising any entity — demon, "angel," spirit god, whatever — *anything*. This is not to be confused with devotional monotheistic or pagan rituals and prayers promising one's god to be good. Please note the difference: Negative work is full of negotiations and pacts, promising to do something *in exchange for* some specific "powerful" service.
4. Threatening any entity with harm if it does not obey.
5. Dancing counterclockwise *as a specific part of the work*. Harmless as it may seem, such dancing involves a traditional occult method of summoning up negative energies. It is known as "widdershins" and is designed to go against the turning of the Earth. Positive ceremonies in magic involve clockwise-directed dances ("deosil," or with the Earth.) (Some religions dance

54

traditionally in either direction, but this has nothing to do with magic circles and energy.)

6.   Any practice dealing with revenge, including so-called "minor" revenge spells — even if the recipient of the spell "deserves it." No true witch or positive magician attempts to right any wrong; we know that the laws of karma will take care of that adequately. *There is no such thing* as a "minor" revenge spell. All revenge is *major*.

7.   Any form of manipulation, including manipulating other people's thoughts, minds, lives, or manipulating a spirit or invisible being. Avoid even the use of recipes, herbs, and love potions to *influence* others in any way.

8.   Any ceremony or ritual involving cursing, "blasting," or wishing harm or bad luck to come about. Witches would extend this even to plants (blasting of crops). Wish no one and nothing ill, specifically *as part of your work*. It's advisable not to wish anyone or anything ill — in any case! However, if you have angry thoughts, you may acknowledge them, and always do work so that these thoughts have no negative power. (See p. 218).

9.   Use of another person's belongings, such as clothing, or an image (doll, photograph, etc.,) or anyone's bodily parts (fingernails, blood, etc.) for magical purposes.

10. Never allow anyone to do any magical work for you which you do not understand or like.

11. Never work in any language you do not understand completely. And never perform any magic unless you understand it completely — *including everything in this book!!*

12. Never go against your own Inner Bell.

The Contemporary Problems And Dangers: Modern Versions of Negative Magic

> There's a sucker born every minute.
> — P.T. Barnum

> True spirituality never advertises itself.
> —Dion Fortune[6]

During this particular Cusp period, negative magic exists in a variety of forms. Some of these may be obvious, the direct remnants of negative occult traditions. Others may seem elusive, disguised as modern movements and teachings of various kinds. I suggest that if you encounter any activity which deals with the human mind and human energies, you can assess its relative safety and effectiveness according to traditional occult definition. Whether it is categorized as a philosophy, mystical discipline, religion, school, technique, theory, therapy, or science, simply ask yourself: IS THIS HARMFUL TO ANYONE, OR MANIPULATIVE OF ANYONE — INCLUDING MYSELF? If the answer is *"yes,"* or even *"maybe,"* I suggest that you avoid it with a ten-foot-pole. There are always more positive ways of working with your life.

Satantic cults still exist (at the time of this writing) in varying degrees of religiosity and seriousness. They may range from theatrical flamboyance, seeming mainly for entertainment purposes, to more organized depravity. Often they pander to a deep need for rebellion. Fortunately modern cults are far tamer than their blood medieval counterparts, and murder is a rarity today. The main lure is perverted power and license for license — some people still seem to feel a need for Satan's say-so in order to have an open and free sex life. Some groups are formed specifically for orgies, mate-swapping, or sado-masochistic activity as part of the "rites." Some groups perform specific negative ritual services for a fee (as opposed to positive ritual services which are traditionally free).

Negative ceremonial groups may still exist also. Some openly call themselves "black" magic and deal (or attempt to deal) with demons. Other groups may call themselves anything from "white" magic to "witchcraft," and may not even understand the negative nature of their work. Please note that it doesn't matter whether the work is spelled "magic" or "magick." Negative or positive work can use either spelling.

Instructions for negative ceremonies may be found in books — again, either directly labelled as such or misleadingly labelled "white" magic or "witchcraft." If you examine the content and style of the work itself you will be able to tell what's what.

Occult "rip-off" refers to the commercial exploitation of magic in negative ways. A (positive) ceremonial magician I know aptly calls this area "occult pollution." In my view, it is a Cusp phenomenon — a Piscean exploitation of an Aquarian trend. You could call it "magic for a price."

Occult shops can provide a delicate area. We need shops in which to buy accurate occult books, appropriate tools and jewelry. But we might well hesitate to buy our candles, incense, pentagrams and other items in any store also selling "voodoo kits" (dolls complete with pins for harming and cursing); recordings of "genuine" Black Masses to be performed on one's stereo; and similar products. I do not want to contribute financial support to a store which perpetuates negative work — even negative paraphernalia solid as jokes or curios. Incidentally, any occult object must be labelled "to be sold as a curio (or souvenir) only." No power resides in an object — a piece of jewelry, a talisman, candle, crystal ball, whatever — except for the power invested in it *by the user*. Positive magicians and witches usually bless their jewelry and tools or consecrate these according to each specific belief. Adepts understand fully that any material object is a symbol of a higher Power and not powerful in itself. Believing that power dwells in an object is superstition.

An occult object or piece of jewelry can be at best a beautifully crafted work of art, to be imbued by your own belief and transformed by your own personal power. At worst, such an object can be a vastly overpriced piece of junk for which the seller claims "holiness," "luck," or some specific power such as the ability to ward off evil spirts or attract love. Examine the price tag. Often the most beautiful magical objects may be found in nature, a seashell or stone. If you come across one that has meaning to you, you may choose to carry it or wear it as your own amulet. Such objects are appropriate symbols for positive magic, which draws upon the beneficent forces of nature.

Watch out for mail-order courses which profess to "make" you into anything, such as a witch or psychic. These are not titles; they are states of being. The proof of magic and the occult lies in the doing, and the power comes from within. Titles come from without.

Beware of manipulative, overpriced psychic readers. See p. 155 for what to look for and what to avoid in a psychic reader.

Try to avoid the inaccurate books; it's hard to know where to begin defining these. The worst are the "instructional" variety which include come-ons such as "MAGIC LOVE POTION RECIPES!" "CURSES AND SPELLS!" "BEND OTHERS TO YOUR WILL!" Also many books may be less dangerous, but a waste of time and money — books claiming expertise that consists of rough conglomerations of sources many times removed from accurate information. The books recommended here as supplementary reading for each chapter should give you a pretty clear guideline to authentic information and enable you to steer clear of rip-offs.

Media exploitation can be filled with blatant misinformation about the occult; unfortunately, film and television can play vividly on human emotions; with sensational impact. Please remember that horror films are simply entertainment, and their goal is to give the audience a good scare and not necessarily to tell the truth about the occult. A genuine coven of witches quietly working their Words of Power in someone's living room do not offer the excitement of "demonic possession," screaming, blood, murder, and much scary music. Horror movies derive their impact from the fears lurking in our culture's collective unconscious. Our society doesn't provide much else in the way of ritual release of this fear, nor of the negative powers within the human psyche, so these are externalized and ritually experienced in the movie theater or in front of the t.v. screen.

"New" cultural phenomena in this Cusp time may not necessarily appear to be occult in form, but they still may be judged according to occult criteria. The forms may have changed, but the essence of the work remains the same: The Invisible World is being used to deal with the visible, World of Form. The new terms may be: self-improvement, self-help, enlightenment, development of awareness, sensitivity training, human potential, and mind training. The new forms may present themselves as social groups, radical psychologies, philosophies, meditation techniques, new religions, new versions of old religions, Western versions of Eastern religions, mystical cults, physical therapies (massage, biofeedback, conditioning devices), psychic training organizations; and others. Such forms represent a burgeoning *industry,* which as yet has not been subject to informed controls of any kind. The information about negative and positive magic in this book can help you to assess these new areas of culture. If applying ancient occult principles to "modern" ideas seems odd, look more closely and you can see that these ideas are not modern. What is modern is the *form* (the trappings) which may provide a disguise: publicity, advertising, public relations, corporate organization, image. Often the price tag is pretty modern too. But what is old as the hills is the lure: quick and easy solutions to life's mysterious problems, a cure for a diminished sense of the self, and promises of power and mystery of the Invisible as it manifests in the Visible.

What is also old as the hills may be the employment of negative occult techniques. For example, the name of Satan, or explicit demons, may not be used. But the concept of making pacts or deals with a power figure may be. Satan's role has been as an authority figure, specifically representing easy personal power. The idea of Satan himself may be ridiculous to us. But today many people nonetheless accept the authority of any person (or organization) making a convincing sales pitch, promising total power and control over their lives in return for money and obeisance. Such behavior is a version of the same veneration and eager acceptance of authority which medieval people felt when they sought the help of the devil to cure all their woes.

Manipulation of the human mind is a negative occult technique. Mind-manipulation may take the form of an outright curse — or the comparatively "minor" form of gaining control of another person for one's own ends. *A curse is nothing more than a combination of hypnotic suggestion and ESP* (extra sensory perception). Other forms of mind-manipulation may also be accomplished silently. Hypnosis and ESP are ancient occult methods, and may be used either negatively or positively. In earlier times, people turned over the control of their conscious minds to the leader, and then subconsciously followed the leader's spoken or silent commands, instructions, moods, ideas, suggestions. I believe that some modern mind-training groups make use of this process today — whether the leaders understand specifically what methods they are using or not.

Group hypnosis may be achieved easily when a roomful of people turn over their individual sense of power (conscious control of their minds) to the leader's authority — even temporarily. Group hypnosis is facilitated by any "ritual" technique — from ancient chants to modern count-down spiels.[7] Then, once this state of group hypnosis is achieved, the group is receptive enough to accept any programming from the leader. The programming need not take the form of obvious commands; it need not even be said aloud; it can be *thought*. This is where ESP comes in. The leader can either think specific commands and directive phrases, or simply transfer any indirect ideas floating around in his/her head.[8]

A witness to such a procedure would not notice any overt "brainwashing" unless he/she were a *psychic* witness. Much can be happening without our hearing or seeing. The message which goes on at this level usually involves a few basic ideas.

1. This group is a wonderful organization, and its leader is wonderful, a genius, a guru.
2. I feel wonderful because of this work, and my life is immediately better.
3. I must now encourage others to join in this work.

Now, some positive input happens here specifically in point 2 (above) "I feel wonderful." That belief alone, experienced at a subconscious level, is enough of a causation to manifest in more positive behavior and consequently a more positive life process. *But the rest of it — and the form of it — is pure manipulation.* And in the grand old negative occult tradition, such work serves to nourish the group's existence by drawing upon human energies (including money) and directing these towards perpetuating the group itself.

A social danger also exists to beware of. It is part of the negative occult tradition for a leader to seek power on a large scale. This psychological pitfall can be a consequence of manipulating other people's energies and minds. Thus a religious or cult leader may have political aspirations. Such a leader may have started out with the simple intention to make money, or even to dispense self-help or enlightenment on a broad scale. But if the work is done according to negative occult techniques, the leader may succumb to a growing "need" for power. So watch, too for hidden — or overt — political industrial affiliations associated with the growth of such a group.

How does such manipulative programming effect the individual? This question can be complex, because often there seems to be some immediate improvement in the person's life. Such a result may be ascribed to the fact that *some positive occult techniques* may be interspersed with the work. For example, it is helpful to learn that we are all responsible for our lives and are not at the mercy of fate. But be wary of the side effects. The very idea of handing over custodial power of one's psyche to *another person (authority figure) — even temporarily — is antithetical to the concept of developing any real power of the inner self.* If the technique involves subtle submission of the self, then the result can be any related side effect: submission, resignation, servility, rigidity — various negative modes of approach to life's problems. If the technique involves physical deprivation or discomfort, then the result can eventually manifest in directly related side effects such as masochism or even physical symptoms. For example, some modern "conditioning" methods in hypnotherapy include *negative suggestions* to combat negative habits such as drinking, smoking, and over-eating. Instructions might include: "Every time you want to drink (smoke, over eat), you will feel nauseated (think of garbage, feel ill.)" These negative associations can create the desired *immediate* effect, but they can perpetuate the problem by leaving the basic emotional cause unresolved. The problem may then manifest in some other "unrelated" area of the person's life.

More dramatically, neuroses and psychoses, including hysteria and schizophrenia, have long been traditional side effects of negative occult work. Most probably the individuals involved were unstable originally, but the speed of psychic transformation involved with negative work no doubt served as a catalyst to set off mental imbalance. Positive occultists know that opening up "unused" psychic areas of the mind must be a gradual process in order to avoid delusionary mental states. Negative occultists categorically sought delusionary states, so that people would believe immediately that they were better off.

Positive occultists have always made serious attempts to evaluate individual emotional capacity, rate of progress, absorption of the techniques, or integration of the work with the entire personality.

Some new organizations encourage work in the astral plane, specifically communication with "imaginary" entities. Anyone participating in such work would do well to have a firm foundation in occult time and space concepts. The person also requires a clear awareness that specific entities might try to enter a person's thoughts in intrusive ways if positive controls (see p. 63) are not clearly set up before such work begins.

I am not saying that all modern groups, organizations, courses, etc. for development of the human energies and mind are dangerous. I am

60

saying that some of them *can* be dangerous, and the dangers are too serious to be ignored. It is important to acknowledge that while an influx of mass mental and psychic activity has emerged in our culture, no controls have been set up to protect the public, no responsible statistical analysis has been made to evaluate the results, and not enough time has yet elapsed to study the long-term effects.

However, if you are exploring some of these methods, watch out for these specific points:

1. Be wary of salespitches. Does manipulation or coercion enter into the way the work is presented? Do you find an eagerness to sign you up, get a commitment (a sizeable deposit), without respecting your right to consider the matter at your own discretion?

2. Note the mood of the organization. Are there hordes of people involved? How much personal instruction is available? Does the organization respect the rate of each person's progress or is it a hurry-up, results-guaranteed affair?

3. What is the group leader like? What are his/her credentials?

4. What are the personal instructors like? What are their credentials? "...former salesmen who have had a few courses in hypnotic programming are not qualified to work in this very delicate area of the human psyche."[9]

5. Speak to others who have already participated. Do they repeat key phrases of praise for their experience? Watch carefully for this, and note that parroting may be a symptom of a well-washed brain. Try to get these people to tell about their individual experiences instead. Are they able to do this thoughtfully? If so, this is a good sign.

6. Does the group require ongoing participation of people who have already "mastered" the work — to the extent of actively recruiting new customers? Do these people provide time-consuming free salesmanship for the organization? If so, ask them *why* they "choose" to do this. (And watch for repetitive key phrases again or an irrational zeal).

7. Does the group place heavy emphasis on a specific (rigid, higher, or "holier") authority figure — guru, leader, teacher? Is such emphasis built into the actual work process? *Can authority be challenged?* Does the group provide ample opportunity to question the methods, techniques, theories of work or does it have an implicit attitude of "we know what is best for you"?

8. Can you observe any negative techniques, especially in the beginning exercises or instructions? These might include obvious personal insults, put-downs, tearing-down of egos — or less

obvious giving of orders, bullying, threatening, and general *reinforcement of diminished sense of self*. (Such techniques usually pave the way for the final illusion of "building up the self" at the conclusion of the work).

9. Does the process involve any severe physical discomfort or pain? Mental or emotional pain?

10. Is *hypnosis* part of the process without being fully acknowledged as such (this includes countdown, see p. 59)? Hypnosis *per se* may be a valid tool, if used by qualified professionals and adequately explained beforehand as integral to the work. (If not, hypnosis is being used in a manipulative manner).

11. Does any aspect of the work "go against" a personal belief, conviction, or religious concept? If so, are your feelings respected? (Always listen to your Inner Bell).

12. Does the process project an air of mystery, secrecy, of things not explained? Are you instructed or encouraged to do any work you do not fully understand (including chanting in another language without adequate translation)?

13. Is there any responsible assessment or screening process of each applicant's physical, emotional, and mental state before admission? Or is money the only prerequisite to doing the work?

14. How do you feel about the people participating? Do they seem intelligent, balanced, thoughtful, aware? Or is there an underlying mood of desperation, or an apparent inability or unwillingness to think things over?

15. Does the group tacitly discourage members from continuing close relationships with nonconverts and encourage members to recruit everyone in their lives?

16. Is any form of intimidation or dominance over others encouraged by the work?

17. Does the group place emphasis on affiliations with celebrities, politicians, industry?

Please think of some questions for yourself. Apply them all to the work in this book, too. Investigate, research, inquire, ask questions. In other words, *use your own mind*. Be responsible to your mind. Do not settle for less than you deserve. Do not compromise yourself in any way. New movements and methods pop up almost at every moment. This is part of the excitement — and part of the danger — of the Cusp time.

I believe that in the Aquarian Age, the concept of self-responsibility and enlightened mastery of one's own life will be common knowledge. No one will be coerced into paying a high price for it, demeaning the self in order to learn it, or knuckling under to some authority figure in order to figure it all out. Meanwhile, in our consumer society, most of us have learned to shop around and assess all our major investments of time and money. We do not fall for the loudest sales pitch. We are careful when we buy cars, television sets, electrical appliances. We are careful when we select *services* also — schools, piano lessons, dentists, doctors, psychiatrists. Now we need to be just as careful, intelligent, discreet and responsible when embarking on each personal occult journey.

Psychic Protection

No matter what form of mind work or occult work you may enter into, or have already participated in, please bear in mind that you can make any experience positive if you take responsibility for the experience and realize that it was your choice. Remember that it is *you* who interpret, assimilate, define, and apply that experience for yourself. Even if you have participated in work you now perceive as negative, *simply take responsibility. Do not judge or blame yourself, and determine to turn the experience to positive ends.* (A simplistic way of saying this is, "We can learn from our mistakes as well as our triumphs.") Then let the whole experience go, giving it less importance in your own life, and turn your attention to serious *positive* work. As the *I Ching* says, "Finally, the best way to fight evil is to make energetic progress in the good" (Hexagram 43, Book One).

Here is a Words of Power Statement (phrased according to the positive Occult Principles in Chapter VIII) which will deal effectively with any problems or side effects resulting from negative work:

Words Of Power For Releasing Negative Occult Work:

There is One Power
Which is positive, infinite Good,
And I, (your name here), am a perfect manifestation of this Power;
I hereby reaffirm my life and total existence as a positive exper-
    ience only.
I now dissolve and release every negative influence, cause and
    effect, Visible and Invisible;
And replace it with positive Good, and turn it to positive Good.
I take full responsibility for my acts, as well as for my receptivity to
any negativity in the past — without judging myself.
And I now redirect my life, taking full responsibility for my positive
    direction — backwards and forwards in time.
According to free will,
For the good of all,

I TURN THIS TO GOOD.
And so it must be!

You will see in Chapter VII how this Statement was composed, and how to compose your own version or make any appropriate variations. For now, note that it applies both to: 1 - the responsibility of having participated in negative work and 2 - having been the possible "victim" of negative work. ("I take full responsibility for my acts as well as for my *receptivity to any negativity...*")

One final point: *Atheism can be dangerous* because it can leave a gap in people's natural psychic protective mechanisms. This does not mean that one must conform to any specific religious dogma. It simply means that it can be dangerous to see one's life as consistently meaningless and as totally exclusive of the rest of the Cosmos. Most religions have built into them some ancient forms of "magical protection." This is why prayers may seem to "work" in moments of danger — even when people pray according to religions other than their own, or turn back to beliefs they thought they had discarded. Every religion includes some sort of Higher Power concept. And any realignment of the self with that High Power (yes, as in prayer) is a powerful form of psychic protection.

In fact, many cases of psychic attack have occurred simply because the victims had reacted so violently to some limited form of rigid religious upbringing that they never paused to investigate or reassess their own personal beliefs. Such people simply dispensed with *all* belief. Hence the "psychic gap" — a complete lack of psychic protection. Rev. John Scudder, a psychic healer, made this point on my radio show. He claimed that a number of such cases came to his attention because these unfortunates actually reached the point where they required some form of exorcism. So if you were born into a religion to which you no longer can relate, please do not entirely remove religion from your life. A person can believe in God, Goddess, Christ, Gods, Power, Life, People, the Universe, Buddha, Krishna, whatever you choose — no matter what you call It.

Since the early Middle Ages, some versions of Western religions may have, shall we say, lost something in the translation. I suggest the reintegration of occult beliefs into, and along with, many existing religious beliefs. Danger may result from renouncing one's religion, trampling on the cross, or reciting anything holy backwards. Positive occult work isn't *instead of* — it's *in addition to* — everything else that's spiritual and uplifting in one's karmic inheritance. Only you will be able to interpret this idea for yourself.

In this chapter, I have explained that which is negative in occult work, in its various expressions. It is naive and dangerous to disregard the negative forces in the Universe, but it is completely unnecessary to fear

64

them, because fear lends power to the feared object. The classic occult technique for dealing with evil is to recognize it, release it, and then "make energetic progress in the good."

The rest of the this book wil be devoted to the practice of *positive, magic.*

¹C.G. Jung, *Aion, Researches into the Phenomenology of the Self, The Collected Works of C.G. Jung,* Bollingen Series XX Pantheon Books, Vol. 9, Part II, New York, 1959, p. 42.

²As Doreen Valiente states succinctly in *An ABC of Witchcraft, Past and Present,* St. Martin's Press, New York, 1973, p. 83: "The belief in a rebellious Satan as the Power of Evil has always been contrary to the text in Issiah, Chapter 45, verse 7: 'I form the light and create darkness; I make peace, and create evil; I the Lord do all these things.'"

³See Doreen Valiente, *An ABC of Witchcraft, Past and Present,* pp. 81-87, and Gustav Davidson, *A Dictionary of Angels,* The Free Press, Macmillan and Co., New York, 1971, pp. xiv-xvii, 261 and 176.

⁴See Doreen Valiente's *An ABC of Witchcraft, Past and Present,* pp. 205-207 for an excellent definition and distinction drawn between invocation and evocation. Note her emphasis on the point that invocation has the built-in goal of raising the consciousness of the magician.

⁵Sympathetic magic is a symbolic act performed in miniature, which is believed to have a larger effect at a distance. The most common example of a negative sympathetic magic ritual is the sticking of pins into a doll in order to affect the represented person.

⁶Dion Fortune, *The Mystical Qabalah,* Ernest Benn Ltd., London, 1974, p. 10.

⁷"The 'count-down' induction procedure used in commercial mind training 'programming' is a classical hypnotic technique." Elmer and Alyce Green, *PSI, The Other World Catalogue,* Regush, Putnam, New York, 1974, p. 149. It may also be facilitated when the entire group energies are focused on one specific mental exercise, on spoken directives by one specific person. (For example, exercises to "close your eyes" and picture this or that).

⁸Ibid, p. 150. This can manifest in "the instructor effect": "Apparently a kind of psychic 'transference' phenomenon can occur, a kind of 'psychic pollution' can take place due to the unconscious receptivity of the subject to 'extra sensory projection' by the hypnotist."

⁹Ibid, p. 150.

Chapter IV

WITCHCRAFT, A LIVING HERITAGE

Witchcraft, as we have to remember when considering any aspect of it, is primarily a religion. It has its creed, its system of ethics, its rituals.....

The story of the beginnings of witchcraft may be the story of the involution of the concept of spirit — non-material power — in human consciousness.

—Justine Glass[1]

Witchcraft is, quite specifically, an ancient Celtic magic-religion. Translated directly from the Celtic *Wicca Craft,* it means "craft of the wise," or "craft of the dedicated":

Probably the term evolved because witches had their own cultural heritage and were among the first literate members of the European community. Some people still call it "Wicca" or The Craft. In the British Isles, where the religion first became firmly established, people often refer to witchcraft simply as "The Old Religion."

Related traditions in Hawaiian, Mexican, and African cultures have been translated inaccurately into English as "witchcraft"; some interesting parallels may be drawn between these and Celtic witchcraft. But the witchcraft I shall be discussing here is Western — the original Celtic tradition which spread with few variations all through Europe for centuries, and has even reached the United States. Witchcraft has existed in the form still practiced today for approximately 6,000 years. It predates all contemporary forms of monotheism and at first glance seems definable as a pagan religion.

But should we classify witchcraft as pagan or monotheistic? Witchcraft is so old that it defies defining in modern terms. First, it is not exclusively a religion in the modern sense because witchcraft dates from that early time when religion, theater, art, philosophy, science and magic were all part of the same package. And as for being pagan or monotheistic: Oddly enough, witchcraft may be viewed as both. It is monotheisitic because it is based on an underlying belief in One Life Force, One Power over all, One Essence or One Energy Source of the Universe. But witchcraft also qualifies as pagan because it acknowledges two primary aspects of deity: feminine and masculine, the Goddess and the God. Further, witchcraft is also polytheistic because it affirms that the One Power manifests in *every* life form — not only deities, but in all human, all animal, all spirit life, and all forces of nature.

In contrast to modern monotheistic religions, witchcraft does not posit a heaven or a hell. The Old Religion acknowledges the Invisible World and the World of Form, giving equal importance to both. Enormous confusion has existed between witchcraft and assorted folk supersitions. Many nonadepts who acknowledge the Invisible World also fear it on some level, and most supersititious practices are often aimed at placating Invisible forces. But witches do not fear the Invisible. They simply accept it as a reality; thus, they can work with it. Much of the work of witchcraft, deemed so mysterious, is actually a detailed system of working with the Invisible in practical ways. The witch's focus is directing the Invisible so that it will manifest in the World of Form — in people's lives — to make life on this Earth Plane more positive. I believe that the techniques and the underlying philosophy are still valid today, workable in modern life, and easily adaptable for any responsible person with an open mind.

However, actually to be a witch requires a certain aptitude as well as full-time dediction, commitment and belief. If someone "thinks" he/she has paranormal powers, or has an unusual telepathic experience, that does not a witch make. The witch's proverbial and much-misunderstood "powers" are a combination of natural psychic aptitude plus careful development according to the Craft traditions.

In contrast to more recent religions and philosophies (of the past 4,000 years), witchcraft somehow seems to have evolved organically; no known teacher or leader initiated the beliefs or the structure of the Craft. In the same way, each witch develops his/her mastery of the witchcraft arts, organically and individually. Numerous sects of witchcraft exist, but they all have certain basic traditions in common: *1 - reverence for all nature; 2 - belief in the existence of Goddess as well as God; 3 - belief in a Power which unifies Visible and Invisible forces; 4 - the use of the Threefold Law.*

1 · Reverence For All Nature: In earlier times, this included an emphasis on fertility. One could say that the roots of witchcraft are similar to many early fertility-oriented nature religions. Obviously, early agrarian life — and survival — focused on fertility and nature. Accordingly, witchcraft addressed itself to the needs of the early European primitive community.

The traditional work of the witch has always included (what is now known as) astrology, telepathy, telekinisis, astral travel, precognition, divination, weather prediction and weather control, fertility control, blessing of plants and crops, spirit contact, psychological counseling, hypnotism and healing, the latter both psychic and physical. Witches studied medicinal herbs extensively and were among the world's first midwives. The early pagans in field and town often found themselves frightened by the vicissitudes of raw life on this planet. Often they found themselves unable to deal with birth, death, sickness, crop failure, drought, etc. Then the people turned to the witch — as expert, helper, or "Wiccan" (wise one).

2 · Belief in the Existence of Goddess as Well as God: Philosophically, this belief represents an understanding of the importance of the female aspects of nature, of the Universe. Many pagan traditions included worship of many goddesses, but in witchcraft there has always been only one primal Goddess figure. In modern times, in the West, a deep reverence for deity as female is still unique to witchcraft; patriarchy never touched the foundations of witch theology. If there is a God, there must also be a Goddess. Neither is more important than the other, both are in balance, together they create a Whole. Both Their aspects are manifest in everyone and in all life.

The belief in Goddess is a source of Power because it helps us to understand and to draw upon a specific source of Universal energy involving fertility and birth. Many nonadepts consider this source very mysterious, probably because patriarchal beliefs have so categorically denied its existence. This Power source, which the Goddess represents, is the inheritance of male and female witch alike.

It is important to realize how compatible witchcraft was with the beliefs of the heathen (i.e., people who lived on the heaths) of early Europe. All the early Western religions worshipped an assortment of gods and goddesses; among these a major female and male deity usually could be viewed as comparable to the witch's Goddess or God.

3 · The Unifying Power — Visible and Invisible: All these pre-Christian peoples believed in the reality of the Invisible World and in the existence of Invisible forces in nature. Witchcraft fit right into all the other forms of early paganism — on the surface. But beneath the surface, witchcraft differed in the basic spiritual and operative concepts which gave the witches their special "powers."

Most pagans who acknowledged the Invisible World both revered and feared the forces of nature. The witches acknowledged the Invisible World, yet revered *and connected with* the forces of nature. The witch philosophy embraces *one cohesive link* between human life and all life, including Invisible forces. Witches believe that the One Power may manifest either invisibly or visibly, throughout nature, and that humans are simply one type of manifestation of this original Power source. Thus the witch has always felt at one with all of life, at the most basic level. The witch believes that no outside source of power need be feared to the extent that it cannot be understood — and dealt with — at the root level of the One, All-encompassing Power.

Craft may be defined as "an art," "a skill," or "an occupation requiring special skill." The Craft of the witch encompasses the heightened use of human energies as aligned with natural forces — for positive ends.

I have often been asked how witches worship. But most witches do not "worship" in the accepted sense. More accurately, a witch considers worship and work synonymous; both are accomplished simultaneously. The emphasis is not on adoration, supplication, or entreaty of a Higher Power. Instead, the witches' focus is on the heightened awareness of their *connection* to the Higher Power. This is often achieved on a psychic level, but it can manifest in physical ways as well.

4 - The Threefold-Law: the basic working philosophy of witchcraft. This Law states that *everything you do comes back to you three times.* For example, if a witch cast a prosperity spell blessing a farmer's crops, equivalent prosperity would come back to the witch in three ways. If a witch cast a spell for harming the crops, three times would harm come back to the witch — each time affecting the witch in the same way as the blighted crops affect the farmer. The number three symbolizes one of the magical processes involved: 1. the spell is said and sent out into the Invisible; 2. the spell comes back into the World of Form to manifest in the desired way; 3. the spell reverberates in the life of the person working the magic (as the "side-effect"). The Threefold Law keeps the magic positive, life-affirming, and harmful to none. Following the Law, one may expand one's psychic energies fully, understanding that no harm will come back and that good will multiply organically.

The Threefold Law is unique to witchcraft and the only statement in the entire religion remotely resembling a commandment or a rule. But the law cannot be considered religious dogma nor abstract philosophy. To the witch, the Threefold Law constitutes a natural, integral fact of life. Witches attempt to live by this Law every moment. Once one has experienced the powerful effects of the Threefold Law for working magic, one cannot forget about it in daily life. The use of this Law offers a huge source of Power to the witch — and anyone can use the Law if he/she believes in it. (See "Cause and Effect" as a basic Principle of occult work, Chapter VIII, p. 251).

Craft Structure

At one time, witchcraft was primarily a family-oriented hereditary religion. Hereditary witch families which trace their ancestry back thousands of years, are still in existence. The Craft has a strong belief in reincarnation, which leads many witches to believe that families may be reunited over many lifetimes. In fact, some groups still do specific work to control their reincarnations, to be reborn again and again amongst their loved ones.

Witchcraft is a sociable religion; witches consider group energy integral to much of the work. Therefore, witches traditionally worship and work together in *covens*. These are usually ongoing groups of thirteen or fewer members; more than thirteen becomes unwieldy for close and harmonious group work. The number thirteen comes from many mystical sources; most obviously it echoes the thirteen lunar months in the year. Nonadepts usually consider the number thirteen unlucky, possibly because they fear witches and all that was associated with the Craft. Actually, the number of members varies from group to group. One ideal coven structure traditionally consists of "six loving couples" to represent the balance of female to male. Since the medieval persecutions, numerous witchcraft sects have evolved with varying customs. Some sects may have a coven leader or two coven leaders: the High Priestess and High Priest. In the case of the hereditary witch families, the position of leader may be inherited. In other groups, leadership may be earned or may be an elected position. The group leaders generally perform an inspirational and symbolic function for the rest of the coven, because there is no hierarchy in witchcraft. The witch leaders do not function as intermediaries with higher powers, as witches believe that "all women are Goddess Incarnate; all men are God Incarnate." In keeping with this idea, many groups take turns, with each member acting as leader for a short period of time. And some covens have no leaders at all.

Witchcraft is a religion which places a strong emphasis on free will. Not every member of an hereditary family necessarily becomes a witch; some embrace other religious faiths. Some witches *(solitaries)* work alone, the traditional "wise woman" or "wise man" in a village, with no coven and not another witch in sight. Today, many people study and form their own covens and groups, re-interpreting the traditions. There is no one official way to become a witch, other than to believe in and do the work.

Basic Beliefs

All work in the Craft centers upon the principle of One Power existing over all and within all beings. This Power is symbolically divided into the female and male principles: the Goddess and the God. In many sects today, the Goddess assumes paramount importance. And it may seem to the nonadept that witchcraft is by definition a matriarchal religion because of belief in the Goddess, a surprising idea for our patriarchal culture! Actually, I believe that the two aspects of deity — female and male — basically balance in the witch theology. Perhaps the Goddess concept in the Craft evolved in some way from earliest matriarchal times. In any case, She goes by many names, including Diana, Keridwenn (Cerridwen), Artemis, Isis, Hecate, Cybele, and Selene, or simply the Great Mother or the Lady. Some of the earliest Christian converts continued to worship Her by the "Christianized" names of Brigid and Mary. Possibly numerous pagans rationalized their conversions to Christianity by believing that they still worshipped their beloved Goddess in the new identity of the Virgin Mary, Saint Brigid, or some personal female saint. In fact, many shrines and places of worship once considered sacred to the Goddess became the building sites of early medieval Christian churches specifically dedicated to the Virgin Mary. The Goddess's symbol is the moon, and silver is Her sacred metal.

The male principal in witchcraft is called the Horned God. No, the God of the witches is not the devil; but His representation is often a man with goatlike horns and feet, and He is often symbolized by a goat.

He is also called the Goat-foot God and clearly evolved from the figure of Pan, the nature deity of classical times. His Craft names include Pan, Osiris, and Cernunnos (Kernunnos). Although this latter name is considered to be secret by some witchcraft sects, I do not feel I am betraying any secrets by naming Him here. Anthropologists have been referring to Cernunnos openly for years as the divinity of some "ancient sects." Ancient, yes — but not defunct. His sects are alive and well, and flourishing today. Often witches refer to Him simply as the Horned One or the Old One. (Christians later picked up these names to refer to the devil.) His symbol is the sun, and fire is considered to be under His dominion.

It is difficult to convey the roles of the Goddess and the Horned God in witch culture. The Goddess has power over fertility in crops, animals, and people. She embodies the female principal of nurturing, protection, nourishment, birth and productivity of the Earth. Her aspects are quite complex. She is also known as the Threefold Goddess — a concept echoed in ancient legend and myth as the Three Fates, the Three Graces,[2] and others. Her three aspects of Virgin, Matron and Crone represent the turning of the seasons, the phases of the moon, the cyclical nature of all life forms. Do witches believe in a literal Goddess divinity? Some do, in the anthropomorphic sense, but most see Her as a symbol of the female aspects of the Power inherent in every woman — *and* in every man.

Similarly, the Horned God may be a literal divinity to some. But to most witches He represents, symbolically, the initiating life-force, that spark of primal fire and the essential phallic, creative energy in all men — *and* in all women. Witches realized long before modern psychiatrists that both male and female attributes belong to each person.

Symbols are very important in the Craft, and the Goddess and the Horned God do function as symbols. Witches who revere the Horned God as the sun, and as the goat, have always revered the Power behind these symbols rather than the symbols themselves. Similarly, the witches revere the Power that moves the moon rather than the moon itself. Thus the symbol serves an important psychological and parapsychological purpose in the work, as it becomes the link between the microcosm (the witch) and the Macrocosm (the Universe). As Justine Glass says, "The witches believe that the symbolic representation of a power forms a channel between men's unconscious and the power behind the symbol, and that his awakened imagination enables him to make contact with it."[3]

Witches believe that we live in two Worlds, the World of Form and the Invisible Realm. The Power exists in both Worlds, and we may move our focus freely between both.

This brings us to the importance of the circle in witch symbolism:

Most of the work begins with drawing a circle used to connect the two Worlds. The witches stand on its periphery or just within. Thus we encompass, touch, connect, and draw upon — *raise* — the Power of both Worlds. Witches realize that we *always* somehow stand between and within both Worlds, but the concentrated use of the circle ritually intensifies concentration and aids in the work.

A cone symbolizes raising the Power — (the Cone of Power). Witches stand "in Circle" and raise the Cone of Power psychically, focus it, and send it out for a specific purpose. Usually, the purpose of the work is to bring about helpful manifestations in people's lives — in the World of Form. This can include blessings, healings, abundance, fertility, love, protection, and safety. The traditional witch's hat also symbolizes the Cone of Power. The principle of using the cone as an energizing shape relates to the concept of "pyramid power," which recently has been rediscovered.

It is important to note the difference between the witch's magic circle and the ceremonial or ritual magician's magic circle. For the witch, the Power emanates from the people doing the work, and the function of the circle is to connect the Visible and Invisible Worlds. Ceremonial magicians usually draw upon power from an outside source — demon or angel — and the function of the circle is to protect the magician from negative forces. In negative, "black" magic, the magician would not dare step outside the circle, believing that no demon would dare to step inside.

Circles also appear in witch imagery in relation to time. The image of the year is represented visually (spatially) as a *Wheel or Yule* (ancient Celtic). As the Wheel turns, the holidays may be seen as the "spokes," in the Wheel, which mark important turning points of the seasons. The eight witchcraft holidays are called the *Sabbats*. They are the same days as the pagan festivals all over Europe, and you may notice that many important Christian (and some Jewish) holidays fall within a few days' time of most of them. There are several reasons for this. Historians believe that the Church placed Christian holy days right on or close to these ancient celebrations because the peasants related more easily to their new Christian celebrations at these times. I believe magic is in the air on these Holidays. Call it spirituality, call it religious feeling, call it the power of the collective unconscious, call it astrological influence — an important invisible force is present, to which we find it difficult *not* to respond emotionally.

Early agricultural communities in Europe considered these pagan Holidays important turning points of the season, but for the witches the meanings of these days are significant on a deeper level. These are the *astrological* turning points, and each one marks important shifts in invisible forces on this planet. These realignments of planetary influences and invisible tides of energy are propitious times to work magic. Each Holiday has inherent specific "vibrations" or attributes which witches draw upon for raising the Power, especially in group work. Also, the male and female forces in nature are believed to shift their balance of power for each seasonal change, symbolized by each Sabbat. Generally speaking, the Goddess rules spring and summer, and the God rules fall and winter.[4]

Here are the basic meanings of the eight witch's Sabbats:

• HALLOWEEN, October 31, or *Samhain*, is dedicated to the idea of eternal life, specifically our connection with those who have departed the World of Form and now live in the Invisible World. The symbolism marks the transcendence of physical death. On this day the "veil" connecting the two worlds is said to be so thin that our loved ones on the other side can easily join us in joyous celebration, worship, and work. Many witches consider this New Year's Day. This holiday also marks the Third and final Harvest of the year.

• THE WINTER SOLSTICE, December 20-23, is the longest night and the shortest day of the year. The fire force of life (the sun) may *seem* to disappear, but it begins immediately to grow stronger as the days grow longer. Thus *rebirth* becomes an important theme at this time. This holiday is also called *Yule* because the Wheel of the Year begins to turn again as the days grow longer. Many traditional "Christmas" symbols — the tree, the Yule log, holly, and red candles are ancient Winter Solstice pagan and witch symbols. This holiday also marks the astrological turning point from Sagittarius into Capricorn.

• CANDLEMAS, February 2, or the *Feast of the Waxing Light*, signifies the first stirring of plant life beneath the earth (plant life symbolizing all life).

•THE SPRING EQUINOX, March 20-23, marks the equality of time — day and night — and the exact balance of female to male forces in nature. It is the astrological turning point from Pisces to Aries.

•BELTANE, May 1, is a super-fertility holiday. The influence of the Goddess flourishes, and all the forces of spring are manifest. This holiday stands exactly opposite Halloween on the calendar and on the witch's Wheel of the Year. I was happy to hear recently that there are deserted country fields where witches still dance and leap on their brooms over seeded crops, symbolically to nourish plant growth. My city coven leaps over a special houseplant on this night to aid symbolically all our indoor "crops" to bloom. You might try this too, and watch your own plants tune into this joyous activity and flourish!

• THE SUMMER SOLSTICE, June 20-23, marks the counterpart of the Winter Solstice; it is the year's longest day and shortest night. It is

the astrological turning point from Gemini to Cancer.

● LAMMAS, August 2, celebrates the beginning of autumn — the First Harvest.

● THE FALL EQUINOX, September 20-23, marks the moment of equal day, equal night, as the year turns to winter. Again, male and female forces in nature stand in perfect balance. It is the astrological turning point from Virgo to Libra and the Second Harvest.

And so the Wheel turns.

Between these eight Sabbats are the *Esbats,* possibly less significant from the viewpoint of cosmic magic but still extremely important in the structure of witchcraft. Esbats are minor celebrations and meeting times, usually based on the phases of the moon. Some witches celebrate the New Moon, others the Full Moon, and some celebrate both times.

Some covens do all their major work on the Sabbats; others save these times for feasting and celebration, and work only on the Esbats. Some covens work on both occasions. Customs vary widely from coven to coven, but it is possible to give a generalized description of a typical coven meeting: In warm weather, witches like to work outdoors under the open sky. The meetings are held at night, generally in full view of the moon, although sometimes the house or apartment of a coven member may be the setting.

The magic circle is drawn on the ground and consecrated. The traditional circle size is nine feet in diameter, but this varies with the size of the coven. The circle must be large enough for all the members comfortably to stand, sit — *dance* — on the periphery. Not all covens necessarily dance these days, but the circle dance always has been an important method for raising energy. Many mystical sects all over the world — from Hasidic Jewish groups to African religions — include dance among their rituals. In witchcraft, the circle dance symbolizes the Wheel of the Year and the dance is always performed *clockwise*, attuning to the turning of the sun, the planets, and the Earth. This is called *deosil*. Counterclockwise dancing is called *Widdershins* and it is a traditional form of generating negative magic in the West, as mentioned in Chapter III. In most occult traditions it is considered anti-life, and no real witch would use it. Some groups raise the Cone of Power directly through the ritual circle dance. Others dance for celebration and release of energy, and prefer to raise the Power by meditation or in other ways.

The four elements are symbolically represented by the witch's ritual tools: There may be *incense*, to represent *air*. A Western witch's incense differs from the Eastern kind. Most witches mix their own incense from seasonal herbs, roots, barks, and spices such as cinnamon. Generally a ritual cup of *wine* represents the element *water*. Sometimes a ritual vessel contains salt and water. *Earth* is often represented by a cake, which is shared. This is, of course, an ordinary cake, having nothing whatever to do with the obnoxious ingredients ascribed (by witch-haters) to witches' recipes. In many sects, the cake is put aside for later, after the work; in this case the element of Earth is represented by seasonal leaves, plants, vegetables, or twigs placed in the center of the circle. *Fire* may be represented by a candle, or a bonfire (outdoors, of course).

Many groups still use a cauldron, to represent the Goddess and the source of all life. Most groups also use a variety of ritual instruments — the knife, the wand, the pentacle, the broom. Some covens work in everyday dress, some in ritual robes, and some work "skyclad" (nude), according to an old occult belief that clothing can get in the way of magical vibrations. Some hereditary groups recite old chants, and many of the newer groups have tried to reconstruct ancient chants which have been long secret or largely forgotten. Some groups compose their own Words of Power or improvise personal rituals.

No matter how serious the work of the night, a mood of gaiety and fun emerges at some point in the proceedings. After the work has been completed, the coven usually shares a meal or a snack; cakes and wine are the traditional fare. Later there may be dancing and singing purely for enjoyment. (In my group, we tell jokes). After the work is finished, witches feel intense joy and relief because the continuity of life has been so deeply affirmed, the positive vibrations still linger in the air, and there is a shared conviction that problems have been solved. The traditional greetings are "Merry meet, merry part" and "Blessed Be."

The Book Of Shadows

The *Book of Shadows* is a witch's personal book, a combination handbook, textbook, recipe book, diary and work journal. Most witches keep one; in some cases the entire coven shares one. Since witches were often the only literate members of their community, especially in the Middle Ages, the contents of the Books of Shadows were easily kept secret. During the Persecutions, however, most of these Books burned along with the witches. Even though many of the surviving witches committed these Books to memory, it is impossible to estimate the amount of occult information destroyed during this dark time.

> Keep a book in your own hand of write.
> Let brothers and sisters copy what they
> will but never let this book out of your
> hand, and never keep the writings of another,
> for if it be found in their hand of write
> they will be taken and tortured....Learn
> as much as you may by heart and when danger
> is past rewrite your book.
> > —twelfth century witch's
> > Book of Shadows[5]

The religious symbol of witchcraft is the *Pentagram* — a five pointed star usually enclosed in a circle. The pentagram has many meanings.

 The five points represent the five human senses. Enclosed in a circle, a human being can touch all the points of the circle with raised head and outstretched arms and legs. The five points also represent the four elements (Earth, Air, Fire, Water), plus spirit (Mind) presiding at the top.

Pentagrams have long been used as symbols of magical work in many traditions. The *Goetia* contains many illustrations of complex pentagrams (ascribed to Solomon, naturally) considered necessary for ceremonial magic. A pentagram turned upside down usually has

78

negative significance. For Craft purposes a witch traditionally draws the symbol with one stroke of the pen. Witches like to wear small silver pentagrams on silver chains. All Craft jewelry is made of silver because witches consider it sacred to the Goddess and the metal of the Moon. Although decorative, the jewelry also serves as symbolic protection, as in amulets and talismans and for ritual purposes to focus energy. For these reasons, when witches first get their jewelry, they consecrate it, according to specific traditions. I was not surprised to hear of recent parapsychology experiments proving silver to be a powerful conductor of psychic energy.

Some covens have statues representing the Goddess and the Horned God, and some witches keep in their homes small altars with statues and ritual instruments for private work.

Witches consider *words* important in all Craft work, making use of chants, verbal charms, and rhyming devices. Blending words with rhythm serves as a triggering mechanism, to draw on powers of the subconscious. Justine Glass says that a spell must "say itself" in order to sink easily into the subconscious mind.[6] But a spell need not be rhymed or rhythmical to be effective; essentially, the meaning of the words is the source of Power. Many witches make up their own Words of Power and poetry for ritual purposes. A nonadept might recite a folk-magic spell by rote, but a witch prefers to create an original spell rather than repeat anything without full understanding.

A candle often aids the depth and focus of concentration in Craft work. The deeper the concentration, the more effective the work. Some modern observers may call this a form of auto-hypnosis.

Some witches communicate by telepathy (ESP), a traditional teaching device on the Craft. Some things cannot be said in words; they must be conveyed in images of sight and impressions of emotion. This brings us to the tradition of the witch's *familiar* — a subject of much confusion and fear amongst the witch-haters of medieval times.

The familiar is usually a small animal of extraordinary psychic ability, generally a cat, small dog, rabbit, mouse or frog. This differs from a "familiar spirit," usually a friendly spirit helper from the Invisible World. Witches always have kept many animals as house pets, even in times when other people saw animals simply as objects to be killed and eaten. Witches evolved methods of communicating with animals in nature, as did many Native American tribes. The animal familiar is a witch's special pet; in fact, its status goes beyond that of a mere pet. It is an animal with a talent and a desire to join in the work of magic. The familiar is a faithful companion, a magical helper, and a psychic presence, able to link natural energies with the witch for various occult tasks.

Because the most well known familiar was the usually a cat, witchhunters in the Middle Ages burned countless cats along with human victims. The supreme irony of this action was that in the fourteenth century, the bubonic plague raged far more widely than it might have, had there been a normal cat population left alive to kill the rats carrying the disease.

Divination, or looking into the future (in fact, looking into various dimensions of time and space), is important to witches. Tarot cards, crystal balls, and the so-called "witches' mirror" are usually part of a witch's personal effects. This black concave mirror is probably the basis of the legendary wicked queen's magical mirror in the story of "Snow White." An all-black mirror must look ominous to the nonadept; to the witch, the black mirror simply offers an alternative to the crystal ball. (No, the mirror does not speak, as in "Snow White," but it does provide an excellent vehicle for psychic concentration).

The use of *herbs* would take volumes to explore and explain. Herbs provided the first medicines on this planet, and still are natural remedies for many ills. Also, herbs lend specifically evocative aromas to various blends of incense (psychic triggering aids) and unusual flavoring to food. Many witches enjoy good food and like to cook. Perhaps in earlier times, such food smelled and tasted strange to the suspicious non-adept. Today however any quasi-gourmet cook knows the "secrets" of cooking with herbs. Herbs once again are gaining favor as mild curative agents in relaxation, digestive aids, headache relief, and many other purposes, as any modern health food store owner will agree. As for love potions, poison potions, or potions intended to bend another to one's will — these have *never* been part of any true witch's work. Remember the Threefold Law? It would be manipulative practice (to put it mildly!) to concoct or use such potions. Similarly the whole compendium of distasteful ingredients — "eye of newt, and toe of frog," and such barbarisms that Shakespeare and others have accredited to witches — have nothing to do with the Craft. Categorically, witches revere all nature. Perhaps this misunderstanding arises from the observation that witches have always kept many odd little creatures (including newts, toads, and frogs) as pets.

Some schools of negative magic believe in the sacrificial killing and mutilation of animals, and in the use of various parts (animal and human) for ceremonies. These practices have been ascribed to witchcraft, when in reality they bear no resemblance to any work within the Craft. Furthermore, the use of such ingredients has no magical effect that I have ever heard of.

No discussion of witchcraft would be complete without some reference to the witch's broom, which has seized the imagination of so many people. Several explanations for the broom exist. There is an element of truth in each of them.

1. During the persecutions, all magical ritual objects had to be hidden or disguised because of periodic household searches. Some sects used a wand for ceremonial work, and what better hiding-place-cum-disguise for a ritual wand than a common broomstick?

2. The broom is a fertility symbol; the phallic symbolism is obvious. Also, trees and woods offer a long tradition of mystical significance (see Graves' *The White Goddess).* [7]

3. Witches have always travelled astrally — or as some psychic researchers would say, "mentally" — i.e., they "thought" they were travelling. A common theory holds that the witches annointed themselves with a hallucinogenic agent such as belladonna and then mentally took off, thinking that they were flying astride their brooms. I disagree with the hallucinogenic-drug theory, because astral travel requires no drugs. Also, astral travel requires no broom!

Why then is the broom assocated with flying? My theory is that the earliest cultures upon which the Craft is based, were technologically advanced, and employed fuel-propelled vehicles which could carry people through the air — much like those which carry modern astronauts. Since these ancient technologies were destroyed, I believe that the witch culture has kept alive the memory of such vehicles. The broom has become a symbol, probably because the shape is similar and because the broom also symbolizes for witches the same transcendant ideas universally associated with flying.

History

The history of witchcraft has been confused with the histories of other occult practices — from the "Witch" of Endor in the Old Testament, to European folk magic, to early encounters by European missionaries with the so-called "witch"-doctors (shamans) of African religions. The history of witchcraft is the history of one tradition only.

To cloud the issue further, the history of witchcraft in Europe has been represented primarily by its "official" chroniclers: the witch-hunters of the Middle Ages. A responsible occult historian would no more accept an Inquisitor's history of witch-craft than a modern religious historian would accept a Nazi's history of Judaism. These medieval sources are so biased — so filled with harsh invectives and bizarre claims — that modern historians regard the entire picture with disbelief. It began to appear as if the witch-hunters were deranged propagandists, the victims anyone in political disfavor, and consequently perhaps no witches at all existed in Europe.

But there were witches in Europe. Historians assume correctly that most of the witchcraft "history" consists of accusations, trials and fantastic confessions extracted under torture. It is true that many, if not most, of the victims were not witches, but there *were* witches in Europe.

Anthropologists and archaeologists have not avoided the challenge of sparse or confused evidence when encountering ancient cults in civilizations less close to home. It is common knowledge that many pharoahs and ancient kings tried to destroy all evidence of their predecessors, especially if those predecessors happened to espouse a different religious belief. But modern historical sleuths unearthed a relic here, an inscription there, and from such evidence — keeping an open mind — piece together a responsible history of the earlier sect.

This same openness of mind finally was demonstrated in relation to Western occult history by the British Egyptologist Margaret Murray in the 1920s. Dr. Murray turned her attention to the pagan traditions in Europe, and pieced together all the evidence which had been just waiting there virtually in her own backyard (England). She concluded that "The witch cult" did indeed exist, that it was not the cult of the devil, and that witchcraft had its roots in a pagan tradition of Paleolithic times. Dr. Murray identified the Horned God as Cernunnos, or Pan, and interpreted all of witchcraft history through a clear and unbiased eye.[8]

Since Margarat Murray's valuable discoveries were made public (in *The Witch Cult in Western Europe* and *The God of the Witches*), many modern witches have confirmed these facts. Most reliable witchcraft books today draw upon Margaret Murray's work. The only problem one could point out in her findings is that the emphasis on the Goddess is not clear enough, and perhaps that Dr. Murray linked other pagan cults too closely with the Craft's practices. But these are minor points.

Before Dr. Murray's findings, two earlier works offered evidence of the pre-Christian witch religion in Italy. Giralomo Tatarotti's *A Study of Midnight Sabbats of Witches*, published in 1749, went pretty much unnoticed. But Charles Godfrey Leland's *Aradia, or The Gospel of the Witches*, 1899, has become something of a classic.[9] These works acknowledge that among Italian witches *(strege)* the main theological emphasis seems to have been on the Goddess Diana, leading to the definition of witchcraft in Italy as a "Dianic cult."

The religion, with little variation, also flourished throughout Spain, France, Scotland, Ireland, Germany, and the Scandinavian countries. Dr. Murray and her followers believe that witchcraft had its primitive beginnings in Europe over 12,000 years ago during matriarchal times. They believe that witchcraft began with the earliest sympathetic-magic traditions of the cave and the hunt. However, witches themselves trace the origins of the Craft to the ancient mystery traditions of Greece, Rome, Crete, Egypt, and even earlier — back to advanced civilizations such as Atlantis. A popular theory within the Craft holds that the religion spread to Europe from almost forgotten Mediterranean cultures after the Great Flood.

In any case, anthropologists and witches agree that for many thousands of years before the coming of Christianity, all Europe was pagan and various sects existed in varying degrees of primitivism. Witches and Druids were the two main tribal groups, considered "specialized" and somewhat apart from all the others. But they were not feared. On the contrary, they were respected and sought after for the spiritual and practical help they offered to their less learned countrypeople. Unfortunately Druidism was all but wiped out in the massive persecutions of the Middle Ages. Modern Druids effectively guard their secrets to this day, but many parallels still exist between the work of the two religions.

The Persecutions

In the British Isles, even though the Druids were persecuted at the time of the Roman occupation (43-410 C.E.), witchcraft survived — probably because of the affinities between witchcraft and the Roman Mystery sects. But when the Roman Empire collapsed and the Saxons occupied the British Iles (43-324 C.E.), the Saxons began the unequivical persecution of all pagans, including witches. After the Normans invaded Britain (1066-1300) there was a brief respite during which the witches were tacitly accepted, perhaps because witch groups in the Gallic countries still flourished. In fact, Margaret Murray believes that the Plantagenets were members of the Craft. But when the influence of the Normans waned (by 1300), the massive persecutions of all pagans resumed. All pagans were labeled witches, and all witches were considered followers of the devil (see Chapter III, p. 84) At this time the European rulers were Christian and the people primarily pagan. More and more people converted to Christianity but the witches did not, nor did their influence in the populace die easily.

In the early fourteenth century the concept of the devil, brought back from the East by the Crusaders, provided the ideal scapegoat and propaganda tool for stamping out minority beliefs. The Persian devil, it was said, personified pure evil. It was depicted as a manlike being with horns. The Horned God of Europe was also depicted as a manlike being with horns. Could this not be the one and the same devil? The Horned God already constituted a threat to Christianity because His worship stood in the way of mass pagan conversions. If He were renamed the Devil (Satan) — if He came to personify pure evil in the minds of the people — they would have to turn away from His worship. Especially if such worship was considered a crime punishable by death.

> The god of the old religion becomes the devil of the new.
> —Margaret Murray

Thus the followers of the Horned God came under merciless attack from the fascistic branch of the Church/State. Witches still refer to the period of 1300 to 1600 as "The Burning Time," for all too obvious reasons. Throughout Europe, over NINE MILLION PEOPLE were systematically tortured and murdered. Volumes of "Satanic confessions," extracted under torture, were categorically documented as evidence by the Inquisitors. In addition to these documented deaths, the peripheral tragedies remain uncountable. The victims included men, women, and children. Along with the actual witches, the alleged "devil-worshippers" included Jews, pagans, gypsies, magicians, physicians, midwives, aged people, infirm people, eccentric people, left-handed people, poor people and rich alike. Ironically, many were Christians. Some rose to notoriety (such as Joan of Arc and Gilles de Rais) due to the dramatic circumstances of their lives and of their trials. All the problems of the society, the culture, the feudal system — everything from sexual perversion to the bubonic plague to poverty and starvation — was blamed on Satan and "his" witches. Since women were considered impure, it became traditional to label most women as witches, especially young beautiful women or old ugly women: the two witch stereotypes. As the persecutions got out of hand, corruption ran rampant, from violent sadism to plain old pecuniary interests. Witchhunting became a profitable business, since all property of a condemned witch was confiscated and local officials always cashed in when a wealthy "witch" was discovered.

It was a persecution governed by hysteria. Any accusation created the victims. One of the goals of the torture was to extract names of other neighborhood "witches"; in this way new lists of victims were readily obtained. There was no recourse for the accused, no defense of any kind. The purpose of the trials mainly was to document the "facts," i.e., the feverish details of devil worship. To confess to this fictional hodgepodge of horrific acts meant to be burned alive. To refuse a confession meant the most grissly torture (for which the dungeons of the Middle Ages became so famous) until the appropriate confessions could be obtained — *and then* to be burned alive. Sometimes confessions were extracted by promising the accused he or she would be merely strangled (and then burned); this was considered a more "merciful" death.

The descriptions of the torture are difficult to wade through; the modern mind pulls back in disbelief.[10] But equally difficult to comprehend is the conclusion that such confessions could have been based on any reality. Yet out of this incredible procedure emerged the popular image of witchcraft which has lingered into modern times. Far too many books still remain available as "sources" which draw upon information from the trials.

Needless to say, the Church at this time was not being led by the followers of Jesus. It bore no resemblance to the original Church of earlier centuries, and little resemblance to the Catholic Church which followed. The Inquisitors and the myriad petty officials who carried out their brutal tasks were not actual clerics. They were either genuinely power-mad types, or people who got pleasure out of violence, or simply people who wanted to save their own skins. If an honest clergyman tried to speak up against all this butchery, he too would be considered in league with the devil and killed. Nuns, monks, priests— no dissenters were safe. It was "evidence" that one was a witch if one defended a witch or questioned the religious value of mass torture and murder.

This reign of terror became official in 1484 with Pope Innocent VIII's famous Bull against witches and sorcerers. The Pope sponsored one of the most powerful propaganda devices of all times, the *Malleus Maleficarum* or "Witch's Hammer." Two German Inquisitors, Heinrick Kramer and James Sprenger, wrote the book, one of the first to be disseminated widely by the newly invented printing press, owned by the Church/State. The *Malleus Maleficarum* became the official handbook for witchhunters, defining a witch according to contemporary "satanic" dogma and including detailed instructions for identifying and torturing witches. The definitions in the *Malleus* constitute primary sources for many witchcraft "historians" and replaced accurate occult lore. All popular understanding of the Craft was replaced by these "official" definitions.

The Craft went underground and most covens lost contact with one another. Many witches continue privately to pass on their heritage through family generations, and have not surfaced to this day. The entire field of Western occult knowledge has yet to recover from The Burning Time.

Witchhunting reached its peak of fanaticism in the seventeenth century. In 1692, America was the setting for an hysterical incident of accusation and murder in the name of the Church, when the tiny village of Salem in the Massachusetts Bay Colony discovered over 150 "witches." Of these, thirty-one were killed because they *denied* being witches, and fifty-five were set free because they "confessed" under torture. The episode subsided after six months, and was later officially denounced as a mistake. Much doubt still exists whether any real witches lived in Salem during that time.

In 1736, England no longer considered witchcraft a capital offense — but it was not until 1951 that the last Witchcraft Law was taken off the books!

Dualism — The Light And The Dark

As with all massive persecutions throughout the ages, the question inevitably arises: why did the victims succumb? Especially in the case of the witches — those beings with such special "powers" — how and why did they allow themselves to be nearly exterminated?

The answers are complex. Not all the victims were witches. Actual members of the Craft formed only a small percentage of the population that was murdered. Although the original targets were religious dissenters — after a short time the choice of victims became fairly arbitary. In fact, it is possible that some of the genuine witches were able to escape, by hiding in remote country areas. However, so many witches were killed, and so much literature was destroyed, that the religion was effectively buried if not actually eliminated. The essential physical structure — small widely scattered covens — was not conducive to forming a unifying defense. There were no large well-organized congregations, no central temples or meeting places. People met in one another's homes and fields — hardly safe ground.

But the best explanation I have heard sounds all too familiar. It echoes the analysis of why most of the Nazis' six million Jewish victims "allowed" the slaughter: *They couldn't believe it.* This may sound simplistic, but the victim's attitude deserves investigating because it holds a key to an important occult concept, that of the Light and the Dark (Positive and Negative).

One of the foundations of Fascism is its need to label evil (the Dark) as "other," always existing outside the self. Totalitarianism acknowledges no evil within the self, either within the chosen community or within the "pure" individual. Evil is viewed as a threat to the entire community, a threat coming from the *outside*, and therefore easily eliminated. All one has to do is destroy the "others" and the community will be pure.

By creating the idea of the devil, "black" magic, Satanism, and demonology, the Church created an enemy who existed outside all true Christians and outside God's dominion itself. Hell was no longer confined to the netherworld. Hell became a free-floating enemy camp and its followers could be anywhere — anywhere except inside the true Christian's heart or mind. This repressive theology left no room for human imperfection. For example, to have a sexual thought indicated being in league with the devil; *someone else* must have planted that thought in one's own brain. The solution was simple: Burn the person who "sent" the thought. As Doreen Valiente points out:

...The Devil played an important part in the psychological

86

development of mankind. The corruption of man's heart has been projected onto him. People have accused his supposed servants, the witches, of doing the forbidden things they wanted to do themselves, in the dark deep hells of their own souls, and then tortured and burned the witches for being so "wicked"...The real powers of hell come not from external devils, but from the unacknowledged contents of man's own mind.[11]

As Jung says, when evil, or the "shadow" is projected outside of the self, it can then overwhelm the self from within. Incidentally, the roots of modern racism may be traced to this mass projection of the shadow, as Satan is repeatedly described by the witchhunters as a "black man" — this at a time when there were virtually no black people to be seen in Europe. The image lingered in mass consciousness waiting to be projected again onto the entire black race, and yet again onto the Jews and gypsies. When the shadow-self is projected, the "master race" is always white; white is considered synonymous with purity, and darkness with impurity.

The *I Ching* warns:

Nor must our own passions and shortcomings be glossed over... the struggle must not be carried on directly by force. If evil is branded, it thinks of weapons, and if we do it the favor of fighting against it blow for blow, we lose in the end because thus we ourselves get entangled in hatred and passion. Therefore it is important to begin at home, to be on guard in our own persons against the faults we have branded.[12]

The witchhunters of the Middle Ages became "entangled in hatred and passion" to the extent that they acted exactly like the enemy they had branded. No diabolical act that they accused the witches of performing could have been worse than their own diabolical acts. The nature of totalitarianism is such that by attempting to get rid of evil, it is overhwelmed by evil. The nature of the Dark is that it sneaks up on you and attacks from within. If you label it outside yourself, you automatically activate it within you.

Negativity does not exist outside the self. It is inherent in everyone, no matter how pure or good. The Dark is potentially there simply because the Light is there and neither can exist without the other. This is standard occult knowledge; witches have always known this, and they simply couldn't believe that others didn't.

The idea of dividing the Power Beyond into two, one good and one evil, belongs to an advanced and sophisticated religion. In the more primitive cults the deity is in himself the author of all, whether good or bad.

—Margaret Murray. [13]

By this definition witchcraft is a "primitive" religion. It can be tragically naive, as in the Middle Ages, to believe that all others are equally "primitive." But the point is that out of this "primitive" philosophy of the witches comes an important occult concept of working positive magic.

Light is the left hand of darkness
And darkness is the right hand of light...

—Ursula K. LeGuin[14]

The witch philosophy of Light and Dark: No duality exists between good and evil. The One Power over all is neither good nor bad; it transcends qualitative thought. The Power contains potential for both Dark and Light. Acknowledging the existence of the Negative makes it possible to work consciously with the Positive.

Thus we perceive life rhythm as cylical: light goes to dark and light again...summer into winter and back to summer...day into night and back to day...life into death and back to life. Everything returns threefold. When we direct positive actions out into the Cosmos, they come back threefold to further the life process. All life is united: as the moon waxes and wanes, and the tides respond, so do the roots and buds, and seeds beneath the ground. Dark thoughts and deeds spring from the same common source as life-affirming ones. All life is *One.*

Since there is no value judgement on either good or on evil, evil is not to be feared. It is easily acknowledged as potentially part of each witch's psyche; as such evil may be avoided. The negative use of the Power is to be avoided as antithetical to the furthering of life on the planet. Since all life is One, "bad" for the people is synonymously bad for the crops; bad for the individual is bad for the community. Negative actions are counterproductive; they come back threefold. Every ritual, every symbol illustrates this principle. Witches do not ignore the dark side of the psyche. They ritually acknowledge it and release its negative power to make way to the Light. The Godddess is accepted in both Her Light and Dark aspects, as symbolized by the light and dark sides of the moon. The God is acknowledged in both His dying and rebirth aspects, symbolized by the yearly "death and rebirth" of the sun. When a soul reincarnates on Earth, the Goddess is celebrated as the giver of new life. When a soul departs from this plane to the next, the God is celebrated as the Lord of the Underworld who will care for the soul until it is reborn in physical form.

From this foundation develops an infinitely powerful use of magic.

Witchcraft, Sexism, and Sex

The sexist nature of the witch hunts provides a rich field for feminist analysts. *All* of the witch hunters were men — no women burned the witches — and most of the "witches" were women.

In a matriarchal culture, the role of magical women is essentially positive, that of priestess. In a patriarchal culture, the magical women is viewed as a negative entity and a threat to the established order. The past two thousand years have imbued the word "witch" with negative meaning, and calling a woman a witch constitutes an insult, even today.

In view of patriarchy, the idea of a woman possessing any power seems to embody a basic denial of the power of the male. For example, it may seem a compliment to call a woman an "enchantress," or to say that she is "bewitching" or "charming." But notice that such descriptions implicitly deny a man's own responsibility in any interactions with such a woman. Even if it is pleasant to feel bewitched, enchanted or charmed, it still defines the male as a passive — albeit often willing — *victim* of some mysterious feminine force.

Some people still use the word "witch" to describe a woman who doesn't fit into the prescribed woman's role in society. Whether the term applies to a wicked witch woman or an enchanting bewitching woman, it still refers to a woman whose own power and energy extends beyond men's understanding. This somehow poses a threat to the established image of men being in control of everything, including their own emotions.

Jung has much to say about this phenomenon, relating it directly to the *anima* or female part of a man's psyche. In its positive aspect, the anima can be viewed as a Goddess or personal muse. In its negative aspect, the anima may appear as a wicked "witch" or cruel siren figure. In either case, it represents a female archetype existing within the man's own subconscious. Jung believes it is important for a man to recognize the female aspects of his own psyche and consciously integrate them into this entire personality. Otherwise, just as with the Shadow side, the anima is likely to be projected outward onto others, specifically onto women. A man who thus projects his anima, denying its existence within himself, imbues it (and the women who seem to embody its attributes) with enormous power.[15]

In a patriarchal society, where men categorically reject, suppress, and deride any possibility of accepting their own female characteristics, we may find the majority of the male population projecting their animas onto women. Such men then ascribe unnatural power to women, and see them as nonhuman creatures to be at once adored and feared. This is what happened in the Middle Ages.

One of the problems of the medieval doctrine of Christianity was that it allowed no explanation for men's sexual desire. Bodily needs were considered the Devil's doing, not God's, and certainly not the individual's. Any sexual activity was considered impure and unholy. Consequently, all women were considered unclean and inferior. They aroused a "non-Christian" lust in men and lured them away from celibacy and pure thoughts. Women were viewed as vile creatures of the Devil — even those who weren't accused as witches.

> By a monstrous perversion of ideas, the Middle Ages regarded the flesh, in its representative woman (accursed since Eve), as radically impure.
>
> —Jules Michelet[16]

Women had to care for their own bodies; male physicians did not deign to heal women, nor even to assist in childbirth. As Michelet further points out:

Medieval medicine concerns itself exclusively with the superior, the pure being (to wit, man), who alone can be ordained priest, and incarnate the living God upon the altar....But does it ever think of children? Very seldom. Does it pay attention to women? Never![17]

By contrast, witchcraft and all the pre-Christian European pagan groups considered women equal to men, and sex a natural and even holy part of life, symbolizing fertility. These ideas made paganism a profound threat to the Christian ideal of the time (remember that witches were among the first midwives). Not surprisingly, most of the accusations levelled at alleged witches were of a sexual nature, such as women "casting spells" on men's sexual parts — making penises larger, making them smaller, making them disappear, and making them come back. (Freud would have had a picnic!) One doesn't have to be a psychiatrist to figure out that in such a repressive and hysterical atmosphere, sexual fantasies would run rampant. But there were no psychiatrists around to explain that these were fantasies. Dreams, hallucinations, and "unclean thoughts" were taken literally as facts and blamed on witches, demons, and the Devil. Certain demons were believed to take the form of an *incubus* (male demon) or *succubus* (female demon) who specialties were to seduce people in their sleep. Dreams of copulation with either type of demon were considered sufficient evidence for any number of people to be burned; the person in the village whom the incubus or succubus happened to resemble, that person's husband or wife, and sometimes even the unfortunate dreamer.

There were numerous "official" accounts of wild sexual orgies in which women were said to have been seduced by the Devil himself. Such alleged seductions alone "defined" many women as witches. The women confessed under torture to every lurid detail their judges could imagine: Satan's penis was unnaturally large, or long, or small; it felt painful to the touch, or pleasant, or cold as ice, or hot as fire, etc.

In the witches' prosecution which took place among the Basques at Labourd in 1609, many witches declared that sexual favors of the devil were very painful, for his penis was as long as an arm and covered with fish-scales. Marie Marigrane, an accused girl of fifteen, asserted that the penis of the devil consisted half of flesh and half of iron; others explained that it was of horn.[18]

Such details are typical of the "evidence" emerging from the trials.

Before being questioned the accused women were officially stripped by their captors, and thoroughly examined for "devil's marks" and various other physical signs of demonic sexual activity. The examination consisted of preliminary torture, frequently of a sexual nature. Rape was evidently frequent, if not always official. Ironically enough, for all their supposed power the accused "witches" were always considered "Brides of Satan" or "Satan's Handmaids," forming a sort of unholy harem. The Big Boss, even of the underworld, was still viewed as male.

But men could be burned as witches too. In the opinion of the Inquisitors, any man who behaved oddly was routinely considered a witch. The husband of a female witch could be guilty, as could the children. If a man was a homosexual, he was considered lower than a witch, and used as kindling material for the witch's pyre; hence the degrading slang term of "faggot" or "fag" for male homosexual.

In reality, the Craft has always included both male and female members. The use of the word "warlock" to define a male witch, is inaccurate. "Warlock" actually means "truce-breaker" in Scots dialect. Within the Craft, men who are witches are simply called witches.

Witchcraft has been associated primarily with women partly because women have always been equal to men at the very least, and partly because it develops the human psyche on levels deeper than ego. The Craft encourages and nourishes the intuitive faculties, used for working magic, which during the past Piscean Age have been associated mainly with women. The practice of witchcraft assumes that this intuitive magical faculty is the domain of men as well as women.

Perhaps people still associate witchcraft too much with sex. The "wild orgy" accusation has lingered to this day, in spite of these sexually permissive times. Enough modern sexual studies provide that many people gladly engage in group sex without witchcraft, Satanism, or any sort of magic at all.

I am disturbed even more however at the association of witchcraft with manipulative magic to ensnare someone, such as through love-spells. Unfortunately, it seems that women are the ones who usually turn to this sort of "magic." I believe that such women are defining themselves through patriarchal eyes as less powerful than men or as needing a specific man, often to the exclusion of all other needs, and requiring an extra "dose" of power (supernatural power) to enable them to "get" that man.

To "get" a man in that way, to "make" him fall in love, is far from a true Craft union on equal sexual ground. Such women acknowledge a diminished sense of personal power by aligning themselves with the supernatural. They seem to want to tip the balance of power back to themselves, to gain power over the man through witchcraft — and in general to act out the witch-as-anima projection which men have put on women in the first place. This is a natural cultural problem arising from social conditioning, and I'm sure it will pass by the time we are into the Aquarian Age. Meanwhile, turn to p. 228 to deal with the need for love via magic.

The Resurgence

Witchcraft is emerging now at the Cusp as a "revivalist" religion. It is taking many forms; it is part of the current general trend away from standard Western theology, and in particular, it is part of a growing return to paganism.[19]

If the modern popularity of the Craft can be traced to one person, that person would have to be the controversial Gerald Gardner. Gardner's book *Witchcraft Today*,[20] originally published in 1954, was the first to explain witchcraft as a positive non-Satanic religion. The author established Gardnerian Witchcraft, a highly organized branch of the Craft based upon his own initiation into a British coven in New Forest in the 1940s. Gardner inspires controversy because some hereditary witches claim that he added his personal version of traditions to witchcraft; these include nudity, token flagellation, the earning of degrees, and the required use of ritual tools. Gardnerian Witchcraft, an organization which a person may *join*, has initiation requirements and bears a striking resemblance to some of the positive ceremonial magic societies of the early nineteenth century.

Since Gardner, several other carefully structured witchcraft sects have been formed, including Alexandrean Witchcraft, Georgian Witchcraft and Seax-Wicca. Many of these groups are ceremonial in style. In addition, many people are forming their own Craft paths. These can be quite eclectic, drawing on numerous traditions including ancient Egyptian and early Welsh. A number of all-women feminist covens have formed, some of which deny the importance of the Horned God and primarily deal with the Goddess. There a number of ecology-oriented covens, many of them communal farms, dedicated to the preservation of the planet according to ancient Craft belief. Some homosexuals, both men and women, are forming their own witchcraft groups. These people are evidently drawn to a tradition which acknowledges the male-within-female and the female-within-male, without bias and without stereotypes.

Unfortunately, a number of publicity-seeking pop-"witches" clutter the scene, some of whom have written "witchcraft" instruction books perpetuating the negative preconceptions about manipulative-magic-as-witchcraft. Some of them have established mail-order schools and groups promising instant witchery for a fee. But with more and more excellent witchcraft books emerging for the public, and with more and more informed people turning to witchcraft as a religion, the sensation seekers seem to be receding in importance.

Some people are converting to witchcraft as a purely devotional religion, choosing simply to worship on the Sabbats and enjoy the rich traditions. Others are involved in serious occult research, and many work magic for their communities as did the witches of long ago. In any case, it seems to me that witchcraft is becoming increasingly less mistrusted and less mysterious, thanks to modern Aquarian spiritual seekers and to recent scientific investigation of the paranormal which was once considered either a dangerous or fanciful domain.

The Burning Time did not put an end to the Craft; in fact, occult lore predicted that witchcraft would re-emerge in the Aquarian Age. All witches believe in reincarnation, and I believe that many people discovering witchcraft in this life, supposedly for the first time, are really remembering other lives as witches.

Which brings us to the occult concepts of Karma and Reincarnation.

[1]Justine Glass, *Witchcraft, The Sixth Sense*, Wilshire Book Company, California, 1970, p. 49.

[2]Robert Graves, *The White Goddess*, Noonday Press, Farrar, Strauss & Giroux, New York, 1970. The most thorough and profound study of the Goddess in Western tradition, including Her threefold aspects. The most thorough and profound *global* studies of the Goddess are by Merlin Stone, *When God Was a Woman*, The Dial Press, New York, 1976, and *Ancient Mirrors of Womanhood*, Vols. I and II, New Sybylline Press, New York, 1979.

[3]Glass, *op. cit.*, p. 57.

[4]Sir James George Frazer, *The Golden Bough*, Macmillan Paperbacks Abridged Edition, Canada, 1969. A detailed study of the pagan interpretations and customs surrounding each of the holidays may be found in these pages, but please bear in mind that these are the pagan folk customs, not the witch customs.

[5]Quoted by Gerald Gardner, *Witchcraft Today*, Citadel Press, New Jersey, 1970, p. 52.

[6]Glass, *Witchcraft, The Sixth Sense*, p. 67.

[7]The magical meaning of trees may be found throughout *The White Goddess*, but Chapters X and XI are specifically significant.

[8]Margaret Murray, *The God of the Witches*, Oxford University Press, New York, 1931, p. 14: "Hitherto, the anthropologist has confined himself to the pre-Christian periods or to the modern savage. Yet medieval Europe offers to the student of Mankind one of the finest fields of research...I have traced the worship of the Horned God through the centuries from the Paleolithic prototypes, and I have shown that the survival of the cult was due to the survival of the race who adored that god... It was not till the rise of Christianity, with its fundamental doctrine that a non-Christian deity was a devil, that the cult of the Horned God fell into disrepute."

[9]It's available in paperback, published by Weiser's, New York, 1974.

[10]Russell Hope Robbins, *Encyclopedia of Witchcraft and Demonology*, Crown Publishers, Inc., New York, 1959. One of the most thorough books on the subject, recommended by Doreen Valiente.

[11]Doreen Valiente, *An ABC of Witchcraft, Past and Present*, St. Martin's Press, New York, 1973, p. 87:

[12]Richard Wilhelm, *The I Ching, or Book of Changes*, Wilhelm/Baynes translation, Bollingen Series XIX, Princeton University Press, Princeton, N.J., 1967, Hexagram 43, Book One, p. 167.

[13]Murray, *The God of the Witches*, p. 14.

[14]Ursula K. LeGuin, *The Left Hand of Darkness*, Ace Books, New York, 1969, p. 222.

[15]C.G. Jung, *Aion, Researches into the Phenomenology of the Self, The Collected Works of C.G. Jung*, Bollingen Series XX Pantheon Books, New York, 1959, pp. 11-22. I would also like to add that the popular "positive" anima production in modern times has often taken the form of female Hóllywood "sex symbols." The anima is always associated with sexual longing. In women, the corresponding archetype is the "animus." Read Jung for details.

[16]Jules Michelet, *Satanism and Witchcraft*, The Citadel Press, New York, 1965 ed., p. 87.

[17]Ibid., p. 88.

[18]Emile Laurent and Paul Nagour, *Magica Sexualis*, trans. by Raymond Sabitier, Falstaff Press, New York, 1934, p. 46.

[19]Margot Adler, *Drawing Down the Moon, Witches, Druids, Goddess Worshippers and Other Pagans in America Today*, Viking Press, New York, 1979. The social implications of the pagan movement are excellently explored in this study. (Recent paperback: Beacon, New York, 1981).

[20]Available in paperback, Citadel Press, New Jersey, 1974.

Chapter V

KARMA AND REINCARNATION

Karma

The buck stops here.

—Harry S. Truman

In the occult frame of reference, the acknowledgement of karma is the ultimate acknowledgement of personal responsibility.

What Karma Is Not

Many people believe that karma is an Eastern philosophy, but for ages karma has also been — and still is — an important part of occult thought in the West. Since the occult has been hidden in the West, and since translations of Eastern traditions, including karma, have been a bit muddled in Western thought, karma has been much misunderstood. Most people seem to believe that karma means destiny or fate, but nothing could be further from the truth. By popular definition, destiny or fate imply predetermined life circumstance — usually of a negative kind — which cannot be changed. Naturally many people reject such an unpleasant prospect. (I reject it too. In the occult view, karma is always changing — and changeable). Also, some Westerners believe that the concept of karma forms an integral link to Eastern religions, and that you cannot consider it relevant to your own life unless you convert to such a religion; that you cannot relate karma to your own Western religion, or psychology, or philosophy or way of life. This also is not true. The concept of karma is practical and universal; it does not confine itself to Zen, or other Buddhism sects, or other specific Eastern beliefs. Karma can become a part of your life view, no matter what your tradition may be.

It is also commonly thought that to believe in karma you have to accept the idea of *reincarnation,* still culturally strange to Westerners (although increasingly less so). Again, not true. Of course, the idea of reincarnation logically extends from the idea of karma. But you do not have to believe in reincarnation in order to understand karma (particularly your *own* karma), or for this understanding to be useful in problem-solving and living your life in the here and now. We may begin by applying the idea of karma to this one lifetime.

What Karma Is

By occult and metaphysical definition, karma means literally "cause and effect," specifically those built up by the thoughts and actions of our lives. In other words, it means that *we create our own lives.* It means that we have been, are, and always will be *completely responsible* for everything that goes on in our lives. It means nothing "happens *to* us," because we make everything happen. And if things seem to happen *to* us, that is simply because we have chosen to make our lives look that way to us — either as a conscious or subconscious choice. Usually the choice is subconscious. We may have accepted without question a cultural viewpoint which says that this is the way things are; that things "happen" to people from some outside force — God, circumstances, luck, chance, or whatever. And we may have chosen to live our lives according to this viewpoint. The very nature of such a viewpoint creates an atmosphere that prevents our awareness that we have *chosen* this viewpoint — albeit subconsciously. And it also may prevent us from realizing that things could be different.

If we have chosen to accept the viewpoint that things happen to us, we can just as easily choose to change our point of view. This time the choice will, of course, be conscious. We can choose to believe that we make life happen for ourselves. You may accept this whole other approach and decide to try it right now — or you may accept it hypothetically, if you wish, and *it can still work for you.* Of course, you can reject the karmic concept too — but it's an important idea in occult work. In any case, the new choice involves a shift of perception.

Within the karmic frame of reference, there are no accidents or coincidences. Nobody does anything to us unless we let them (or invite them). People do not wander into our lives at random. We draw them to us, invite them into our lives. We do this either directly (Let's have lunch"..."Let's keep in touch"..."Let's get married") or indirectly by creating the circumstances which are conducive and nourishing to the kinds of relationships we have around us. One way or another, we encourage relationships in our lives. But of course the people in our lives have their own karma, too. If people choose to leave us, there is nothing we can do to stop them; if they choose to stay, they contribute equally to a karmic interaction. If the karmas of two people "mesh" — presto, a relationship.

Some events may appear to be accidents, but on closer investigation we can see that we provided the atmosphere for their occurrence. We either created each event, or drew it to us, or participated in it. Coincidences are never arbitrary happenings. As Jung says, they are "significant" (i.e., a deeper meaning exists behind each event).

Resignation to a situation perpetuates that situation by personal choice, even if the choice is subconscious (which is often the case). Sometimes perpetuation of a situation involves the chosen belief that no other choice exists. Within the concept of karma, you have a great deal of choice involved, more than you may be able to believe (at first, anyway). No one creates your own karma but you, yourself.

If you choose to believe otherwise, *that* is your karma; according to the definition of karma, you chose that view.

The choice is the cause. The effect is the result of that choice. Choice is another way of saying "cause," of saying "creating."

Now, karma is *cumulative* by nature, referring to accumulated causes and effects. Already you have accumulated much karma, and this determines the choices now readily available to you. Of course, when you consciously work with karma, you can change it all; you can actually transcend the choices already available to you. To transcend and transform karma on a massive scale, it is necessary to understand the concept of reincarnation (p. 113). But usually this takes time and study, and most often we begin with the "given" choices around us (i.e., karma within this one lifetime).

Many sayings of folklore offer pearls of karmic wisdom: "Reap what you sow"..."Live by the sword, die by the sword"..."Troubles come home to roost"...etc.

Karma is not passive, and it does not imply resignation. The karmic philosophy means: "I have created everything in my life so far; I have participated in it, or chosen it, or drawn it to me, or perpetuated it." Because karma is active, it furthermore means: "I can now *change* any part of my life, of my karma by creation, participation, or choice." In other words, you have the option of setting up new causes and getting new effects in your life.

If you remain unaware of what you are (or have been) subconsciously creating in your life, this can also be a cause. In this case, the effect looks as if events are happening to you — or that events are somebody else's fault.

99

There Is No Blame with Karma

If you blame somebody else for anything in your life, that negates your responsibility for your own karma. On some level you must have participated, even if you only perceived that another person had the power to alter your life adversely. Or you may continue to perceive another's influence as powerful enough to leave bad effects, even long after the negative influence has passed. This often happens with negative conditioning by parents, teachers, and other childhood influences. But it is equally important not to blame *yourself* when you accept the responsibility as yours. Responsibility is not synonymous with blame; blame slows everything down.

The essential way to work with karma is to:

1. be aware that you created your life and are continuing to do it, and...
2. be aware that you can choose to change it — for the good.

This process is the foundation for working transformations in your life, as delineated in Chapter VIII.

For now, a good way to get used to working with karma is to examine your life and your actions — without blame! — and to watch what you do. It will become apparent to you that you are responsible for far more than you may have thought. If you see that you are creating causes, drawing things to yourself, feeling resigned, participating in situations, or perpetuating them, ask yourself:

* What have I been doing?
* What am I doing now?
* What have I been getting out of it?

As each new event in your life unfolds, stop and think: Is this really fate (God's will, destiny, the way things are, etc.)? Or what have I been doing to get things that way, or to help things stay that way, or to make things appear "locked into" being that way? This approach may be difficult at first, and it may be difficult not to immediately start blaming, but try.

Here are some examples in everyday life, of karma that can be changed easily, simply by watching and accepting responsibility:

1. *A woman who always has "bad luck" with men.* By karmic definition, she is drawing negative relationships with men to her. She has also been participating in negative relationships and perpetuating them. Possible causes: Such a woman may not believe she deserves better relationships. She may be using negative relationships to avoid

concentrating on other areas of her life — such as creativity, fulfillment, or work. Possible participation: The woman may stay in negative relationships and continue to interact with men in unhealthy, self-defeating ways. Possible perpetuation: She may be resigned to "bad luck" with men. Resignation creates an atmosphere which perpetuates a situation and keeps you "stuck" in it.

2. *An accident-prone person.* Most accident prone people subconsciously put themselves in dangerous situations. An objective observer, such as a psychotherapist, usually can point this out. But even if you are not habitually accident-prone, you can trace the karmic cause for an accident by asking yourself: What benefit (however odd it may seem) did I get out of this accident? What negative feelings — such as anger or vulnerability or helplessness — did I experience *before* the accident? These would be karmic causes. By acknowledging them, you can cut down on accidents or even eliminate them entirely.

3. *A person whom "nobody understands."* What is that person getting out of "not being understood?" What is that person doing to remain "misunderstood?" Who are the people that person surrounds himself/herself with? People who have their own personal karmic reasons not to be understanding?

And on and on with other examples: The man who can't sustain a meaningful relationship with any woman. "It's my mother's fault," he may say. He believes it, even though his mother may have ceased to have an active part in his life for decades. A person who always loses things, who says, "I don't have anything to do with it, things just disappear." A person who can't keep a job, who says, "It's the boss's fault."

It seems easier to blame another person, or the system, or the Universe, or *anything,* than to blame the self. But karma does not involve blame, it involves responsibility. Of course conditioning, especially early conditioning, creates many of the causes and effects in our lives. But right now, in the present, we may stop the negative chain of causes and effects by taking our own karmic responsibility for any given moment. Then we can begin to change things — with psychotherapy, with common sense, with positive magic — with whatever means we choose. Many of the new therapies and human-potential systems have pounced upon the idea of self-responsibility, although they do not always call it karma. Often, however, they mingle the idea of accepting responsibility with dramatic self-abasement, self-accusation, or the summoning of some special act of bravery.

It's no big deal to accept responsibility. You need no trappings, no extra emotions, no special bravery, nor even effort. It can simply get to be a new healthy habit: "Now, what did I do to bring this situation about? And next, how can I begin to change it?"

Changing karma can be very simple.

Karma And The Occult

The occult recognizes a variety of Unseen forces which influence us. In the karmic view, we can choose these influences and work with them. Just as with an understanding of karma in the World of Form we can consciously choose tangible influences in our lives, so can we do this in the Invisible World and the occult domain.

This awareness becomes very important, specifically in divination and prediction. Interestingly enough, many nonadepts misunderstand this aspect of occult work. They may say, "No one's going to tell me what my future will be like; I want to create my own future!" Or they say, "No bunch of stars can dictate my life!" Of course, such people are right. It is superstition, not occultism, to believe that any prediction is irrevocable, that any given set of circumstances such as those shown in a horoscope, cannot be changed, worked with, transformed, or influenced.

All predictions are subject to change. Any valid occult system has been set up to show you the direction towards which your karma is heading. Once you become aware of this, you can change it. You are creating your future right now. Your actions and thoughts right now are the causes. The effects lie ahead, in your future. In an astrological chart, these karmic trends may show up in the Houses representing karma, the fourth, eighth, and twelfth Houses, or in the positions of the Nodes of the Moon. In tarot readings, such trends usually show up in the "future" and "outcome" cards. In palm-reading, any good palm-reader will tell you that the lines on your hand, indicating your future, can change! The lines reflect the causes you have created and are creating now. In fact, any reputable soothsayer will say your sooth with the full understanding that it doesn't *have* to turn out that way. The future consists of your accumulated karma, indicating the trends you have created by your own behavior and ideas, your own conscious and subconscious choices. You can change these trends — yes, change your future — at any time (see Chapter VII, "Divination" p. 149).

Karma And Death

According to the occult concept of karma, *every person chooses his/her own death* — startling as this may seem. But perhaps this idea is not so startling if we stop to think about it. We've all heard stories of wise old folks who simply "knew when their time had come," announced it to their loved ones, and departed this plane peacefully. We have also heard stories of people who "pined away" after the passing of a loved one and shortly thereafter died themselves of no apparent cause other than a desire to "join" the departed person. And of course people can commit suicide. These are examples of obvious conscious choices of time and circumstances. However, many other deaths do not seem to be choices: accidents, illnesses, murders, the deaths of young people. So many deaths seem arbitrary and beyond human control. But in the occult view these deaths were not arbitrary nor beyond the control of the people involved. The death-choices were subconscious choices, but choices just the same for any of a myriad of reasons. If a person knows that he/she can choose the circumstances by which to depart this Earth Plane, that person has the freedom to choose the circumstances consciously. And nothing and no one else can interfere with that choice.

In ancient occult books such as *The Tibetan Book of the Dead*, we are given a very clear picture of cultures which knew how to control the death process. But we must make this point clear: controlling the death process (choosing circumstances, including time and place) does not mean avoiding physical death, nor being afraid of it. In order to choose one's death consciously, a person must first accept the idea that "death" is not the end of everything; it is merely a transition to another form of life. The next part of this chapter will deal with reincarnation, but for now we may simply make this point: We choose our own deaths. Those deaths which seem arbitrary are deep subconscious choices by people unaware that they may choose consciously. Such people may feel resignation, fear and helplessness about death, and their death circumstances are then the effects of such conscious beliefs.

Conversely, we have all heard stories of sick people who were told that they were dying and who refused to accept the news — at that point, they chose *not* to die. At such a point the person may choose to draw to himself/herself circumstances which reinforce the effectiveness of the choice to live. Thus we hear of "miraculous" recoveries of an "indominatable will to live." Many psychic healers save people's lives simply by convincing the afflicted person (often telepathically) that a choice exists.

However, if a person wants to leave the Earth Plane, nothing and no one can stop such a death. One often hears of people who "give up," who "lose the will to live." These cases are obvious examples of resignation or the feeling of helplessness. Less obvious are the cases of seriously ill people who reject any spiritual, religious, or psychic help. Such people may not want to know that they do have the conscious choice; so one might say that their choice was not wanting to know that they had a choice. Sometimes a person seems to want to live and yet dies. In the occult belief, such a person wanted to leave, although the desire may have been on a deep subsconsious level.

Reasons for death are complex and individual. The subject requires a full occult book. It may seem impossible to believe that anyone would want to die, especially a young person with a full life. But in the occult view, please remember, this Earth Plane is not the only place in the Universe, this life is not the only time-span that exists, and this space is not the only space in which a soul can experience life in a positive way. This Earth Plane, this World of Form may be the best that we know; it may even seem to be all that there is. But myriad other possibilities for life exist. Even though our conscious minds may not be aware of these possibilities, even though our culture may deny them, even though contemplating them may seem strange — *our subconscious minds, our souls, know.* And our subconscious minds, or our souls, are left to make our death choices if our conscious minds remain limited.

In the occult view, death is neither horrible nor frightening. We believe in the eternal life of the soul, and we work with the concept of contact between the Worlds. The change-over from this physical form may seem mysterious, but it is not final. This belief does not mean witches and other occultists do not mourn their loved ones. The physical loss of a person from this plane is painful for most people, even the most enlightened. But we believe that when a loved one leaves, the separation is only temporary. We respect the free will of the person involved, and that alleviates our own pain to a large extent. We do not fear our own deaths (even though we may not always like the idea that our time will come), because we know that we can direct our own circumstances. We believe that death is not destiny — it is karma; and karma involves choice.

Karma And Western Theology

Since many people wish to work with the occult and still remain within their own religion, the idea of karma may require some careful thinking to reconcile it with one's existing religious beliefs. This is, of course, a personal process and your own Inner Bell will point the way for you, but I can make some suggestions.

Does karma fit in with a Western belief in God? I think it does. First of all, it's important to figure out Who (and What) your God is. Everybody has a different concept of God. Even within one religion, most personal views differ. Atheists might even discover a residual, personal God lurking somewhere!

"What the hell are you getting so upset about?" he asked her bewilderedly in a tone of contrite amusement. "I thought you didn't believe in God."

"I don't," she sobbed, bursting violently into tears. "But the God I don't believe in is a good God, a just God, a merciful God. He's not the mean and stupid God you make him out to be."

—Joseph Heller[1]

To the adept, God is not an outside personality or force in which to be believed or not believed. To the adept, no deity, no destiny, fate, good or bad luck *takes the place of* personal responsibility, or karma. Many nonadepts, nonreligious, "rational" people — perhaps psychologically oriented or even atheistic types — will agree. So far, so good. But the adept does believe in a God (Goddess) Power, or a Force, or an Energy, a Unifying Life Spirit, a Universal Mind, a "Something." In contrast, the atheistic, rational Westerner:

1. might dispense entirely with all God-belief (hence the saying, "God is dead").

2. Or such a person might think he/she has dispensed entirely with the God belief, but might still retain some vestiges of a traditional God concept — in the sense that some things still somehow express God's will ("I am personally responsible for everything in my life, except for certain things which are beyond my control").

Other people might describe themselves as "semi-religious"; they may believe that personal responsibility holds true up to a point, and the rest is literally up to God ("I am personally responsible for everything in my life, except for certain things which are God's will"). In fact, "An Act of God" is still a legal term, used to define large-scale manifestations of nature such as hurricanes, earthquakes, and floods. And certainly many openly religious people in the West still clearly acknowledge a belief in God and believe that He is responsible for everything — including their own lives.

How can we deal with these varied ideas of God and still work with the occult concept of self-created, self-perpetuated karma? First of all, karma is not an atheistic idea. It is true that according to karmic law, a God does not punish us or reward us directly. We take care of that ourselves, by creating our own causes and by reaping our own effects. But this does not deny the idea of a Higher Power; it simply changes the point of view, and the definition of this Power, into a more abstract, holistic concept.

For most people, the traditional anthropomorphic, Piscean-Age version of God is viewed as punisher and rewarder. Meanwhile, within the Christian and Jewish traditions, small groups of scholars and mystics always have viewed God as an idea, a moving force, a totality; as all-knowing, all-powerful, all-present, all-being. This does not mean "in charge of" everything and everyone. It means *manifesting within and through* everything and everyone.

> Bear in mind that the soul is actually a part of God....It is a general rule that the parts of a whole and the whole are similar, and thus applies to the soul as part of God.[2]

Instead of feeling separate from God and wanting to please Him, these mystics have essentially perceived their own Oneness with God and endeavor to know that Oneness more fully.

> There is no single substance existing in the world, whether it be that which we experience through the senses, or that which we perceive through the mind, which is not comprised in the Creator ....All abundance springs from the One Origin in which no differences are discernible.[3]

On the other hand, in popular religious dogma as presented to the masses, God was rendered knowable, understandable, and easily visualized — often in a literal, humanized form: a King on a throne, a heavenly Father, etc. The drawings of Blake exemplify this vision, which the mystics and saints accepted as a symbol but then recognized the boundless qualities beyond that symbol.

> The ignorant man goes no further than the concept of God as an old man with a long white beard who sat on a golden throne and gave orders for Creation.[4]

In primitive society, a very effective means of enforcing morality has always been a belief in a powerful — even fearsome — deity, which punishes and rewards. In the Piscean Age, the entire structure of the Church, and also most of the Jewish religion, evolved to support popular belief in such a deity. Many people believed literally that they lived their lives on this Earth with the sole purpose of pleasing God. The clergy interpreted exactly what would please God, as most people either could not read or did not have access to religious literature. Thus the religious establishment supported the social structure.

Such an arrangement seems too simplistic for many people today, but at one time it seemed to have all the answers. For example, if God's ways seemed arbitrary, if human suffering seemed mysterious, the theological structure contained clearly detailed explanations: heaven, hell, the Devil, evil, original sin, laws and codes. The structure also included instructions for specific prayers, specific rituals, what to eat, how to dress, when and how and with whom to have sex, how to conduct oneself, *how to please God*. The people were assured that anything which seemed difficult to understand would become clear, later, in heaven. Essentially this view precluded personal responsibility, but it did provide a sort of idealized morality. As we have seen, the morality proved too strict and human barbarism erupted anyway.

Unfortunately our popular heritage of the Judeo-Christian tradition comes from the strict, primitive exoteric vision of God, rather than from the inner, evolved *esoteric* vision which was held so secret. In any case, the primitive religious structure which emphasizes pleasing God is now publically up for re-definition. Within the established religions, the process of change has already begun. Christianity and Judaism now seem more personal, more human, less awesome, and less strict. Now, religious services have been abbreviated and translated into the vernacular; several "pop" Bibles are even available. The role of the clergy is loosening up in many ways, and religious leaders involve themselves more directly and realistically in communal needs than ever before. These are all Cusp phenomena.

But for some people, this popularizing process hasn't been effective enough, hasn't happened quickly enough, and the old monotheistic structures still seem too rigid. Today, when "God's ways" seem arbitrary, many "old-fashioned" religious types can easily hold onto some version of the old religious structures, finding solace and even valid explanations. But for many others, orthodox religions no longer remain meaningful nor relevant to modern life. As a result, many people proceed to throw out the entire package — the specific religion plus any idea of God.

I do not believe that rejecting all is a thoughtful act, nor even an effective one, in terms of personal development and psychic health. Too often people who discard their God may then simply transfer their (primitive) "religious" feelings of awe, fear, and devotion over to science, or psychotherapy, or to any authoritative system which still denies people's own sense of power, inventive thought — and personal responsibility. Or such people may lapse into atavistic superstitition and free-floating fear. They may feel empty, generally worried about who or what is in control, and chalk it all up to neuroses. Some people feel haunted by guilt at having totally left the religion into which they were born; they experience conflict because they no longer "believe in it." Like the character in *Catch-22*, such atheists may find that even though they "got rid of" God, they are still secretly afraid of Him. ("I'm probably just as good an atheist as you are," the lady tells Yossarian. Later she adds, "You'd better not talk that way about Him....He might punish you.)[5]

Somewhere along tne way, people seem to have forgotten that they had the *right* to personally question, interpret, and analyze the God-force in the Universe. They somehow got the idea that to do so meant to reject God (and Goddess) totally. But the mystics, poets, saints, esoteric scholars and innovators of every faith have always struggled, debated, and redefined their own personal views of God. They didn't question their right to do so. Even though many such people came under severe persecution, still they persisted. They managed to find access to books and they respected their own minds. These people didn't understand nor find it meaningful. It seems to me that now, in the Aquarian Age, we can all do this. All of us can deal with God in any way we wish. We can define Him, Her, It, or Them in any way we choose, and still we can remain within our won "inherited" religions. Books of divergent religious beliefs are no longer banned; they are easy to find. No longer will anyone be burned at the stake for heresy. We can reinterpret our old religions, we can make up our own new ones, or we can evolve our own versions of existing religions. I do not mean conversion *per se*, although that remains an option too. I mean making our own ideas of God personal, meaningful, and workable according to all our other beliefs. This includes (should we choose) a belief in karma and personal responsibility. Such choice is our Aquarian heritage. In the Aquarian Age, the God concept is within, and no one can tell us what God "should" mean to us nor how we are to envision or deal with God. Thus we do not have to feel hyprocritical or afraid, or in turmoil or in conflict, or empty in a life devoid of any God at all. Nor do we need to fear God any more. (As we shall see, in the occult view fear can be a karmic cause actually creating problems in our lives, problems which can manifest in tangible ways). I think it is better to believe in a God who is your friend than to be afraid of a God you no longer believe in. And that goes for a Goddess too.

Therefore, does the concept of karma fit in with a Western belief in God? I think so and in this way: If we can accept the responsibility for finding, defining, and understanding our own Gods (make that Deities), then we can accept all our other responsibilities as well.

Group Karma

Here is another much-misunderstood subject, and I shall deal with it in occult terms. If we are all linked as parts of one Divine Whole (called God or what you wish), then we may note that some people seem to be more closely linked than others. I refer to people of the same race, the same nationality, the same tribe, etc. The lives of these people are interwoven, literally seem to be joined by shared events. For example, an entire nation may go to war, suffer a famine, or be invaded by another nation (most often group karma is recognized in its more "disastrous" aspects). A large group of people may band together in response to external events which seem unavoidable. But group karma also applies to people who choose to band together according to similar internal promptings. Such groups include people who form research institutes, study groups, clubs and even religions. The term "group karma" applies when numbers of individuals make personal karmic choices leading in the same direction, to the same set of circumstances, and the same time and space. The karmic choices may be conscious and planned, or they may be subconscious (even in the sense of resignation as a choice, p. 217). The people within such a group usually experience their mutual karmic links, and share their experiences on a profound level. The outsider may find it difficult to understand how or why these people are linked. The outsider may also find it difficult to determine his/her own connection to such a group, especially if the group is experiencing a karmic misfortune. Such confusion often manifests in a feeling of separateness, which can lead to the common copout: "That's their karma; I will leave them to fulfill it."

But such a selfish attitude can prove very harmful to one's *own* karma! Karma is not synonymous with passivity, nor with separation, nor with indifference to the life of any other creature. The only kind of separation indicated in the idea of karma is *free will*. This simply means that it is not a positive act to interfere with another being's free will. This does not mean don't help; this does not mean standing by and letting people suffer. It is a negative act to force someone to do anything; according to karmic law, such behavior reaps negative effects in one's own life. (According to the Threefold Law of the witches, this reaps negative effects in one's own life three times). When confronted with group karma, it may seem that a thin line indeed exists between interference and help. When confronted with this dilemma, rely on your own Inner Bell. No one else can tell you what is right. I can only reiterate that karma is not synonymous with passivity. Your own karma may require you to help a group karmic experience; in such a case you may discover an indirect karmic link with such a group.

Occultists and metaphysicians often hear profound questions when the subject of group karma arises: "Did all the people of that country *choose* to suffer such-and-such a tragedy?..."Did all the people on that airplane *choose* to crash and die?" It seems impossible for me to answer such questions without knowing all the circumstances in each case. The reasons for pain in group karma, as well as in personal karma, can be quite complex and differ each time. This book emphasizes the individual: the basic understanding of personal karma, and the practical applications of working with karma in one's life. The same principles extend to understanding and working with situations involving group karma. But it is important to realize that because of the nature of free will, no mass changes can be worked out effectively unless every member of the group chooses to participate. However, you need not be resigned to remain part of a negative group karma experience. If you belong to such a group — an oppressed minority, a nation under seige, or victims of any adverse situation — you may consciously choose to emerge from the situation. You can accomplish this in a positive, healthy way, and work Words of Power (see Chapter VIII), for this goal, including in your work all who wish to participate. Whenever we hear of people who were "miraculously" thrown clear of a dangerous accident, who emerged unscathed from fires and other disasters, who jumped from trains and escaped the Nazis, who in the face of all odds escaped from any negative situation, in the occult view these people *chose* not to participate in a destructive group karmic experience. They may have made this choice subconsciously. However if a person makes the choice consciously, he/she can then openly invite others to be saved also (i.e., to save themselves) and can help them do so. But you cannot *force people* to do anything, even to escape danger.

Karma and Suffering

On the individual level, it may also seem impossible to understand the workings of karma in severe personal tragedy. How does karmic law explain such painful experiences as the loss of a loved one, serious illness, poverty, or any other occurrence which seems to be far from one's personal choice?

I can only say, although it may sound simplistic in the abstract, that many painful experiences are based on someone else's personal karmic choice; if such an experience seems painful for you, you may be viewing the other person's karmic choice with a limiting perception.

A limiting perception of another person's karmic choice usually involves some idea that the other person's choice *must* affect you — in fact, must affect you negatively. For example, when a person plunges into despair because a lover or spouse choose to terminate a relationship, the despair to a large extent exists in the "victim" perception. Such perception could be turned eventually into an open-minded outlook, which could then lead to a more positive relationship, perhaps with another person. Another example is the potent despair many people feel if a loved ones dies. But in the karmic view, that loved one chose to die. Of course, there may be periods of sadness, but that does not have to make life unalterably worse for the person remaining on this Earth Plane. Such a belief — that life must now be "worse" — constitutes a limiting perception of another person's choice. In the midst of personal tragedy, it may seem difficult to believe that one's own responsibility is involved. But the whole point of working with karma is not to stop there; not merely to assume responsibility and grind to a halt. The *next step* is to assume responsibility for the change-over, the karmic transformation, the change into the positive. In this

110

way, the principles of karma, applied consciously, can help us surmount just about anything.

Instead of speculating in the abstract, we can best start in the here and the now. We can begin by working with the present events and circumstances in our lives. Such work includes being aware of our *perceptions* of our present circumstances and separating these perceptions from an objective view of the circumstances themselves. Such work also includes acknowledging any resignation to our current state and changing such resignation into the awareness that we *can* change our circumstances. Even if working with karma in this way seems impossible or unrealistic, it's like the old joke about chicken soup: *It can't hurt.*[6]

However, some life circumstances present a more complex picture than this explanation of karma provides. If you wish to delve into karmic concepts on a more advanced level, I recommend that you study *The Nature of Personal Reality, A Seth Book* by Jane Roberts, (Prentice-Hall paperback, New Jersey, 1974). This book is also an excellent source of profound self-help techniques.

Finally, when confronted with circumstances which seem incomprehensible or even impossible to have chosen (circumstances of birth, including birth defects, congenital physical disorders, slum environments), I don't think that we can explain these fully within the context of the karma of one lifetime. In order to work with occult techniques on these — or any unexplainable "given" circumstances — it is necessary to extend the concept of karma into a broader occult background: *reincarnation.* And even with general everyday problems, the idea of reincarnation can prove to be an immeasurable help.

Reincarnation

It seems we stood and talked like this before,
We looked at each other in the same way then,
But I can't remember where or when...
—Rodgers and Hart[7]

Birth is not a beginning: death is not an end.
There is existence without limitation; there is
continuity without a starting point....
—Lao Tzu (604 B.C.)[8]

Reincarnation is an infinitely helpful concept in which to find explanations — and solutions — for problems when all else seems to fail. In order to apply reincarnation as a frame of reference for self-help, *you do not even have to believe in it literally.* You may use it in the metaphorical, or shall we say poetic sense. Most witches believe in reincarnation quite specifically and literally, as do the followers of many Eastern religions and philosophies, and adepts of most schools of occult thought. But it is not as well known that both Judaism and Christianity have always included the tradition of reincarnation (also called "metempsychosis" and "transmigration").

The doctrine of transmigration has been secretly
taught from ancient times to small numbers of
people, as a traditional truth which was not
to be divulged.
—St. Jerome (340-420 C.E.)

All souls are subject to the trials of transmigration....
—The Zohar, Vol. II, fol. 99 et seq.

For the purposes of our work, we may view reincarnation as the logical step following the applications of karma within one lifetime. Reincarnation makes it possible for us to deal with karma over many lifetimes. Life may now be viewed as *one long lifetime* divided into many individual "lives"; that is, one eternal life of the soul demarcated by a series of physical births and deaths and rebirths.

The memories of former lives may be hazy, or they may be quite clear. In cultures where reincarnational memory is encouraged from an early age, less is "forgotten" of past lives. Often dramatic examples exist of young children remembering certain houses, locations, even people — all of which they could not possibly have experienced in their present lives. From time to time, such stories come to us from India, Tibet, or other places where reincarnation is accepted and such memories are not categorically ignored or discouraged. These stories may seem bizarre here in the West, where at best they are classified as "psychic phenomena." However in our own culture I would not be surprised to find large numbers of children able to remember past lives if such an idea were not repressed by so many societal influences. Childhood provides the easiest time to draw on these memories because:

- the child is closer, in linear-time perception, to the earlier life experience, and
- the child is usually more psychically open than an adult. Any limiting "screening-out" process of extra-sensory impressions has not yet become solidified by the personality.

But not to worry! An enlightened (and sane) adult has many ways to draw upon reincarnation (karmic) memories and use these memories to gain understanding of the circumstances of this lifetime. And perhaps it is even more valuable to come to an awareness of one's past incarnations at a mature and reasoning age. One is less likely to get embroiled in the emotional impact of such information if one is analytical and even perhaps a bit skeptical. Also mature people can readily distinguish the important difference between karmic memory and fantasy.

Actually, as yet we cannot "prove" whether such memory is accurate — but then what do we mean by "accurate"? I consider a karmic memory accurate if it makes enough sense to explain, work on and effectively solve a specific situation in this life. The "memory" needn't be taken literally. It can be used as imagery, metaphor, or allegory, as a way of gaining insight beyond the confines of this one set of life-circumstances.

The concept of reincarnation thus provides a helpful frame of reference:

- if a problem seems unexplainable within the context of everything you know about yourself in this one lifetime (including early conditioning, past events, etc.),
- if a pattern of a type of problem recurs repeatedly, taking various forms each time — again, of unexplainable origin.

Reincarnation: The Frame of Reference

Just as the idea of karma within one lifetime involved taking personal responsibility for making all life-choices within the circumstances in which you were born, this idea extends into the area of *many* lifetimes. We may now say that even the circumstance into which you were born were also personal choices. They were personal choices on a larger scale.

Everything is viewed as the accumulated causes and effects of personal choices. We choose each life and everything in it. Most of these choices may have been the subsconscious activity of the eternal soul. In other words, we can assume that our souls live through eternal time and space, but our personalities are reborn numerous times into different physical bodies. Our souls usually make each rebirth decision, between lifetimes, while living in the Invisible Realm. When we return to the Earth Plane as babies, we usually have "forgotten" much of our past data — but it remains within us on a deep subconscious level.

We may bring some of this information to a conscious awareness, if we choose. We may begin by acknowledging the basic concepts of reincarnation, specifically as seen within the perspective of this one life. Now, let us acknowledge that each choice in this life was indeed ours, and (just as with karma earlier) we may now accept personal responsibility for all these choices.

At first this idea may take a certain stretch (or possibly leap?) of credibility, but please bear with me if you've gotten this far. You see, the more fully we are able to understand and accept responsibility for these life choices, the more effectively we can now cause major changes in this lifetime (as well as in other lifetimes).

To be specific: We chose our birth, we chose our parents (i.e., we chose parents whose choices of a child meshed with our choices), we chose our race and our religion. We chose the place of birth, the time of birth, and the planetary configurations of that time — so we chose our astrological influences as well. We chose our sex, and our physical appearance, and our talents. We always choose every "given" circumstance of every lifetime (one might say that we "give" these to ourselves). However, karma has accumulated for us by means of our choices. So the choices were never arbitrary, and they were always based on other choices. We chose — and continue to choose — everything we have (and don't have) in this one lifetime here and now *as a direct result of how we lived the last life and the ones before that.* This is "karmic inheritance" — the accumulation of personal karma stretching back in time over the course of many lifetimes.

Karmic inheritance is not irrevocable. Any preconceived notion of karma as something one is "stuck with," or which "has" to be worked out painfully, is neither appropriate nor accurate in the occult view of reincarnation.

What we do now about all those accumulated choices is up to us, in

114

the here and now. True, we may have to begin with certain given circumstances (i.e., the circumstances we find ourselves in now, in this life) but since even these resulted from our own choices, we may now choose to use them and/or transcend them. How and why did we get to be where we are and the way we are? Obviously, information about our past lives can help us to figure this out. But the process of unearthing such information is not one of rationalizing or jumping to conclusions that "seem" to fit (which usually means making them up — or allowing someone else to make them up for us). At best, this process involves personally uncovering ideas and reasons which make sense, which provide enough information to work with, to aid us in making the changes we need and want now.

The point is that is we accept the theory that many of our current problems could have originated in former lives, then the reason we chose our current circumstances was to solve these problems. Some people mistakenly think that if they accept painful current circumstances as their karmic inheritance, they must somehow "deserve" their misery! Such people may conclude that they must have done something "terrible" in their karmic pasts; they must have been bad people and must now reap their karmic punishments. They may end up wallowing in free-floating karmic guilt and resignation. This is ironic, because often the karmic cause of present-life pain is not some "terrible" past deed but a feeling of unjustified guilt or inordinate resignation to personal suffering.

Working constructively with reincarnation involves viewing adverse circumstances (or any "given" circumstances) as opportunities for solving problems which may have been around for a long time. The emphasis is on the solving, and no resignation need be involved. Usually a problem solved is a lesson learned. Working with reincarnation resembles working with karma within one lifetime; a problem can be solved (a choice can be made) either consciously or subconsciously (generally speaking, consciously is faster). With awareness of reincarnation, we do not have to wait hundreds of years to work something out on a subconscious level; we can choose to bring it to consciousness and work with it now.

Sometimes all that we need to work out a problem is the simple realization that it could be of an ancient karmic nature. This removes the element of mystery and confusion which often intensifies such a problem and thus frees one to tackle it in practical ways. Instead of saying, "This is a weird problem which seems to have no cause," we can simply say, "This problem seems to have originated in another life." Once circumstances can be explained within this new frame of reference, the problem often loses its potency. Then we can proceed more easily to apply any method which works to solve it, from

psychotherapy to positive magic (see Words of Power, Chapter VIII).
Here are some common karmic problems:

1 - irrational fears or phobias which cannot be traced to any source in
this lifetime's experience;
2 - guilt patterns or feelings of unworthiness (often in some specific
area) which do not relate to anything in this one lifetime's experience;
3 - sexual problems or even recurring sexual fantasies which seem
unexplainable. (Of course, fantasies aren't necessarily problems, but
sometimes the problem might be that a fantasy seems compellingly
real, in which case it might not be a fantasy at all, but a karmic memory);
4 - personal prejudices which seem unreasonable and even irrational
in the context of one's present ideals, morality, etc. (They may have
been "valid," long ago);
5 - identity problems, feelings of uncertainty about who one "really" is,
or the pervasive feeling that one is an imposter, or is playing a role;
6 - hypochondria and/or a fear of death, which does not seem to relate
to any conditioning experience in this lifetime. (Vague memories of
dying in another time can be the cause of many a karmic neurosis. Also
the way in which one may have died in the past can leave one with a
related phobia — fear of fires, heights, etc.);
7 - difficult or unexplainable relationships.

Many if not most of the important relationships we have in this life
have been set up in earlier lives. Such karmic relationships usually
include family, friends, lovers, mates — even pets! We literally knew
these individuals before, and most often we have a specific karmic
situation to work out with each one. Conversely, they have a karmic
relationship — whether it originated in this lifetime or centuries ago —
in a two-way street, a mutual agreement between two individuals, to
stay involved on some level and for some purpose(s).

Did you ever meet a person for the "first" time and feel that you've
known him/her for your whole life? Well, probably you have — except
that it may have been during another life. Some indications of long-
term, other-life relationships include: love at first sight, hate at first
sight, mistrust at first sight, and the less dramatic but just as tangible
instant feelings of friendship or of kinship. Sometimes the intense
feelings are more evident to one person than to the other. Sometimes
feelings are mutual. Sometimes the other person feels similarly but
won't admit it because the feelings seem too weird. In any case, it is
important to note that it is the *quality* of the past relationship, not the
specific details, which is remembered — and it is that quality which is
important to us now. Karmac relationships vary. Some may date from
only one or two shared lifetimes; and some may have been repeated,

often with variations of roles, over numerous lifetimes. What is the "purpose" of karmic relationships? That varies too. Often, there is some specific "unfinished" business to be mutually worked out. Some relationships are repeated in order to become deeper and more meaningful; others are repeated in order to be ended, once and for all.

The belief in one "soul-mate" and the subsequent search for such a person, is usually karmic in origin. But in the occult view *several* potential karmic soul-mates exist in each of our lives. And there is probably a karmic inheritance of a deep personal nature to be worked out with each. We choose the one we want for this life, and it is up to the other person whether he/she will participate at this time. In addition, we have the option of several karmic love experiences within one lifetime, all equally meaningful.

Roles in relationships may change over the various lifetimes. Most of us have lived many times as men and as women. In heterosexual love relationships, it is possible that the person who is the man in this lifetime may have been the woman last time, and vice-versa. Sometimes a person can be one's former mother, father, child, husband, wife, love, sister, brother or friend! Love has many aspects, many faces. We get a chance to experience them all. And after each lifetime, the quality of love is always remembered rather than the specific role. Over the centuries, roles are secondary to the nature of people's feelings for each other.

In different lives, we may have belonged to many different cultures, races, and nationalities. Often one brings into this current lifetime some unaccountable affinity which seems unrelated to present circumstances. For example, a person may have a strong feeling for a different culture, language, country, or city — other than the one he/she was born into, in this lifetime. Such a person may still be identifying with the circumstances of a past life or lives.

The concept of choice in reincarnation does not conflict with our understanding of heredity or genetics. A strong feeling of identiy for one's current religious, racial, or national heritage may indicate having been reborn numerous times within that particular group. We choose our entire heritage, ancestors included, with each life-choice.

The concept of choice in reincarnation does not discard the importance modern psychology places upon both early environment and conditioning within this one lifetime. We simply take a larger vantage point and note that one chooses all the situations of this one lifetime; also one makes choices about how to *react to* the influences of early environment.

In each life we choose our sex, race, and social identity for a myriad number of karmic reasons. Sometimes we choose a role which is *a priori* difficult. Why? To work out old problems, to solve karmic situations. For example, often homosexuality reflects such a karmic choice. Homosexuality in itself is not a problem. But if one chooses to be born into a society in which homosexuality brings attendant cultural pressure, it would be worth looking into the karmic causes, which may still need to be understood. The same holds true for choosing to be a woman in a culture which subordinates women, or any minority in the midst of an oppressive majority.

Now, at the Cusp, many of us seem to have chosen "downtrodden" roles simply to establish a firm stance for working positive social changes from within. By transcending the culturally negative connotation of the chosen role, one may effectively help many others to do the same.

The reasons for choosing any life-role may have broad, social implications or they may be more personal. For example, many transexuals or transvestites may be longing for other lives in which they were happier in other sexual roles. Most sexual role-playing — in fact most role playing of any kind — may be attributed to karmic memories. Similarly, perhaps the feeling of being older than someone you know to be older than you are — of feeling younger than someone who in this life is physically younger than you — is karmic. Perhaps in other times, the ages were reversed and you remember this.

"Child prodigies" may simply be remembering other mature lifetime experiences and years of study. Even though they may not remember the circumstances of other lives, child prodigies remember the content of their talent and their work.

Thus many explanations of present circumstances lie in an understanding of past lives. If we now live in pleasant circumstances, it is helpful to know the past causes so that we can make the most of what we have. If the present is unpleasant, we now have an added tool to make effective changes, to make this life more positive.

For most people, karma is worked out slowly, and problems are solved gradually over many lifetimes. Generally speaking, the soul of each person thereby evolves to a higher state of awareness and fulfillment. This process continues even if karmic memory is hazy, in fact even if it does not seem to exist at all. Now, the entire process can be speeded up with proper use of karmic memory, but reincarnational memories *must be dealt with very carefully!*

It is important to pay attention to the reasons most people "forget" so much material from other lives. Our culture does not teach us *what to do about* such memories, and it is not healthy to remember them unless we understand what to do about them. When we bring important karmic choices to consciousness, we do this in order to take responsibility for each choice and to work with each choice. Consequently we remember only as much as we are capable of working with.

When we do not know how to work with a karmic memory, we may take the memory too literally. This is not appropriate because in effect it denies some of the validity of our lives on this Earth Plane, here and now. We may place more importance on a past life — by remembering it without knowing what to do with it — than on the life we are now living.

Re-enactment is a common problem that comes with karmic memory. If the memory of a former life is pleasant, we may lapse into re-enacting that pleasant memory over and over. For example, one might say, "I was a happy soldier of fortune in that lifetime. So now I'll quit my job, leave my family, join the French Foreign Legion, and be a happy soldier of fortune again." *But the purpose of karma is growth.* If you really were a happy soldier of fortune once — you already *did* that! And now probably you need to translate what you have learned from that experience into a different situation, preferably one that presents a new set of circumstances for karmic growth. Re-enactment — especially of pleasant former life circumstances — can be seductive. But if we allow ourselves to keep doing the same things over and over again, we may very well come back again into the next life to do what we could have accomplished in this lifetime! It's like repeating the same year of school over and over.

If the karmic memory of the former life is unpleasant, one could slip into a neurotic pattern of re-enactment also. In this case a mood of negative resignation might prevail that could slow down the process of karmic growth. Freud gives a classic example: A woman had a Victorian neurosis of feeling compelled to spill red ink every time she saw a white tablecloth. Freud figured out that the woman was re-enacting a painful memory of her first sexual experience. She felt compelled to re-enact the trauma symbolically, over and over. I think the same tendency could occur with traumas of other lives. We could feel compelled to live out symbolically the same problem over and over — even though we now have a new set of life circumstances in which to grow beyond that original trauma.

If the memory of the past life is extremely painful, one might give in to it all over again, granting it too much importance and too much negative power. One might get depressed and suffer again in response to an experience which has already been transcended and now is actually irrelevant. Finally, if you do not know how to work with a karmic memory, its discovery might lead to an ego-trip. One could trip in either direction: "I was so wonderful, I can just sit back now and be smug," or "I was so terrible, I must now suffer and punish myself." Neither conclusion is valid. If you take a memory too literally, the conclusions could be too simplistic — especially when taken out of context of all your past lifetimes, all your accumulated karma, and mainly all your present life circumstances.

Keeping in mind these potential pitfalls, we can now turn our attention to *remembering other lives:*

Guidelines

1 · You may experience your karmic memories in vague, hazy impressions. Do not expect your memories to be necessarily literal, graphic, or detailed. You will remember only as much as you need and are able to work with.

2 · No matter what methods you use, the best way to get your information is from within. Triggering devices can help and other people can sometimes help — but no one knows your own karmic truths better than you. They are already stored deep within your eternal soul. Your own Inner Bell always remains the final authority for accuracy (i.e., what works for you).

3 · I would advise tracing your memories by subject matter rather than by sequential, all-over lifetime experiences. In other words, trace and work on each *subject* specifically (a relationship, a phobia, etc.). In the process you may trace the problem back through several lifetimes, leaving out other details of of each lifetime but nonetheless fully dealing with the problem. Whenever possible, follow the mood of the subject matter.

4 · It's not who you were at each time that is important to you now, and it's not what you did, as much as *what you learned* and what you do about it now.

5 · Concentrate on the idea of responsibility for each life-choice, and for each cause and effect set in motion. Do not blame or judge, simply accept karmic responsibility. Always concentrate mainly on the idea of *choice in the present* to change the effects of any other lifetime causes. You can change these now.

Suggested Methods

Pay attention to the phenomenon of *deja-vu* ("having already seen"). We all get this feeling from time to time; an event may seem literally to have happened before. As Lorenz Hart put it:

Some things that happen for the first time
Seem to be happening again...

As soon as possible after you experience such a feeling, write it down. Think about the feeling and make notes of associated ideas and events surrounding the experience. Keep a notebook of such experiences. Also, pay close attention to your dreams. Keep a record, and particularly watch for recurring themes which do not seem to bear a direct resemblance to circumstances in this life. Compare these to your *deja-vu* notes. Write down all you can of past dreams and past *deja-vu* memories. Do not censor anything as irrelevant — it might be a key.

Here is an example: I have had recurrent dreams of lush tree foliage which did not bear resemblance to any I have seen in this country, in this life. When I travelled to Europe as a teenager, the trees looked oddly familiar (*deja-vu*). They seemed identical to those in my dreams. At that time I was not involved in karmic memory. In the years since I became involved in this research, I have kept a dream record and noticed details. Those lush trees in my dreams grew in a park, but the park didn't resemble any I had ever seen. Many years later I travelled to Europe again, and this time in a certain city I passed what looked exactly like that park. I have since pieced together other details, all having the same mood as the *deja-vu* experiences and as the dreams. I have uncovered in the process some past-life experiences related to that park — karmic explanations for problems in this life. I have allowed the memories to emerge gradually; I did not force them. I simply kept notes and followed the trail of the mood of the memories. The process took several years.

A wonderful method for unfolding karmic memories is the use of tarot cards (Chapter VII, p. 176). If you have another person read for you, be sure not to tell your exact purpose. Simply say, "I am trying to figure out a story (or event)," but do not spell out that this may lead to information about other lives. It's always good to check out one system with another system; every method of divination helps. Check out the tarot with the *I Ching*. Check out your dreams with the tarot and the *I Ching*. And have your astrologer check out the fourth, eighth, and twelfth Houses, and the Nodes of the Moon.

I recommend that if you wish to investigate your past lives, use a combination of all the above methods. Set up your search beforehand with a careful Words of Power Statement. Here is an example of such a Statement, subject to your rewording after you learn the Principles in Chapter VIII.

Words of Power For Karmic Memory

There is One Power,
This is all time, all space, and all wisdom,
And I (your name here), an individualization of The Power,
Now draw upon my heritage of my own time, space, and wisdom,
Specifically by remembering *what it is appropriate for me to*

remember about my karmic past —
Specifically in relation to (name problem).
I now solve this situation in an easy, natural, and positive way;
I draw to me all the memories I need and all the ideas which I need,
    Specifically in relation to (name problem).
    I now solve this situation in an easy, natural, and positive way;
    I draw to me all the memories I need and all the ideas which I need,
And use these in all the most perfect and creative ways,
To bring about that which I need and want in this life,
According to free will,
And for the good of all,
And so must it be.

This statement is particularly helpful, especially if used before going to sleep. The Words of Power will help you direct your dreams towards karmic recall. Or you may simply say, before going to sleep, "I now instruct my subconscious mind to reveal helpful karmic memories to me in positive ways."

Please be very careful about information that comes from outside sources. I would like to recommend a good psychic reading, but it may be difficult to find an accurate source (see "Psychics," p 155). Many psychics claim to be able to read past lives, but may instead actually read their own projections, fantasies, neuroses, — or pick up your subconscious expectations, projections, fantasies, etc. Some psychics garble or interpret the information they read — even the accurate information — in an inaccurate way. Reading past lives is a highly technical job, and any psychic who claims to do it easily or who is eager to do it for you is probably irresponsible. Psychic reading should never be undertaken lightly. Also, remember that spirit guides can be either very helpful or very irresponsible (p. 29).

However I am not discounting psychic readings for the purpose of karmic recall. I have found several friendly spirit guides to be most helpful — but it took years of wading through pompous and inaccurate spirit contacts (and garbled human readers) before I met the right ones. (See "Spirit Contact" section in *Earth Magic, A Dianic Book of Shadows* by the author, Earth Magic Productions, 1980, pp. 42-45. Please note that this is advanced work).

Another popular method for tracing karmic memory is *hypnosis*, and this I mistrust most of all. The idea of hypnosis is not unequivocally terrible. But the variables built into the process, especially when dealing with past lives, simply can run too rampant. There is no way to tell for sure whether the subject is remembering his/her own past lives, or picking up the hypnotist's past lives, or picking up the past lives of someone else (by ESP), or piecing together inaccurate data in an effort to please, and influenced by the hypnotist's suggestions.[9] Self-hypnosis does not seem to prove much more reliable. I would not rule out hypnotic regression entirely; you might work out just the most perfect method. But I do urge you to be extremely careful.

I have heard numerous stories about karmic recall, and have had many personal experiences, as have most of my friends. We have found working with karmic memories to be an intriguing and incredibly helpful way to work on contemporary problems. But I have also heard *and experienced* some off-the-wall, out-into-the-wild-blue-yonder karmic blunders. I would like to warn you so that you can benefit from these:

- Beware of other people trying to pull you into their karmic trips.
- Beware of trying to coerce others into your karmic memories. (As in all occult work, *no manipulation!*)

For example, in some occult circles you may encounter a come-on equivalent to "come up and see my etchings," i.e., "come up and be part of my past karma." I have actually heard this line, as have some of my women friends: "We were lovers in another life; you are my soul-mate." Please don't fall for that one! Some self-proclaimed guru types have been known to assemble a veritable cast of karmic characters around themselves. Such a cult leader may claim to be the reincarnation of Jesus, Buddha, Krishna, or another spiritual leader. All the loyal followers who then cluster around may also claim to "remember" their past identities. These are shared delusions. At present, alleged "reincarnations" of Jesus seem to be quite popular. You may have read about such cases in the newspapers.

It is equally irresponsible to involve even one other person in your own karmic memories, however real they may seem to you, unless of course both karmic memories (independently recalled) mesh. And even so, please take it all as frame of reference. It if doesn't help things now, it is not a useful karmic memory; possibly not even an accurate one. Even if a karmic memory appears accurate, even if several people share the memory — using all the responsible methods delineated in this chapter — the memory still serves merely as a frame of reference for working on the present. It is still not more important than the present.

Reincarnation is a fascinating area, deserving much more study than we have so far afforded it in this culture. Such study is likely to reveal far more important information about the nature of life than we have imagined.

Witches believe that we reincarnate in the following ways:

1 · on this Earth Plane
2 · in the Unseen Realm
3 · on other planets.

We also believe that there is a "waiting period" in the Unseen Realm for each soul, in between each Earth-life experience. We usually choose to reincarnate with our loved ones again and again, and Halloween is the holiday which is dedicated to this idea. I believe that anyone can get to the point where he/she can consciously direct the next incarnations.

Now, hold on to your hats: Witches believe that we can reincarnate in the Unseen Realm (2, above). At first glance that may seem to mean that we can reincarnate in spirit form. That idea may be sufficiently strange for anyone. But it means much more. Remember that all time is coexistant. Past, present, and future are all happening together at one time; human consciousness merely *preceives* time as sequential. Consequently there must be other levels of existence than we are able to perceive ordinarily while we are here in the World of Form. There are myriad, multidimensional soul activities — including our own lives in alternate universes. (Some theories go so far as to suggest that our souls — or some "part" of them — may be living parallel lives in alternate universes right now). In fact, within this context one could say that *all our incarnations* are not necessarily sequential. Past, present, and future lifetimes — which is which? In a sense, they are *all happening right now,* and we are simply choosing to perceive this one. If we have gone as far as the ideas in this chapter, we have now extended our perceptions *in a linear fashion* through "past" incarnations. Thus we can plan for "future" ones — even glimpse them.

But we can also change all of them (past included). If you wish to work on this advanced level, I suggest you read *The Nature of Personal Reality* and other books by Jane Roberts. For our purposes here (basic occult self-help in daily life), we may simply repeat that sequential memory of past incarnations can be extremely helpful — as a frame of reference for this life — if one works with the memories as choices, and if one identifies and solves each problem and then moves on. *Karma keeps on moving.*

And now let us move on to PART II of this book. We have established our occult foundation. Now we can begin to work with the techniques.

[1]Joseph Heller, *Catch-22*, Dell Publishing Co., Inc., New York, 1973, p. 185.

[2]Rabbi Levi Isaac Krakovsky, *Kabbalah, The Light of Redemption,* The Press of the Yeshivat Kol Yehuda for the Dissemination of the Study of the Kaballah, The Old City Jerusalem, Israel, and Research Centre of Kabbalah, New York, 1970, p. 104.

[3]Rabbi Yehuda Ashlag, *Kaballah Ten Luminous Emanations*, Research Centre of Kabbalah, New York, 1969, p. 28.

[4]Dion Fortune, *The Mystical Qabalah*, Ernest Benn Ltd., London, 1974.

[5]Heller, *Catch-22*, pp. 183-185.

[6]This joke is attributed to the events surrounding the death of a famous actor on the Yiddish stage. In different versions of this joke, it's often a different actor. In any case, the actor suddenly and mysteriously falls down and dies during a performance. The curtain rings down. The manager of the theater makes a sad announcement: "Ladies and gentlemen, I am sorry to inform you that the play cannot go on. Our leading actor has just died."
From the balcony comes a small, hopeful voice. "Give him some chicken soup."
"I don't think you understand," replies the somber manager. "Mr. —— is *dead*."
"That's all right, try some chicken soup anyway."
"But he has passed away. Chicken soup can't help him now."
The voice grows defiant. *"It can't hurt!"*
I once referred to this joke during a radio show in relation to doing occult work in circumstances which one might ordinarily be resigned to. An angry vegetarian listener called and said: "You're wrong about chicken soup; *it hurts the chicken!*" Of course I conceded that he was right. But the joke is a metaphor, and when working with positive magic, no negative sacrifice of a chicken is involved.

[7]"Where Or When," copyright Chappell Music Co., Inc., 1937.

[8]All the quotes in this section of chapter VII with the exception of the one by Rodgers and Hart, may be found in *Reincarnation in the World's Religions*, compiled and edited by Joseph Head and S.L. Cranston, A Quest Book (paperback), The Theosophical Publishing House, Wheaton, Ill., 1968. THis book is a fascinating compilation of 400 quotations which traces the subject through most of the world's religions by the writers and philosophers of many cultures.

[9]It has been proven possible to create fictional past lives. This is described in *Psychic Discoveries Behind the Iron Curtain*, by Sheila Ostrander and Lynn Schroeder, Bantam Books, 1971. See Chapter 12, "Artificial Reincarnation."

PART 2

PERSONAL APPLICATIONS

Magic and Occult Techniques for Daily Life

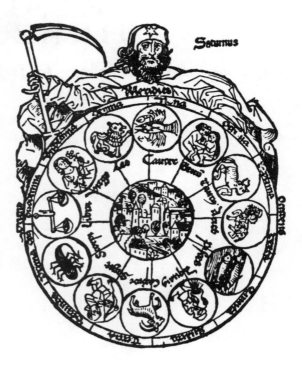

Chapter VI

ASTROLOGY

When you wish upon a star
Makes no difference who you are...
When you wish upon a star
your dreams come true.

—Jiminy Cricket[1]

Men at some time are masters of their fates,
The fault, dear Brutus, is not in our stars,
But in ourselves...

—Shakespeare[2]

You don't have to be an astrologer to reap the benefits of this ancient art; nor do you have to be a credulous, gullible believer, suspending all logic. I consider astrology to be a unique blend of science and spirituality (or, we may say, a blend of the "rational" and the "relational"). You can come to it from either viewpoint.

In earlier times, astrology was applied mainly to matters of survival. Lately it has emerged as a powerful tool for personal growth and fulfillment. I shall be concentrating here on the use of astrology as a personal tool.[3]

If you are an astrologer, probably not much in this chapter will be new. But I hope you will agree that a professional astrologer serves an informed public far more effectively than an uninformed public. If you are not an astrologer, there is no need for you suddenly to become one! I am not an astrologer either. But I have acquired sufficient understanding of this field to make use of astrology in my life in positive ways. I recommend that you too increase your familiarity with this subject, and I will provide some guidelines for you. You may then decide to become an astrologer or you may not. In any case, astrology need not be a mystery to you. Some nonadepts equate all occult work with astrology, and assume that anyone involved with occult study must automatically be an astrologer as well. This is not the case. Astrology is perhaps the most specific technical branch of the occult arts. It involves a certain aptitude in math and a precision of deductive thought. Many gifted scholars in other occult areas have found that they cannot be (or do not wish to be) astrologers. Conversely, many astrologers do not become involved in any other occult area. (I am speaking for today. In earlier times, a working knowledge of astrology was linked inextricably to other occult fields, such as ceremonial magic and alchemy). Astrology is definitely a specialty.

History

The origins of astrology have not yet been pinpointed. Most historians agree that the study seems to have originated in the Fertile Crescent area of the Babylonian Empire, approximately 6,000 years ago. By 3,000 B.C., the astrologer-priests of Babylonia drew up horoscopes according to the complex zodiacal/planetary system which is the foundation for our astrological work today. How did the ancient Babylonians develop such a system? The accepted theory is that these priests spent centuries correlating planetary observations with corresponding events in their society. Using statistics, they deduced casual relationships between the specific movements of the heavenly bodies and trends in people's lives and in the culture. The Babylonian priests led secluded lives devoted to this work, and spent their nights on towers built near the Persian Gulf — an area endowed with incredibly clear views of the skies. The Jewish tribes then carried the study of astrology into Egypt, and the Egyptians established their own branch of the work. The Greeks evolved astrology to a more developed state, and next the Romans took up the study. By this route the Roman conquerers eventually brought astrology to Europe, where the study survived the confusion of the Middle Ages and had a resurgence with scholars in the Renaissance. However, this accepted historical explanation is a bit too neat because it fails to take into account the following facts:

• Northern European pagans had built astronomically accurate monuments — such as Stonehenge — thousands of years *before* The Romans invaded Britain. Possibly the pagans constructed these monuments at the same time that the Babylonians arrived at their deductive statistical system of astrology. How did the European pagans get their information about the stars? Their own skies were not as clear as those in the Persian Gulf area.

- A sophisticated astrological system had been in use for centuries in South America, as the Conquistadors noted before they wiped out the Aztec, Inca, and Mayan cultures.
- In the Orient, specifically China and India, astrology has flourished for thousands of years in a variation on the origina' Babylonian study.

Thus the history of astrology can be traced up to a point, but the exact origins are as yet unknown.

Astrology has received its share of public misrepresentation. Early in my acquaintance with this field, I felt repelled by the vague and simplistic pap which passes for astrology in the media. But I felt equally discouraged by the time-consuming, intricate and technical approach in the more reputable textbooks and courses. I finally found that one of the best ways to get a foundation in astrology — adequate for all practical and personal purposes — is to be friends with a good astrologer! Better yet, be friends with *several* good astrologers. So I recommend this to you. Even if they do not consider themselves professionals, even if they consider astrology a hobby — if they can erect a natal chart, if they can read transits and progressions (all terms we shall discuss in a minute) — I suggest that you invite them over for coffee and danish. And talk.

I suggest that you provide yourself in this way with an ongoing, friendly, pleasant, conversational exchange about astrology, as part of your life. However this friendship is not a substitute for the hiring of professional services; it is *in addition to* it. Another suggestion is to read one or more of the basic texts — if you have the time and aptitude.[4] I would also like to suggest that you investigate any basic astrology courses available in your community. If you read one of the texts first, you will then be able to assess the value of the course and instructor. All of the qualifications of a good astrologer apply to a good astrology teacher also.

In any case, I strongly recommend as much of a foundation in astrology as you can possibly muster. It's a highly technical field, and the more information you have, the more astrology can serve your needs. You also will become less dependent on an astrologer, although the more you know about the subject, the more helpful the services of a professional astrologer will be to you.

Most occultists agree that of all the occult arts, astrology is the one which qualifies most definitely as a science. Many skeptics have been won over by the empirical nature of astrology once they took the time to investigate. The basic system of measurement — the astrological chart — is essentially standard all over the world. It is based on standard *astronomical* data taken from an *ephemeris*, a chart listing

131

the exact astronomical positions of all the planets (for midnight of each day over Greenwich, England). Astrology uses the same information about the planetary movements which is compiled and used by planetariums and astronomical observatories throughout the world. You can observe the movements of the planets, if you are fortunate enough to have the exciting opportunity, through a high-powered telescope. Astrology calculations involve precise mathematics; calculations drawn up by any astrologer on any subject can be checked against the corresponding calculations by any other astrologer or any computer. If accurate, the calculations will be identical.

Of course astrology also has its spiritual side; it graphically demonstrates the Oneness of all life. By working with the influence of far-off planets on our own Earth life-forms, we are able to experience the interrelationships of all life in the Universe. An element of *interpretation* also comes into the practice of astrology. With the basic information as a foundation, an intuitive, thoughtful astrologer can add a deep philosophical dimension to the interpretive area of his/her work.

However this spiritual, interpretive side can lead to serious errors for any astrologer not sufficiently well grounded in the precise, empirical side of the field. An astrological reading differs from a psychic reading. Too many astrologers have been known to, shall we say, "go off into the blue" when they reach the interpretation of a horoscope. It is very important for astrologer and layperson alike to remember that *every* planet, *every* aspect, and *every* configuration represents a *traditional principle* of energy, which allows for a range of traditional meanings. For example, the influence of the planet Mars represents the principle of initiating or physicalized action, which could manifest in a number of wars including: warlike ("martial") anger, sexual activity, or realized creative projects. The choice of which one of these meanings applies is often indicated by other aspects in a chart — and is sometimes best determined by the intuitive or psychic faculties of the astrologer. However, you don't have to be psychic in order to be a good astrologer — if you've studied enough, had enough experience (i.e., seen enough horoscopes), and have enough respect for the free will of your clients.

Free will is perhaps the least understood element in this field. Even among the better astrology texts, those which are based on techniques from earlier periods may still reflect the so-called "medieval" influence. Medieval philosophy, backed by religious dogma and life conditions, emphasized the idea of destiny — which was usually of a harsh nature. In those dark times, preordained fate seemed irrevocable for most people. People were generally locked in to their life circumstances. Most diseases were fatal. Violence was an everyday occurrence and life was short. Thus a "negative" astrological aspect appeared to be inescapable. Many astrological configurations once considered "dangerous" or "malefic" may still appear in a person's chart. At one time people had little or no hope of surviving such aspects. Today, the forewarned individual may make use of such a "negative" indication as a learning experience, and can emerge from the experience unscathed and actually in better condition. Today a person can tune in on the potential positive side of the aspect. For example, the planet Saturn provides a dramatic illustration. Saturn used to be known as "the great malefic." People would shudder in horror at a Saturn influence in a chart. Today Saturn has gained a more realistic reputation as "the great teacher." Free will and personal choice have always been operative in astrology; and in the current cultural context, they are more relevant than ever. Every planet, every aspect, and every influence has at least two sides — two or more basic choices — that are totally up to the individual. The awareness of these choices is an essential philosophical starting point from which to approach your personal use of astrology.

As with any other occult technique, you can cause profound changes by using Words of Power. Here is a typical Words of Power Statement which is designed to work directly on any astrological influence you wish to change. (When you study Chapter VIII, you will see how to revise the following Statement or to compose your own).

Words of Power For An Astrological Influence

There is One Power,
Which guides the stars and the planets,
Which moves through the Universe
And which guides me, and moves through my life.
I (your name here), am a perfect manifestation of this Power;
I hereby use it now, for good,
Specifically to turn this astrological aspect, (name aspect), into its most positive expression in my life.
I release all negative power out of this aspect,
And affirm only positive Power —
For the good of all,
And according to the free will of all,
And so it must be!

Another of the main misconceptions surrounding the field of astrology involves the use of *Sun signs.*

Sun Sign Definitions

Sun sign definitions do not represent astrology any more than Boy

Scout (or Girl Scout) first aid represents medicine. And yet some people believe that Sun sign definitions — the most simplistic area of astrology — represent the entire field! Sun sign definitions may be the most widely known area of astrology, but they are only a starting point! Twelve signs of the zodiac make up the astrological year. Everyone has to be born under one sign. This represents the position (the constellation) which the Sun was in at the time of your birth. Each sign represents a list of traditional personal characteristics *which may or may not apply to you.* Your personality characteristics are described more accurately by the position of *all the planets*, rather than just the Sun, at the time of your birth — and by the *aspects* (or mathematical angles) which the planets form in relation to one another.

For example, here are some popular Sun sign characteristics usually ascribed to people born under the sign of Taurus (April 20 to May 20). Taureans are said to love money, to be skilled with their own finances and the financial affairs of others, and, in general, to be naturally acquisitive. But the truth is that many Taurus people don't love money particularly, don't understand anyone's finances very well, and don't give a hoot about valuable acquisitions. This is because at the time of their birth the other planets balance out and/or significantly alter the way "typical" Taurean qualities manifest. It's simply not accurate to assess a person by his/her Sun sign.

> I've had too many people guess my sign. They take twelve guesses.
>
> —Robert Klein[5]

I used to say unequivocally that all Sun sign astrology was simplistic and invalid. Lately however I have discovered some Sun sign books and individual Sun sign pamphlets (books for each sign, published every year) that have been written so responsibly that I must revise my harsh remarks. Now I'll say that you may find *some* helpful Sun sign information.[6] But I must emphasize that Sun sign work provides a good starting point or beginning frame of reference in astrology, nothing more.

Unfortunately some people actually seem to believe that you can predict events by Sun sign astrology, or that you can determine the compatability of two people with different signs. In fact, too many newspaper and magazine columns would lead us to believe that astrology is mainly a mass of vague and arbitrary predictions and warnings: "Today is a good day to ask for a raise, but stay away from all people named Elmo." Unless you are one of the very few classic astrological cases born exactly at the time on which the (usually syndicated) Daily Blat astrologer based his/her calculations — Sun sign indications for each day are totally meaningless. And never, *never* base your marriage, love affair, dinner date, or any other partnership on these generalizations (such as "Aries people should not get seriously involved with Sagittarians," etc. *Nonsense!)* The most effective responsible, intelligent and informed way to make use of astrology in your own life is to have the most accurate *natal chart* drawn up for you, by the very best astrologer you can find.

First, we'll discuss the natal chart — later, how to find the astrologer.

The Natal Chart, or Horoscope

The horoscope is your basic personal chart, erected by a competent astrologer who works with your birth information. This includes the *time* preferably to the exact minute of birth (unless your mother has perfect recall, you can get it from your birth certificate, local bureau of records, or from the hospital where you were born); *date*, including the day, month, and year; and *place* — town or city, and country.

If you cannot obtain any of this information, you may give the astrologer various other data of significant events in your life, including the times, dates and places of each such event. Significant events could include marriages, births and deaths of relatives, major moves or job changes. The astrologer then arrives at your birth information by a process called *rectification*. If done correctly, the natal chart then can be as accurate as if you had supplied the pertinent birth information.

The outer circle contains the traditional symbols for the signs of the zodiac in astrological order. The markings inside the circle represent the planets with their exact positions indicated. The circle is divided into twelve astrological sections, called *Houses*.

The planets represent principles of energy. The signs represent the ways in which those energies are expressed. The Houses represent the different areas of life.

Every one of these pieces of information is important; so are the aspects (the configurations which these pieces of information form in relation to one another).

The natal chart is actually a map of the sky at the time you were born. It serves as a sort of portrait, a mirror, a blueprint of your life *(as potential).*

The astrologer may spend several hours or even several days preparing your chart. Then the astrologer will proceed to interpret and explain it. I recommend that you try to meet with him/her and ask as many questions as you wish. Tape the session or take copious notes. As with any other occult reading, do not "feed" any information! Let the astrologer deliver the information to you. If the chart is accurate, all the information you need will be readily available. Remember that all the

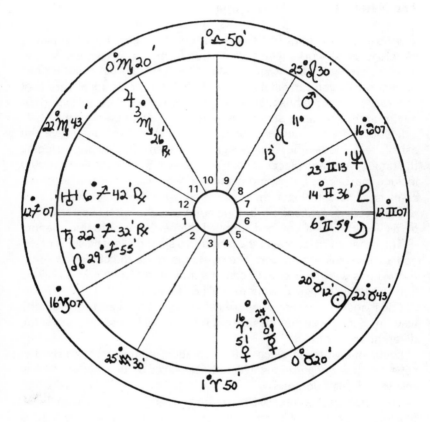

Fred Astaire
May 10, 1899
Omaha, Neb.
9:16 pm

planets, Houses, and aspects in your chart have traditional meanings. A range of interpretive choices exist within these meanings, but no matter how intuitive, psychic or imaginative the astrologer may be, he/she cannot — with any accuracy — go too far afield from these basic meanings. Thus a good astrologer never has any need to fake anything.

A well-drawn natal chart can be mind-boggling in its accuracy. But more important, it can prove to be priceless by revealing important information about facets of your personality and your life. The horoscope indicates what you have, what you need, what you can readily have (and may not be aware of), what may give you problems, what needs work, and how best to work at improvements and changes. The basic natal chart is an in-depth portrait. It does not predict; it indicates life-long trends. So-called "predictions" (actually, *future trends*) come later as *transits* and *progressions*. A good basic astrological reading includes the natal chart plus important transits and progressions. Usually the basic reading session (one to two hours) includes the entire package.

The astrologer's *fee* usually allows for the preparation time as well as for the personal reading session. This service used to cost approximately $15 to $25, and it still does in some places. But do not be surprised if the service costs from $50 to $100. The lengthier the session and the more in-depth the forecast segment of the reading, the more expensive a reputable reading is likely to be. I am referring here to the basic, standard, full natal chart. Follow-up services, such as yearly check-ups, solar returns, progressions, etc., usually cost from $10 to $15 an hour.

Some astrologers prefer to write the information and mail it to you; some record it on tape cassettes and mail it. Of course these latter methods are necessary if your astrologer lives far from your home. But even if your astrologer works long-distance, if you have any questions I recommend that you either call or write for clarification. This is part of the service! Everything must be entirely clear to you. Astrologers are human and can make mistakes, but the service they provide can ideally be thorough and accurate. So always speak up, especially if you have any doubts; *never rationalize to make the reading fit you.* I once had a chart drawn which placed my Moon in the wrong sign, the only part of the reading which did not make sense to me. It was my first real chart, and I didn't yet know where my Moon was — but I suspected that the attributes of the given Moon-placement did not apply. At that time I was consulting the astrologer for career guidance, and the inaccurate Moon-placement confused me in this regard. I'm glad that I mentioned it to the astrologer, and he was delighted as he then could correct a tendency to error which might have turned up in other people's charts. *Never, never accept the information as gospel.* Ask questions, debate, discuss! It's your chart; it's a service for which you pay.

And speaking of payment, if you can't yet afford an astrologer, or don't wish to, or haven't located the right one — you might consider using a reliable computer service.[7] Some computer services supply purely mathematical data with no interpretation; often astrologers use these to check out their own math or actually to do the math. (There is also a growing trend — as computers get less unwieldy — for astrologers to work with their own computers).

Computers have the disadvantage of not being able to conduct a conversation with you, the interpretation is usually at a minimum. But computer charts do have certain advantages: they are usually reasonably priced ($2 to $15) and they are usually extremely accurate in their calculations. I recommend of course only computer services which work with the *exact* time, date, and place of birth. The word "computer" does not automatically mean "expert" or "accurate." Beware the computer rip-off which purports to tell all without individual synthesis of your birthdata. At the time of this writing, too many disreputable astrological computer services exist. Specifically, watch out for astrological companies purporting to do "research" and offering low-priced "reprints" of your natal chart. These are usually hooks to bring in further payments. Our culture seems to have a strange reverence for computers. I suspect this is a transference of primitive religious feelings — but that's another story. In any case, please remember that a computer is only as good as its programmer. If a good astrologer (human) was not involved in the programming, the computer is a dud — no matter how accurate its math. A further word of caution: Watch out for computers offering only partial information. For that matter watch out for human astrologers who give only partial information! A standard, basic complete natal chart includes *eight planets* (Earth, of course, is excluded) *plus the Sun and Moon, twelve signs,* and *twelve Houses,* plus *a variable number of aspects,* with a clear explanation of every planet, House and aspect.

If you can afford it and feel like being particularly thorough, you might consult two different astrologers, or one astrologer and one computer service (or even more computers and/or astrologers) and correlate your own results. If you do this, keep the information from each consultation to yourself and draw your own conclusions.

To help you understand everything in your basic natal chart, try to memorize not only your Sun sign, but your *rising sign* and *Moon sign* as well. This will help you to deal with the transits yourself, and if you happen to come across any technical information in books, magazines or conversations, you will be more likely to relate to such information in a personal way.

Progressions and Transits

Progressions are the secondary or yearly trends, and may be applied to your life in a specific and personal way. I hope that your astrologer gives you a year's worth of progressions in addition to your natal chart, as well as pointing out to you the important transits coming up. The progressions provide excellent guidelines to indicate propitious times and less beneficial times for specific projects and goals. Yes, there are times which are "better" than others to plan marriage, vacations, business ventures, moving, and changing jobs. Of course, these are not mandatory. You are not doomed if you "disobey" the indicated advice, but forewarned is forearmed. It is helpful to know what times to be on guard against *possible* illness, emotional stress, and other problems. You can then take practical precautions for these times, and often actually *prevent* such potential problems from occurring. Of if they do occur, you will be prepared and equipped to handle the problems easily, and to tune in on the positive side of the experience. This way, you will always come out ahead. And as for propitious times — why not take advantage of them? Anything which you undertake at the appropriate astrological time is bound to be more successful.

Transits are the daily (tertiary) passing trends of each planet through the various Houses and signs, the specific planetary positions in the sky for each day. The transits are astronomically accurate and standard; they are found in the ephemerides for each year. You may find transits in the better astrology magazines for each month[8] and in yearly Moon calendars. The transits indicate broad trends, very much like a weather report. Typical transits for a specific day read:

> Monday, the Full Moon day, opens with events that show echoes of the early-month Uranian restless initiative. Mercury enters Capricorn, our mental abilities are centred on practical work. Watch out for a quarrelsome Mars. Friendship has a great significance for us now. Seek the smaller pleasures as insights grow dull. Full Moon gives luster to surface beauty. Avoid profundity. Stability means peace.[9]

As you can see, the transits may be applied in a large-scale cultural sense, on a national level, and on a personal level as well. A basic knowledge of the traditional meanings of the planets and the Houses will provide added insights. You may correlate the transits for a specifically important day with your own basic natal chart information. Or you may simply note the obvious personal applications, such as watching the position of the Moon.

For example: The *Full Moon* every month is usually an emotional time for anyone (lunacy, loony, lunatic, etc.). It is a time when feelings seem more intense, it is a time to drive carefully and to watch your emotional reactions. Also note that the Full Moon may affect others around you who may not be as aware of the astrological implications. The *New Moon* is an excellent time for beginning projects. It is also an excellent time to deal with plants — even houseplants; it is a time for all growing things. After the New Moon, haircuts grow in more quickly; in fact everything seems to flow more quickly as a general rule.

The *Waxing Moon* is the two-week period between the New Moon and the Full Moon. This is the growing-period. After the Full Moon comes the two-week *Waning Moon*, the time to turn inward, make plans, and allow things to germinate. During the Waning Moon, things may grow more slowly and energy may be low. Some people feel depressed and/or physically depleted when the Moon has waned to its lowest point, right before the New Moon begins again.

This example involved only one planet, the Moon. But notice how it can affect anyone in a personal way. Simply knowing about the Moon's phases in advance provides enormous help for making plans. Many of the old-fashioned farmer's almanacs are based on lunar cycles.

When you consider the other planets also, the transits are even more helpful. For example, the movement of the planet Mercury often affects people in the communications fields. When Mercury goes retrograde, communications slow significantly, including mail, radio and television broadcasting, publishing, and business contracts. When Mercury goes direct, communications speed up again. I have found that when people know about any difficult transiting aspects in advance, they become less negatively affected. And when transits indicate propitious times, people are able to take advantage of these times and accomplish more. Also, the more you know about your natal chart, the more specifically you will be able to relate the daily transits to your own life. Always check the transits for any important day, just to see what's cooking in the sky. Such a check is not meant to dictate your actions; it's to tell you what you might well take into consideration. As I said, the transits are like a weather report — and wouldn't you like to know ahead of time if you'll be needing an umbrella and boots?

Comparison Charts

The natal charts of two people may be astrologically compared, noting the points of harmony, the points of similarities, and the points of contact where problems might occur. The technical name for this process is *synastry*. Usually an astrologer charges the standard fee for each natal chart, but not necessarily anything extra for the comparison *service.*

Comparison charts are most helpful. I find them indispensable for any partnership or important relationship: marriage, living together, business ventures, creative collaborations. A comparison chart also makes an ideal wedding gift or anniversary gift. Unfortunately some astrologers may jump to conclusions when they see negative indications between two people in a comparison chart; the astrologer may conclude that such a relationship is doomed to failure. But this is not necessarily the case! Problems revealed in comparison charts are valuable indications of areas needing work in the relationship, with clues pointing out *how* to do such work together. In fact, many couples with difficulties in love relationships have been helped enormously by comparision charts. It's amazing to find out what makes one's partner "tick" astrologically; such knowledge provides deep mutual understanding with guidelines for better communication. I'm not saying that astrologers should *replace* marriage counselors. But I am saying that a competent astrologer can provide an equally effective service which can supplement other counseling. (This goes for individuals seeking personal insight as well as for couples).

Shopping For An Astrologer

Now, how do you find a competent astrologer and one who is right for you?

Recently much consideration has been devoted to astrological licensing, astrology boards (tests, like medical and law boards), and official qualifications. Such consideration makes an effort to establish competence as a prerequisite for anyone who decides to hang out a shingle as an astrologer. Several states are attempting to license astrologers, but this is still a chancy proposition. Who will do the licensing? What should the qualifications be? Upon what basis could we establish standards? These questions are among the major issues confronting astrologers today.

For now, no one system satisfies me for choosing a competent astrologer. I suggest several methods:

● Arm yourself with as much research as you can handle (good books and astrological magazines, as well as astrological information from knowledgeable friends). Then get several names from reliable sources.
● Which of your friends or acquaintances has had a good natal chart reading lately? If anyone whose opinion you respect was favorably impressed by an astrologer, get the astrologer's name.

- Check out occult magazines as well as astrological magazines (not the silly, dippy ones, please. Go for quality). Magazines usually provide an astrological service, or you may write to the magazine for staff recommendations in personal astrology. Check out the classified ads, but avoid the splashy ads (see Ten-Foot-Pole checklist #1, p. 143).
- When you see a sound article on astrology in a magazine, you can write to the author in care of the magazine. Often astrological writers have private practices which they do not advertise.
- "Underground" newspapers, small local newspapers and specialized magazines often list astrologers in their varied "services offered" classified ad sections. Look carefully. You may find astrological services offered on the same page as paperhangers and babysitters.
- Occult shops and bookstores often know local astrologers or have resident astrologers. Most occult shops provide bulletin boards with local astrologers' names and addresses.
- Adult education groups and colleges often include astrology courses. Check the teachers and the graduates. If there is an astrological school in your area, check out graduates and faculty members.

Seeking out an astrologer remains a relatively unstructured activity, and I think that is appropriate for an occult venture. My basic system would be to get as many names as you can from various sources and then depend on your Inner bell to pick the right one. You may also use Words of Power (for an exchange of services, p. 230) before you begin your search.

However do not just sit back, and expect your Inner Bell to ring loudly at the mere mention of a name. If possible make a phone call; try to talk with each astrologer you are considering before you engage his/her services. It is important that you eliminate such potential communication problems as personality clashes or incompatible points of view. For example, some astrologers may have a strong, specific religious background, or may be zealous followers of a particular mystic school, to the extent that this might color their outlook and their work. Some astrologers might be too tradition-bound to understand the needs of strongly individualistic clients. Some young astrologers might not be able to deal effectively with older people; some older astrologers might have difficulties relating to young people. An astrologer's personal life need not necessarily affect the reading, but keep the possibility in mind. Ideally you and your astrologer should be basically compatible. It's entirely possible that a twenty-year-old hippie astrologer could be perfectly in tune with an eighty-year-old conservative client — there are no rules. The initial phone call will help to set off your Inner Bell and determine your rapport.

Here are some further guidelines to help you with your search:

Ten-Foot-Pole Checklist For Astrologer-Avoidance:

1.   Watch out for heavy publicity. If you're answering an ad, avoid the big sell: "Sam Stellar, The World's Greatest Living...." Skip these ego-oriented types and look for the more modest approach. Actually you need only a name, address and/or phone number. The same applies for in-person or on-the-phone conversation. One astrologer kept assuring me that he was "worth a million dollars." A good astrologer has no need to boast. Distinguish self-confidence from egotism; the latter is not an asset to the reading.

2.   Avoid judgemental personalities. I have heard of one astrologer who unequivocally disapproved of drink and premarital sex; another who disapproves of witchcraft (!); and some who are still locked into a sexist view of women. A competent astrologer keeps personal bias out of the consultation.

3.   Be wary of the gossipy type. An astrological reading, like a psychiatric consultation, is by definition strictly confidential. Not one peep about another person's chart should escape your astrologer's lips — and not one peep about your chart should reach another client. If the astrologer gossips about other clients to you, you can be fairly sure you too will be the subject of similar gossip to others. And no matter how famous, how important, how notorious his/her clients may be, a good astrologer will never mention the names of any clients. No one need know that you or anyone else has sought astrological guidance — not that it's anything to be ashamed of, but it's simply nobody's business! This is different from the practice some astrologers have, of erecting charts of presidents, politicians, and other famous people — for "demonstration" purposes. Some consider all public officials to be fair game, as the people have a right to know about their leaders. And some astrologers enjoy tracing trends in the charts of movie stars, writers, etc. — public people who have not specifically consulted the astrologer, but whose birth information is readily available. Perhaps it's the price of fame. In any case, anything harshly personal — even in such a "fair game" famous person's chart — should be kept private by the astrologer.

4.   Contrary to popular belief, a good astrologer does not encourage dependency from clients. In fact, a good astrologer *discourages* such a relationship. When you hear about people who won't make a move without consulting their astrologer, I would say that's not such a terrific

astrologer; that's an astrologer on an ego-trip. Fostering dependencies has nothing to do with planets! This statement does not contradict my earlier advice to use the progressions and transits and to ask copious questions. We need a balance. The good astrologer always gives you guidelines, and you have a right to ask for these. But he/she does not tell you *what to do* about the information. The choices are always up to you — and usually several equally feasible choices may be made.

5. Watch out for a heavily *interpretive* reading. A clear technical explanation should back up every interpretive statement. For example, it does not suffice for an astrologer to tell you, "Beware the Ides of March!" the astrologer should add, "Be especially careful on March 15th, because Mars conjunct your natal Sun, and square transiting Uranus, potentially could cause a susceptibility to sudden personal danger. It would be safer to try to stay inside and rest during such an aspect." Tape the session or make notes. If you don't understand all the material, you will be able to check it out later with your own textbook.

Make sure you receive a copy of the chart itself (see illustration, p. 136) with every planet, House, and aspect clearly marked. Even if it's "Greek" to you at this point, some day you may be able to study it an refer to it. You may show it to an astrologer in the future, or a friend. You will then be able to figure out for yourself from what *facts* the astrologer drew each interpretation and conclusion. According to occult belief, the chart is always open to further interpretation, ever expanding in its potential as you yourself grow. If you consult the astrologer personally, ask to be shown the technical data on the chart backing up each interpretation. Even if you don't comprehend all of it, you still come away from the reading with a new knowledge of how astrology works — as well as of your own chart. If the reading comes via the mail, make it known up front that you expect a copy of your chart in the mail also.

6. Beware of heavy advice. Suggestions, trends, insights, and answers to questions — yes. But advice can border on judgment and may come from the astrologer's own psyche rather than your planets. By heavy advice, I mean sweeping statements such as "Never marry"...."Marry immediately"...."Quit your job"...."Move to Europe," etc. The responsible astrologer gives you guidelines and explains their basis in the chart as well as in the transits and progressions — and leaves conclusions, decisions and actions up to you, respecting your own judgment and free will. Watch for this also in comparison charts.

7. Watch out for heavy predictions! True, sometimes an unusual trend can loom ominously, such as the Kennedy trip to Dallas, and, of course, a responsible astrologer will speak up in such a case. However as a rule informed astrologers do not believe in destiny, fate, irrevocable karma or predetermination. Everything that *might* happen,

no matter how obviously indicated astrologically, also *might not* happen — according to your own free will and choice. Good astrologers are aware of flexibility in future events. Watch your astrologer's use of words: Instead of saying "negative," "dangerous," or "bad," the responsible astrologer will say "potentially difficult," "possibly problematical," or better yet, "*challenging.*" And "malefic" is really old-hat; "malefic" is a word that belongs in the Middle Ages.

8. I repeat: Do not "feed" information to the astrologer. Also do not rationalize any information which the astrologer gives you *if it does not feel right.* This is particularly important in your natal chart, in which the astrologer possibly may have made a basic mathematical error (as happened in my early Moon-misplacement). A good astrologer will be all too glad to seek out and admit to any errors![10]

New Horizons In Astrology

As time goes on and the human life-span on Earth grows longer, our culture grows more complex and we find more possibilities in our life experiences. This is paralleled in the study of astrology. Planets further away from Earth reveal their influences upon us, and astrologically we are confronted with more complexity and more latitude for personal growth. Also the "new" planets clearly reflect social and cultural change. Until the eighteenth century, astrologers recognized only seven planets in a person's horoscope. When Uranus was discovered in 1781, its influence in a chart indicated new areas of socio-political revolution and sudden change. In 1846 Neptune was discovered, and its influence revealed new areas of psychological insight, dream research, and understanding of psychic phenomena. Pluto was discovered in 1930; it rules mass consciousness, the personal subconscious, and the power of transformation.

Now we have nine planets (including Earth) officially acknowledged in our Solar System — and recently the astronomers acknowledged that a possible tenth planet lurks in the distance. In fact, several reputable astrological systems use "hypothetical planets" in natal chart delineations and forecasts today. The most popular is *The Uranian System*, which employs eight hypothetical planets postulated to exist beyond Pluto. Alfred Witte, an early twentieth-century German astrologer, founded this sytem. Perhaps with the aid of advanced telescope technology and space probes, the presence of these hypothetical planets will be proven by scientists — an exciting prospect!

Meanwhile, closer to Earth, some astrologers are beginning to work with the four major *asteroids* (or "minor planets"): Ceres, Pallas, Juno and Vesta. These asteroids have been recognized by astronomers since 1801, but astrologers were unable to place the asteroids in a chart until the use of the computer enabled their positions to be located accurately. These asteroids represent four aspects of feminine life-qualities, and their presence in a chart balances out the predominantly masculine attributes of the other planets. It is no coincidence that their influence became noted exactly at the time of the new Women's Movement, corresponding to the changing sex roles in society. Astrologer Eleanor Bach pioneered the use of these four asteroids.[11]

Medical astrology is a new field — actually a very old field, but recently coming into public awareness. Jung pioneered in astrological therapy; he had a chart erected for every psychiatric patient. Astrology is proving to be a helpful adjunct to all kinds of therapy, from medical to psychological. Astrological charts indicate physical stress areas and time periods, and prove valuable in personality analysis and dream interpretation. I would say that even if your own doctor, dentist or psychotherapist does not "believe" in astrology, try to correlate your other therapies with your astrological information in terms of insights and important trends (including timing).

Political astrology is an important field. It applies not only to government leaders who have often used astrologers (publicly acknowledged or privately), but for the people as well, especially in democratic societies where the leaders are chosen by vote. I think that every politician's chart should be available to the public, as should comparison charts between the official and the group he/she represents. (For example, a comparison chart between the U.S. President and the U.S. itself). Governments and other institutions can have natal charts too. Such charts are calculated from the moment of inception. Businesspeople and businesses have been using astrologers for years; perhaps this will become more widely acknowledged.

Radical astrological systems occasionally surface, often in books which claim to "revolutionize" or even "invalidate" all previous astrological study. So far, all these have proved to be Piscean Age rip-offs and far from valid in themselves.

Astrology can indicate trends and events of large-scale importance: weather (including major upheavals such as floods and earthquakes), elections, government conditions, and cultural changes. These all classify as *mundane astrology*.

Occasionally scientists rally against astrology. Invariably such scientists turn out to be people who have not studied real astrology, but have been horrified by the pop-nonsense in the media. Astronomy and astrology were once one and the same field; astrological truths are compatible with modern scientific ideas. Perhaps some day soon scientists will investigate astrology in a rational way.

The future trends for specific situations can be charted under the

146

guidelines of *horary* astrology. Remember, these are not predictions but trends, and are meant to be used wisely.

Meanwhile, I must agree with Jiminy Cricket: "When you wish upon a star...." (and when you're working *with* your stars), your dreams come true. Astrology is a wonderful help; it helps you to perceive your link with the rest of the Cosmos. Enjoy it.

¹"When You Wish Upon a Star," lyric by Ned Washington, Bourne Co.

²William Shakespeare, *Julius Caesar*, Act I, Scene II.

³All references in this chapter are to the field of Tropical Astrology. Sidereal Astrology is an alternate system, as yet not widely used. See Dal Lee's definitions of Sidereal Astrology, *Dictionary of Astrology*, Paperback Library, New York, 1968, pp. 85-86 and p. 180. Or any good text about the two systems.

⁴My astrologer friends recommend Marc Edmond Jones, *How to learn Astrology*, Doubleday, New York, 1971; Jones, *Astrology, How and Why It Works*, Penguin, Baltimore, 1971; Dane Rudhyar, *The Astrology of Personality*, Doubleday, New York, 1963, John Anthony West and Jan Gerhard Toonder, *The Case for Astrology*, Penguin Books, Baltimore, M.D., 1973.

⁵*Mind Over Matter*, Brut Records, Froben Enterprises, 1974.

⁶Specifically *Linda Goodman's Sun Signs*, Bantam, New York, 1968, and Sidney Omarr's individual yearly pamphlets for each sign, published by New American Library's Signet Books. You may come across others. Note that a reputable sun sign writer will acknowledge up front the limitations inherent in sun sign work and will not claim that his/her book "tells all."

⁷My astrologers recommend *Astral Portrait*, Box 7, Laneville, IL 01930, and *Astro Computing Services*, Neil F. Michelsen, 129 Secor Lane, Pelham, NY 10803.

⁸My astrologers recommend the magazines Dell Horoscope, American Astrology, and The Mercury Hour.

⁹Transits for December 6, 1976 from *American Astrology Magazine*, December, 1976, Clancy Publications, Inc., Vol. 44, No. 10, p. 84. When locating the daily transits in an astrology magazine, do not confuse them with the daily Sun sign information — which is also available in the magazines, and is usually far less significant. Also, if you acquire a familiarity with the astrological symbols, you will be able to ready the "technical" transit information which will make your reading more accurate.

¹⁰Watch out for astrologers who rationalize and stand by their errors. My favorite example of this is one internationally known pop-astrology figure who publicly predicted that the recently widowed Jacqueline Kennedy would never remarry. Within months she married Aristotle Onassis. The astrologer, confronted by reporters, refused to admit any error. His answer went something like this (my paraphrase): "I said she'd never marry again, and I was correct. Look at their age difference! Do you call *that* a marriage?"

¹¹Eleanor Bach, *Ceres, Juno, Pallas, Vesta*, Celestial Communications, New York, 1973. Bach's book includes the Asteroids' Ephemerides as well as instructions for their interpretations. Their use is recommended for any astrologer who wants more detailed personality traits to show up in a natal chart, and for more detailed progressions and transits.

147

THE I CHING AND TAROT CARDS

Divination

> To know the seeds, that is divine indeed....the seeds are the
> first imperceptible beginnings of movement, the first trace of good
> fortune (or misfortune) that shows itself. The superior man
> perceives the seeds and immediately takes action.
>
> —Confucius[1]

"Divination" is the word used to cover a variety of occult techniques for
looking into the future, as well as into the past and into present events
which may be happening far away. Divination is not to be confused with
folk customs of "fortunetelling," because fortunetelling is based on
superstition, ignorance, fear, and a limited comprehension of the future.

Divination is not to be confused with spontaneous *precognition,*
which sometimes gives us a glimpse of the future, often in the form of a
vision or "hunch" (or even a dream). Spontaneous precognition is a
natural psychic talent which we all possess in varying degrees. Some
people experience such precognition more often than others, some
people ignore its occurrence, some people develop their gifts of
precognition by paying careful attention to their intuitions. Most
often, spontaneous precognition is set off by events or persons
involving intense emotional content; by definition there is little
conscious control of how and when it will occur.

Sir Stephen King-Hall had a sudden clear premonition that a man
would fall overboard in a moment. He decided to act on the hunch
and gave orders about mustering the boat crew. As the
commodore was asking him what the devil he thought he was
doing, there was a cry of "Man overboard" from a ship behind

them in the convoy, and then, immediately after, from another ship; their boat was in the water within seconds and both men were pulled aboard. Here it may have been the fact that it was a double emergency that somehow triggered the intuition.[2]

Most of us have either experienced or heard about similar premonitions. But few people know how to control them, to call upon them in a consistent way.

Divination, on the other hand, embodies a vast occult tradition available to everyone. All the techniques of divination involve the conscious study and use of triggering devices which develop the dormant precognitive abilities of our subconscious minds.

In ancient Egypt, Greece, Rome, and China, divination was a respected art, valued for practical as well as spiritual ends. The root of the word (and the verb itself) is "divine"; as Confucius says, "to know the seeds" is divine, or godlike.

Accurate divination was once the domain of the few wise adepts who understood how this form of magic worked. Now it has become available to all of us, as part of our Aquarian inheritance, if we can understand the occult principles on which this art is based. Divination differs from fortunetelling in that divination involves specific occult principles:

• **Integral, Action, or Personal Responsibility.** As Confucius says, the purpose of divination is to provide a perception upon which to base action. The uninitiated have often been afraid of knowing the future, because they thought that if they should happen to find out something negative ahead of time, there was nothing they could do except perhaps worry in advance. But adepts have always sought to see the future, precisely because they understand that they can do something about it. That's the whole idea! Action is integral to the process of divination.

The adept has always known that personal action is what originally "created" the future. Specifically, one's own actions have already created — and continue to create — one's future circumstances. And one's own actions can thus be directed to change the future for oneself. When you look into the future, what you see is not irrevocable, inexorable fate — but *trends*. These trends are "the seeds," the first beginnings of movement — perceptible through the diviner's art, yet still unformed and potentially changeable.

• **We Are The Creators Of Our Own Futures.** Remember the concepts of karma in Chapter V? See how all this comes into play now. We often create our futures subconsciously, but thanks to the divination process, we get a chance to intercede and create the future on a more conscious level. Now, just because a process has been subconscious does not free us from responsibility. Sometimes we may find difficulty in accepting responsibility for an unpleasant future (or present). But remember that accepting responsibility does not involve self-judgment or blame. It is a purely objective fate: "I am responsible," and that's that. (Not "I am responsible; how terrible," or "how wonderful").

Some people are convinced that the future is arbitrary — the choice of fate, destiny, or some mysterious unavoidable outer "force." No matter how Oedipus tried to escape fulfilling the prophecy of killing his father and marrying his mother, he couldn't get away from his fate. The stranger on the road whom he killed just happened to be his father, and the lovely older lady he decided to marry — that's right, you guessed it. Oedipus couldn't outwit the future. Many legends follow a similar pattern. Let us remember that they were handed down from the point of view of the uninitiated. Such legends are based on a misconception of the Universal Law of Cause and Effect. This is a law of the Universe, which (for all practical purposes) cannot be changed — for every cause there is an effect. (In all but the most advanced and esoteric occult work, the Law of Cause and Effect cannot be changed).

This idea may seem inexorable — a law of nature which cannot be changed! And perhaps the workings of this Law are difficult for us to avoid. But *the Law is neutral.* We are not in bondage to its whims, the Law does not set things up for us — *we do.* The Law has no whims, or ideas, or direction, or will — or qualities of its own. We ourselves supply each Cause for our own futures and the Law merely carries it out to the next step: Effect. We can just as easily work consciously, with a full understanding of this process as live in ignorance of it, or in fear of it. In fact, the Law of Cause and Effect is so predictable and trustworthy in its function that it makes the process of divination possible.

Here are the other factors which make divination possible:

Occult Time and Space. *All time is now.* It is our perception of time which defines an event as "future" — to be experienced later. But we can choose to experience the event "ahead of its time" — by seeing it now. Then we are free to choose again — to re-experience the event later in its original form, bypass that form entirely, or experience it in changed form. Divination is one way of transcending our linear perception of time; and perceiving time from the occult frame of reference, the overview, in which linear time does not exist. (This is what psychics mean when they say, "The future has already happened.")

All space is here. Here we sit in the World of Form, and the future is in the Invisible Realm. But since all space exists together, then we are in the Invisible Realm also; conversely, the future is somehow also here with us in the World of Form. Divination techniques tune us in to the Invisible Realm and bring both Worlds together in our consciousness. We transcend our perception of space as limited to all we can see — and then we are able to see more. In other words, divination makes the Invisible become Visible.

• **The Importance of Being Objective.** There are as many techniques and methods of divination as there have been cultures on this planet. Most often, a shaman, expert, or seer, has been appointed to do the seeing for another. But in its ideal form, divination is done by the person whose future is involved. Because of the process of integral action, the seer is ideally also the doer. I strongly recommend that you learn how to read the future for yourself.

It is important to avoid fear, worry, or anticipation. You've heard the term "self-fulfilling prophecy?" Sometimes the fear that something negative will happen becomes a *cause* to "make" it happen. But we can control this tendency, when embarking on divination, by telling ourselves firmly:

1 — With true divination, there is no judgment — nothing is "good" or "bad."
2 — Nothing is irrevocable.
3 — There is nothing to be afraid of! We can control our own futures ultimately — with personal responsibility and the aid of the Law and Cause and Effect.

Sometimes you may wish to consult an expert, or even a friend, to see something for you or to confirm your own divination work.

Consulting a Seer or Reader (Without Awe)

• Even if you consult someone, you will benefit from having mastered some basic divination techniques — to be able to check things out, to have an understanding of how the process works, and to strip away the mystery.
• Every good look at the future includes a vision of the *past* as well. This must be accurate and clearly understood as the foundation for the future trends.
• The seer should be aware of the concepts of integral action, personal responsibility, and Cause and Effect (not necessarily in these words, but definitely these ideas). If the seer does not acknowledge these concepts, then what you probably have is a fortuneteller.
• Watch out for belief in fate, destiny, and irrevocable karma — all fortunetelling also.

152

- The person who reads for you must be objective, or the reading is worthless. If the person loves you (or hates you) too much, has a vested interest in events in your life, or judges anything as good or bad, the reading is not objective.
- Make sure no fortunetelling ego gets in the way. "Look at me, I can see the future!")
- Make sure no pecuniary interests are getting in the way either. ("Cross my palm with silver, and I will tell all.") Of course a good reading by a professional is worth a fee. At the time of this writing, the typical going fee for most psychic readings may by anywhere from $15 to $40. There are, of course, exceptions, usually depending on how much material is covered, and how long the reading takes. But anything over $50 is probably exorbitant (astrology not included), and those little $2 readings are most often worthless. Disreputable "storefront" fortunetellers know this, and never dare to charge more than a few dollars for a so-called reading. They rely on extortion and swindles for their principle income (such as "bring me your life-savings so I can put a magical spell on it...take the evil eye off it...etc.")
- Watch out too for the reader who is simply out to please you: "You will meet a tall (or short), dark (or light), handsome (or lovely) stranger." Such a reading usually relates to the above-mentioned pecuniary interests.
- Watch out for readers who try to convert you to any particular religion or belief-system. They can believe in anything they wish, and this need not interfere with the accuracy of vision. But if they try to lay their beliefs on you, they are denying your own free will and personal responsibility.
- Watch out for readers who obviously try to foster dependencies ("Don't make a move without consulting me first.") or who *subtly* encourage dependencies.
- Watch out for readers who sneakily pump you for information. This is even worse than simple-minded fortunetelling — it is trickery and charlatanism! "A client is drawn into providing information about himself that ends up looking as though it came from the seer. No hypnosis need be involved, but the technique is very similar."[3] It is amazing how a skilled con-person can elicit and work with scattered tidbits of information.
- Don't expect a valid, in-depth reading to take place at a restaurant, cocktail party or any other social gathering. The reader may be sincere, but the crowded ambiance usually is not appropriate to psychic concentration.

Techniques

There is a vast body of folkloric traditions all over the world for looking into the future. Usually performed by the uninitiated, these traditions were based on superstitious beliefs and designed mostly to allay fears of the unknown, or provide entertainment long before the days of radio and television.

The Golden Bough is the definitive study of such customs.[4] Turn to almost any page and you will see a series of quaint traditions and interpretations — tossing beans over one's shoulder by moon light, scattering pebbles, gazing into the fire, counting twigs, cracking nuts. Some of these method work. Why? They provide effective triggering devices. But most often such folkloric methods are severely limited by prescribed traditional and simplistic interpretations. In true divination, all interpretations are creative and flexible by definition.

However an interesting overlap area exists between folkloric fortunetelling and occult divination. A typical example may be found in the popular custom of reading tea leaves. If you read the dregs in the bottom of a teacup by following the instructions in a folkloristic handbook, you would be following specific rigid interpretations for what you happen to see. Thus, you might hit or miss "foretelling" the future — probably miss. But a person with psychic gifts, without following any particular method, can accurately see future trends by looking into the same cup of tea leaves. You probably could do this too, if you understand the principles of divination delineated thus far. All you would have to do would be to concentrate on the leaves, open your mind, and state your impressions. In this way you allow the tea leaves to serve as a triggering device for your subconscious. I have known people who could effectively read any personal form patterns in this way — even odd choices such as cracks in someone's ceiling plaster or folds on a beach towel in the sand. These ideas are cute, but limited in their application for self-help. Divination is more than amusement. The important thing to understand is that any "random" pattern can serve as a triggering device to link the reader's subconscious with future trends.

Now, at the Cusp, an important overlap area is developing between divination and science. Two excellent examples are *graphology*, the study of handwriting, and *palmistry*, the study of lines in the palm of the hand. Both fields, long considered exclusively occult, now have scientific approval. They provide adjuncts to standard psychological testing for personality analysis and indicators of an individual's physical health, and serve as clues to past, present and future trends.[5]

However, some standard divination systems have not yet been

recognized by science and are still considered exclusively occult. These are not folkloric nor superstitious; in fact, they require a certain degree of study and expertise.

Traditional Divination Systems

• *Scrying* is the occult term for peering into a crystalline object such as the ever-popular crystal ball. Some experts explain this process (when it works effectively) as a form of self-hypnosis. Sometimes the reader may see an entire tableau acted out — much as on television — and sometimes only a static symbol may come into view. Either process requires objective interpretation. Scrying is also traditionally practiced with a bowl of water, a bowl of oil, a plate of oil, or a mirror lying face up and covered with oil. Ancient tradition often required one to be a virgin (male or female) to use any of these devices (with the exception of the crystal ball) — but if you didn't classify as such, you had to hire a virgin to do the scrying for you. (This is one of the few occult facts that still mystifies me). An old Celtic favorite for scrying was the fisherman's floating glass globe ("witch-ball"), less costly than crystal and just as effective. Today, modern plexiglass globes eliminate the need to invest in a heavy crystal antique. Scrying usually is not for the amateur, as there are too many variables: reflection from objects in the room and reflection from within the seer's head.

• *Spirit aid* takes various forms. Such divination requires a basic understanding of spirit life (see p. 29,30) because the tendency is usually to believe anything, as long as the information is allegedly coming from a spirit. When you consult a psychic reader who has a spirit guide (or familiar spirit), you not only have to make sure that the psychic is accurate and reputable, you also have to be sure that the *spirit* is accurate and reputable. Spirits can be on ego-trips too! You may have to employ your own methods of divination to check both out. Spirits may speak through the psychic reader (trance), or to the psychic (non-trance), who then narrates to the client.

When you contact a spirit by yourself (or with a friend), you may use a *ouija board or automatic writing*. The latter consists of holding a pencil lightly and letting the spirit direct your messages, similar to dictation in the secretarial sense. Usually I do not recommend these methods to beginners, because often there's no way of knowing from whom or from where the messages are coming — or whether they are accurate.

• *Psychic readers* work in various styles. Some will hold an object such as jewelry up to their head, or clutched in their hand, as a triggering device (more commonly effective, though, for reading the *past* of the object). Some will read photographs. Others can answer

155

questions by holding a piece of paper with the question written on it; the paper is folded so the writing doesn't show. The psychic holds it up to his/her head — more dramatically, the psychic may be blindfolded. Often a spirit guide helps with this, whether the psychic knows it or not.

Some psychic readers require the very minimum of triggering devices. I know one excellent reader who merely has to play a few bars of her favorite music on a battered old phonograph. Then she takes the record off, closes her eyes, and launches into an accurate life reading — past, present and future. Other triggering devices include candles, flowers, incense, prayers, and chants.

• The *pendulum* is a popular do-it-yourself triggering device — a small weighted object suspended from a length of string. You allow the pendulum to swing to a "yes" or "no" position in answer to various questions. Some occultists believe that spirits help with this. I feel that pendulums are reliable only when they are personally consecreated ritual tools in accordance with a specific spiritual system, such as the crystal pendulums used by some witches. Otherwise again the variables are too great for the novice to count on.

• *Numerology* may follow any of a number of traditions, most of which are based on the Caballah. Numerologists generally start out with your name and birth date, assigning various numerical values to each letter. If you are interested, you might try studying this yourself rather than relying entirely on a reader.[6]

• Total *sensory deprivation* is a rediscovered method and not to my taste at all — it forces the seer to deal with nothing but the Invisible Realm. Some psychic and scientific experimenters think this is the latest and the greatest. They have devised complex tanks of body-temperature water, and cushioned, blackened rooms, to block out all sensory input. Actually, this is one of the most ancient of methods for psychic work — as well as for torture — and I mention it specifically to warn you against it. Even *partial* sensory deprivation, using a black molded face mask, may be dangerous because of the possibility of going mad. Not worth it.

• The *tossing of shells* is the method favored by many Oceanic and African adepts. This also relates to the tossing of bones, sticks, stones and specifically the Celtic and Nordic *runestones*. These techniques often prove extremely accurate, but they usually require a complete understanding of the particular culture they come from. Our *tarot cards* are the current Western European equivalent.

• Then, of course, there is the old standby, *dream interpretation*. Neither time nor space permit a detailed discussion of this area in this book. (For now, I can only recommend that you avoid standard "dream interpretation" fortunetelling books with a ten-foot-pole. If dream-divination interests you, I recommend a study of Jung's symbolism, as well as J.W. Dunne's classic work on precognitive dreaming techniques, *An Experiment With Time).*[7]

The techniques of divination which we are going to concentrate on in this chapter are accessible to everyone and can be used effectively for self-help. They are the *I Ching* and tarot cards.

I have chosen to begin with the *I Ching*, the ancient Chinese method which has been so effectively adapted for Western use. I believe this is the ideal starting point for dealing with the future, because personal responsibility, integral action, and objectivity are built directly into the process.

> ### THE I CHING, A Personal Oracle
> It is also unique in being free of harmful aspects; close study of it can do nothing but good.
> —Colin Wilson, discussing the *I Ching.*[8]

The *I Ching*, or *Book of Changes*, is an ancient Chinese system of divination, widely accessible today in book form. Its traditional use is for personal *decision-making* and *problem-solving*.

Anyone who still approaches the idea of looking in the future with some trepidation can easily solve this problem with the help of the friendly *I Ching*. Anyone who doesn't believe that it's really possible to see the future — and to change the future — is probably in for some surprises now. In fact, it still surprises me when people are taken aback on their first encounter with the *I Ching*. When they exclaim, "It seemed to read my mind!"...."It answered my question exactly!" and so forth, I wonder, "What do they expect from an authentic oracle?"

What amazes me the most is that so many people don't seem to know about this book! It seems important to let people know that it exists, and that it is easy to locate and to use. Perhaps the *I Ching* has been lost in the shuffle of the general Cusp occult rip-off. Many "versions" of the *I Ching* abound in stores these days — you may see *I Ching* paperbacks, picture books, calendars, and even playing cards. You could walk right by the shelf where the real *I Ching* sits, peruse the fortunetelling imitations, and deduce that's all there is.

The edition that I recommend is *The I Ching, or Book of Changes*, the Richard Wilhelm translation, rendered into English by Cary F. Baynes, Bollingen Foundation, Princeton University Press. It may be the most expensive of all, as it is still published exclusively in hardcover. (Approximately $12.50 at the time of this writing). The Bollingen edition of the *I Ching* is not always on the "Occult shelf." You may find it under "Philosophy" or "Oriental Studies." It seems that no attempt has been made to popularize the Bollingen edition.

History

Most scholars concur that the *I Ching* originated in China at least 4,000 years ago, probably much earlier. No one is certain who wrote the original material. Since the *I Ching* consists primarily of diagramatic symbols, it is possible that the book wasn't written at all, but devised before the institution of writing as we know it came into being. A legendary figure, Fu Hsi, is assocated with the invention of the oracle. He is also said to have invented cooking during the prehistoric time when hunting and fishing first became established in China.

The other three men who may be said to be "authors" of the *I Ching* are King Wen, the Duke of Chou, and Confucius. Their earliest elaborations on the oracle have become integrated into the text. Generations of scholars added a wealth of philosophical and spiritual thought to the original material. This section is known as "The Commentaries," and is included in the Bollingen edition.

The *I Ching* seems to be but one remnant of a huge body of advanced Oriental culture, lost thousands of years ago. There are legends of tragic library-burnings at that time in the East, probably for political reasons. The *I Ching* itself contains clues and references to related areas of study which seem to have vanished without a trace, perhaps in the book-burnings. (For example, see Hexagram 52, p. 200, referring to a lost school of Chinese yoga).[9] Why did the *I Ching* survive intact when so much else was destroyed? My theory is that the ancient scholars simply asked the book itself how best to hide and save it. And the book — being a most practical oracle provided them with a foolproof answer, which they followed.

As you familiarize yourself with the book, you will note that in certain periods the *I Ching* was used exclusively by rulers to govern their kingdoms wisely and enlighten the people. In other times the oracle seemed mostly in the domain of the scholars and religious leaders. Later the *I Ching* became more accessible to the general public. But because of widespread illiteracy, for centuries the oracle's actual usage was limited mostly to consulting "oracle-readers" who stood on street corners with their copies to help the common folk in their divination.

The *I Ching* reached the West in 1899, when it was translated into English by Sir James Legge for the Clarendon Press, Oxford, as part of a larger work, *The Sacred Books of The East*. It seems that most current versions other than the Bollingen have been taken directly from Legge's translation. Today, if you see a book cover with claims such as "Never before, the one, the only, original *I Ching!*"...."The first, the best!", you can be quite sure it is the Legge translation or some version of it. The Bollingen by contrast is unostentatious, looks like a textbook, and makes no claims — either on the book jacket or elsewhere.

What's "wrong" with the Legge translation? It is flawed by the fact that Legge himself never seemed to value — or even consider — the *I Ching* as an oracle. There is no indication that he ever consulted it! So his vantage point in translating the book was not for practical use, but simply to render it into English. This was of course an important accomplishment, and the Legge translation has historical value. It was the only English version available for fifty years. Readers knew the book as the *Yi King*, and occultists used it mainly for meditation on the diagrams of the hexagrams. If you compare a Legge-based translation with the Bollingen, you will see that much seems to be missing in the Legge. You might also note a slightly deprecating tone on the part of Legge as translator. This contrasts distinctly with the Bollingen, in which the *I Ching* is regarded as a living, timeless oracle. Jungian scholars worked on this translation, people deeply involved with the untapped resources of the human mind: myth and the collective unconscious. These scholars saw the problems with the Legge translation and returned to the original Chinese source. Richard Wilhelm, a German expert in Chinese studies and close friend of Jung, carefully translated the book from Chinese into German between 1911 and 1923. Wilhelm lived in China and devoted his life to the study of the oracle's philosophy and its application. His main instructor was the Chinese scholar Lao Nai-hsuan. Shortly before Wilhelm's death in 1930, he enlisted the aid of his friend Jung to continue the translation process into English. Jung chose Cary F. Baynes, then a student of analytical psychology in Zurich, to carry on the work. Baynes also worked closely with Lao Nai-hsuan with equally impressive dedication.

World War I interrupted the translation from Chinese into German. The translation from German into English was interrupted by World War II. The present edition came out in 1950 as a two-volume set, reprinted as one volume in 1961. This is the version that caught on with the flower child crowd of the 60's, before the paperbacks deluged the market. Numerous attempts have been made to improve, simplify, and elaborate on the Bollingen — but it would take a confrontation with Confucius himself to convince me to change to any other version.

The Bollingen Edition

This edition provides complex, scholarly work, and many people may find it difficult to get used to at first. But the other versions simply are not the real thing and if you settle for one of these, you'd be missing out on the wisdom, power and magic of the *I Ching*.

I am going to attempt to make the Bollingen as easy and approachable as I possibly can. But neither I nor anyone else could impart the full benefits of this incredibly enriching and comforting oracle. You will see for yourself that the more you seek to understand it, the more you use it, the more you study it — the more helpful it will be.

Most of the information in this chapter may be found in the Bollingen edition itself. If you have the time and energy, you could sit down all alone with the book, figure how to use it, practice it, study it, and become an expert without anyone's help. But the pleasantest way to learn about the *I Ching* is to have a friend teach it to you. I first came to know about it in this way over fifteen years ago. Since then I have taught it to many friends who have passed it on to other friends. Now I'm happy to have this opportunity to pass it on to you.

Approaching the *I Ching*

I recommend that you approach the oracle with as much sincerity and openness of mind as you can muster. It is not a parlor game. If you approach the oracle lightly or with a prove-it-to-me attitude, much of its beauty and effectiveness for your own life may be tragically overlooked or even lost.

There are two valid methods of consulting the oracle — the coin method and the yarrow-stalk method. I shall be concentrating on the coin method because it is simpler to master and quicker to perform. You will need three pennies. Three ordinary American or Canadian pennies will do or three equally weighted, medium-sized coins of equal denomination from any other country. Some purists prefer to use three antique Chinese coins, but as far as I can tell this is only personal taste. Since my own taste leans toward personal translation of occult techniques, I feel that our coins are more appropriate for Westerners. For those who wish to try the more complex yarrow-stalk method, I refer you to page 721 in the text, "The Yarrow-Stalk Oracle."⁹ Yarrow-stalks grow wild in many areas. They are also obtainable in occult and Chinese shops. If you can't find yarrow-stalks, you may use fifty large wooden kitchen matches of the same length. Some people have missed the practicality and immediacy of the *I Ching* by insisting on imported yarrow-stalks or ancient coins (even a special container to keep them in), or they wait to achieve a specific frame of mind in which to ask the question. Such reverance is pleasant, but unnecessary. Just be sure that your three coins are equally weighted, and that you can easily distinguish heads and tails. (See p. 165 for instructions in using the coin method).

You may ask the *I Ching* any question! No question is too

insignificant, or too momentous, or too abstruse, or too *anything.* You can usually expect a clear, insightful, and immediately applicable answer. The oracle may be used wherever you happen to be. No elaborate rituals need be performed, and you need no middleman or middlewoman to interpret your answer for you. Sometimes discussing the answer with a friend helps, but it's not a necessity.

You do not require any special background in Oriental philosophy or in anything else. People of all religious backgrounds have found parallels to their own beliefs in some parts of the text. People of various philosophies and schools of psychiatry and psychology have also found compatible points of reference. The content of the oracle is so universal that it does not seem to clash with any belief system. Whatever background you bring to the *I Ching* will only enhance your usage of it. For those with special interests, certain themes may emerge: Taoism, Confucianism, Jungian psychology (specifically myth and the collective unconscious), even statistics and physics.

The best kind of question to ask the *I Ching* is one which acknowledges your own role in resolving a situation. Remember that you shape your own future and create your own karma. One asks, "What is the best way for me to deal with this situation?" or "What do I need to know about it?" rather than "What is going to happen to me?" You need not feel helpless about the future because your own responsibility, not destiny, determines the course of events.

Some people may ask, *isn't that the same as using plain old common sense?* Well, not exactly. Perhaps it is the same as using plain old *psychic* common sense. Because the *I Ching* formulates its answer according to pertinent information — not only the information to which you already have access, but also information from the Unseen Realm. This includes the area which Jung terms the collective unconscious — the vast cumulative wisdom of the human race — and information from your own subsconscious. Thus the *I Ching* provides information you may not otherwise have any way of directly knowing. Such information is neither arbitrary nor mysterious. The *I Ching* actually singles out from the Unseen Realm that specific information which is most pertinent to you and your situation.

Some people have asked me if it isn't antithetical to the concept of personal responsibility to "ask a book what you should do." But even though it might seem that way, you are not asking a book what to do. You are applying a technique which enables you to tune in — by your own efforts — to your own subconscious plus the vast collective unconscious which exists for all to use. The *I Ching* is a binary computer,[10] and an efficient system of tapping a Universal memory bank.

Basic Ideas

I Ching literally means "Book of Changes." Its system is based upon the concept that the Universe is a series of intricate patterns, all constantly moving through time and space. All of creation is woven into these patterns: everything and everyone — Visible and Invisible, from atoms and molecules, to you and me, to planets and stars; from thoughts and ideas, to past events, to present circumstances of every living being, to all the future trends. These patterns are at once infinitely complex and perfectly harmonious in their structures, substructures and interactions. These are all continuously shifting and *changing*.

How can we visualize this conception of the Universe? We may use images. Picture them animated and moving in various multilayered designs. Or picture the view through a giant kaleidoscope of intricate, shifting patterns and colors. My favorite image is a huge, rhythmic Busby Berkeley production number in which we are all participating. Our participation is the key.

This view defines the state of the Universe as harmonious. The goal is to get the details of our own lives in tune with the entire Cosmos as much as we can. Our free will has made it possible for us to get out of step with everything else. Another way of saying this is that our limited perceptions of ourselves in relation to the rest of the Universal Design may have caused us to feel out of step. We may have forgotten the Invisible Realm and our relationship to it. Using the *I Ching* is a way of knowing what's going on in the Invisible, so that we can relate directly to it.

In the occult, reverting to the pattern of things means becoming aware that we are all intrinsically a part of the pattern anyway; the most harmonious way to fit back into the pattern is to fulfill our own natures on every level. From our vantage point here on the Earth Plane, it may be difficult to see ourselves as part of the rest of the Cosmos. But our Inner Bells tell us when we are in tune with it and when we are not. When we feel out of tune, we need to find out how our situation (the microcosm) fits into the Universal Design (the Macrocosm). So we get our pennies and pick up the *I Ching*.

We approach the oracle with a question such as, "What is the best way for me to deal with this matter?" What we are actually doing is determining how our specific event, the microcosm, fits into the larger, changing Macrocosm of the rest of the Cosmos. No question is too insignificant, too "silly" or too anything if it feels important; anything that feels like a meaningful question for you at any moment is valid.

As you concentrate on your question, you toss the pennies and let them fall (specific instructions are coming up). You write down the

traditional diagrammatical line for each heads-and-tails combination. The resulting diagram represents your question "frozen" here and now, isolated from the rest of time and space so that it can be clearly contemplated. The ancient sages who devised the *I Ching* concluded that *every situation a person could possibly get into* is one of sixty-four situations. You use your notation to see which of the sixty-four applies to you right now. It is your answer.

There has been much speculation, from the viewpoints of physics and statistics, as to how an answer elicited in this way can "happen" to apply to one's question. The answer may seem like a coincidence. (In the occult, we do not believe in coincidence. This is another way of saying that all coincidences are meaningful — or "significant.") In Jung's theory of "significant coincidences," he says that coincidences have meaning. Even if coincidences appear to be arbitrary or due to chance, actually there exists an interdependence, a meaningful relationship of large and small events in a person's life. Jung calls this *synchronicity* (the *I Ching*, p. xxiv) and suggests that paying attention to these coincidences can be helpful to a person's psychological development. Some people find this idea weird (even Jung did sometimes), and perhaps even frightening. But I think it is comforting to know that nothing happens arbitrarily, and there there is harmony in the Universe.

Contents

I think that no introduction to the *I Ching* would be complete without a reading of Jung's "Forward," which may be found in the preface to the

163

Bollingen text. Here Jung gives his theories on the way the oracle works, and also consults the book itself about the prospect of being translated into English and published in the West.

The Bollingen consists of three separate books:

Book One is the Oracle itself. When most people talk about the *I Ching*, they are actually referring to Book One. In fact, many of the paperback versions contain nothing more than Book One. This is the portion of the *I Ching* which is used for divination. It is divided into sixty-four hexagrams which are believed to encompass all human experience. Each hexagram is further subdivided into six specific situations. These are the *"Moving Lines."* When you consult the oracle, you draw a hexagram which includes a calligraphic image, a linear design, a "Judgement" and an "Image." Each hexagram is approximately two pages long and contains philosophy, poetry, historical commentary, psychological symbolism, and religious ethics. All these directly relate to your question. The Moving Lines, if any are drawn, refer to specific details of your situation.

Book Two, located in the middle of the text, is called "The Material." It includes the Ten Wings, or Commentaries. This section of the book presents the great body of thought surrounding the *I Ching*. I have found it to be extremely technical. The section explains how the oracle works, and places the content of the *I Ching* in historical, sociological, philosophical and religious (spiritual) perspective. Book Two is complete with diagrams of the structures of heaven and earth as drawn by the hexagrams and their interrelationships. This section may be heavy going, but you may enjoy it if such study is your cup of tea. However this sort of scholarship is not necessary for your use of the oracle. I suggest that you don't entirely avoid this section; within it you will find wisdom which can enhance your understanding of the *I Ching* as a whole. Perhaps you may choose to deal with Book Two as I did — slowly, reading portions of it over the years.

Book Three is officially labelled "The Commentaries." Some people unwittingly turn to Book Three when they consult the oracle — at first glance it looks like Book One. Structurally, it echoes Book One, because Book Three contains specific commentaries on each of the sixty-four hexagrams and the Moving Lines. But it is not meant to be used as an alternative to Book One. Book One is the primary function of the oracle. Book Three may be referred to *after* you have a firm foundation in the use of Book One. The procedure is usually to look up your answer in Book One, and then turn to the same hexagram in Book Three to see what additions the ancient scholars made.

The purpose of isolating The Material and the Commentaries in Books Two and Three was "out of respect for Western minds"...so perhaps the translators were aware that many Westerners would choose to deal only with the Oracle in Book One. In the East, the tradition includes much of the additional material along with the consultation. Wilhelm has been particularly considerate, I think, by carefully weaving some of the oldest and most relevant commentaries directly into Book One, so that we can absorb these selected portions along with our answers.

Many people avoid Books Two and Three completely. I do not recommend this, but it does not seem to hamper the richness of the *I Ching* experience to deal exclusively with the Oracle in Book One — as long as you are aware that the other sections exist.

How To Consult The Oracle

Instructions for consulting with coins (Chinese) are given in the *I Ching* text on page 724. (If your Bollingen text varies, check the Table of Contents for "The Coin Oracle.") I have worked out the following method, using three American pennies:

- Concentrate on your question.
- Toss the three pennies on any convenient flat surface (such as a table), concentrating all the while.
- After the coins have fallen, notate them according to the following values:

2 tails, one head =	7	———————
2 heads, one tail =	8	——— ———
3 tails =	6	——— ———
3 heads =	9	———————

This process of tossing and notating is repeated six times.

List your notations in a column, reading from the *bottom up.* This is your hexagram.

Here is a sample hexagram:

6th toss, two tails, one head... 7	———————	
5th toss, two tails, one head... 7	———————	UPPER
4th toss, two heads, one tail... 8	——— ———	TRIGRAM

3rd toss, three tails... 6	——— ———	
2nd toss, two heads, one tail... 8	——— ———	LOWER
1st toss, two tails, one head... 7	———————	TRIGRAM

Once you have your hexagram, consult the matrix, or chart "Key for Identifying the Hexagrams," usually a fold-out page at the back of the book. (Some Bollingen editions do not have a fold-out page, but the chart is always at the back of the book.)

Match your upper trigram with the column that reads "Upper Trigram." Do the same with the lower trigram in the appropriate column. To match these trigrams, just move your fingers along the columns, as you would read longitudes and latitudes on a map. The number that you get when your fingers meet is the number of your hexagram (remember, this is not the page number, it is the *hexagram* number). The corresponding page number may be found in the index of the hexagrams at the back of the book. Match it visually with the illustration. Look this up in Book One; our sample is Hexagram 42. Recheck the visual image when you turn to the hexagram chapter. For example, Hexagram 42 looks like this:

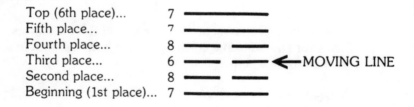

Read your hexagram up to the part where "The Lines" begin.

If you have drawn any sixes or nines — combinations of all tails or all heads — these are your Moving Lines.

If you have drawn none of these (if you have only sevens and eights), do *not* read any lines.

If you have drawn any sixes or nines, read *only* that line or those lines which you have drawn. The lines are numbered from the bottom up.

Thus, in our sample hexagram, the only moving line is six in the third place.

Top (6th place)...	7	━━━━━━━
Fifth place...	7	━━━━━━━
Fourth place...	8	━━ ━━
Third place...	6	━━ ━━ ←MOVING LINE
Second place...	8	━━ ━━
Beginning (1st place)...	7	━━━━━━━

As you toss, if a coin happens to fall on your lap, on your shoe, on the floor — anywhere — you can leave it there and notate it along with the others. I recommend this because the whole procedure is "random," so wherever each coin happens to fall affects the outcome. You do not have to "aim" the coins specifically. In my house, guests have been seen crawling around on the rug from time to time to find out which way an arbitrary penny has fallen, heads or tails. Some people think that if a penny falls out of reach or out of view it somehow doesn't count, and they have to start all over. But I think that wherever a penny falls, it counts!

166

Now you have concentrated on the question, tossed your pennies, notated and looked up your hexagram, and studied your answer. If you have drawn any moving lines, you have studied these in addition. And some people stop right there. But there is an "optional" additional step, often called "The Future of the Situation" — even though it does not necessarily spell out the future (futures being subject to changes which we exert). When we take this extra step, the original hexagram is viewed as the "starting point of a development, leading by reason of the (moving lines)...to the final situation..." (see page 723 in the text).

This step gives rise to an additional hexagram. Is this new hexagram actually "the final situation"? I think that is too sweeping a statement. We may say that this additional hexagram *helps to amplify the implications of the situation*. Remember, this step only applies when you have Moving Lines. Here is how the lines move, or change:

Re-draw your original hexagram, changing all nines to sixes and all sixes to nines.

ORIGINAL HEXAGRAM   NEW HEXAGRAM
#42   #37

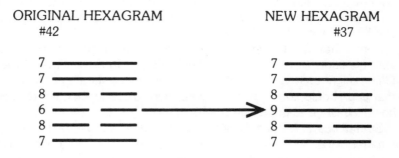

In this example, the six has moved to a nine. Now you have a new hexagram — without a new coin toss. Look up this new hexagram in the chart at the back. Read your answer, but this time *do not* read the Moving Lines. (Instructions for this step are also to be found in the *I Ching* under "The Yarrow-Stalk Oracle," page 723). This new information can be taken into consideration along with the original hexagram.

Some Tips on Asking Questions

Is it necessary to ask the question aloud? Not at all. Just think it, concentrating as you toss the coin. If someone else is present, you may prefer not to make your question known. If someone else enlists your help in consulting the *I Ching*, it is usually best for that person not to ask the question aloud. This is especially important if you intend to look up the answer for him/her, or guide and help in any way. If you don't know

167

the question, your help can be totally objective — and also the other person is less likely to suspect that you had anything to do with the answer! (Many people suspect manipulation on the part of whomever knows how to consult the oracle, especially when the answer is dramatically accurate).

Try not to talk about next month or next year; ask about *right now*. As we shall see in Chapter VIII in Principles, all occult work is done in the present. Remember the occult precept in Chapter II, "All time is now."

Ask about *yourself*. The *I Ching* is primarily a personal oracle, meant to guide your own actions. If your actions relate to other people it is best to keep your focus on your own responsibilities, instead of getting hung up on what another person "should" do. However in some instances it is appropriate to ask about your role in relation to another person. You might ask, "How can I be of help to Louise?" or "Shall I send my child to The Little Green Schoolhouse?" However, if you are asking about a relationship, phrase the question so that your focus is on your own role. Not "Will Fred fall in love with me?" Instead ask: "What do I need to know about a relationship between Fred and me?" or "How can I best relate to Fred?"

Sometimes the *I Ching's* answer will guide you to the proper focus of your question. (So if you ask whether Fred will fall in love with you, the *I Ching* might answer to the effect that your focus should not be here, that you should concentrate on your own role, and then will tell you how to best go about doing that).

Sometimes, in fact, a mistaken focus is what has *caused* a problem in the first place. So try not to be rigid in holding on to your definition of the problem. Be open to the possibility of the *I Ching* redefining the problem for you — by redirecting your focus.

Many times I have seen the *I Ching* "ignore" the question at hand — and address itself directly to another, more pressing issue. I have seen it do this when someone was playing games with the oracle and asking something meaningless. But this has also happened when a questioner was seriously asking something which he/she thought was important. So don't be surprised if the *I Ching* occasionally skips your question and refers instead to a more important issue in your life. In such a case, again the oracle is directing your focus. It is saying, "First concentrate on this matter, and deal with it in this way...."

Some people think one should use the *I Ching* only for asking "spiritual" or lofty questions. I would say, yes, ask spiritual and lofty questions; also ask practical and immediate questions. Ask anything you want; no question is too insignificant if it has meaning to you. The *I Ching* provides excellent practical solutions for problems involving decision in business deals and money matters. There are rumors that the *I Ching* has been used on Wall Street to great advantage. Please bear in mind however that the vantage point of the *I Ching* — as in all valid occult systems — is "for the good of all." So the *I Ching* can help you to make money, but never in a way that is bad for your karma and never in a way that will bring harm to anyone else. (For more about money and the occult, see Chapter VIII).

Some people like to toss a general *I Ching* without asking a specific question. For some, this may even be a daily practice — a "morning-toss" allowing the *I Ching* to direct one's focus to the most important daily issue.

Some people feel it's more spiritual or open-minded or somehow commendable not to define the question, nor to ask about specifics. I do not agree. Some people prefer very specific questions. For example, if your question involves a choice between two or more specific courses of action, you might do best to ask separate questions, each question relating to each choice, and then compare the answers. Usually one will stand out as more favorable. Sometimes it doesn't really matter which course of action is followed if your attitude is adjusted in a certain way (shift of focus) — which the *I Ching* will indicate.

Some people gravitate to "what is going to happen" questions. If you feel you must ask such a question, I would suggest this focus: "How does this situation bode for me?"

The *I Ching* is not designed to give a simple "yes" or "no" answer. This does not mean that you shouldn't ask a yes or no question; it means that your answer will contain more than a simple yes or no. Your answer will include information, ramifications, and explanations about *why* any course of action is suggested.

If you don't understand an answer, try rephrasing the question, and ask again. Sometimes you may ask, "What can you (meaning the *I Ching*) tell me so that I may understand that last answer more fully?" Or you may ask peripheral questions surrounding your situation.

Here is my answer to the inevitable question, *Can you get too dependent on the I Ching?*

There are rumors about people who won't make a move without first consulting the *I Ching*. (I heard of one man who wouldn't answer his doorbell until he asked the oracle. He used the yarrow-stalk method. It took fifteen minutes for the person on the other side of the door to wait until the answer was drawn and read). I suppose that with enough determination to evade personal responsibility, it is possible to misuse any occult technique. Needless to say, the *I Ching* is not meant to be a substitute to one's own self-determination. I suspect that people who lean on the *I Ching* do not read their answers carefully, because the *I Ching* has built-in controls. There are several specific lines which indicate that you have asked too much, already know the answer, and should stop consulting for now. I speak from experience! I have drawn these lines over the years, when I was getting too *Ching*-bound.

Keep a Record of Your Major *I Ching* Work

I suggest that you keep such a record in diary form, listing questions, answers, and the dates asked. If you already keep some sort of diary or journal, you could just include your *I Ching* notes. You don't have to wait until you have the time to write your answers in detail; just a quick note about the question you asked, and the numbers of your answer — including hexagram number and line number, and future hexagram number, if any.

Tips On Interpretation

Some people may be put off at first by the unique language of the Bollingen translation. This problem is easily and naturally resolved as you consult the Oracle more frequently and get accustomed to its style. It's like getting to know a person who has an unusual speech pattern, or an unusual turn of mind.

Do not "skim" your answer. Read it carefully. Some people skip around, reading only what they immediately understand, or bypass the general hexagram and go directly to their Moving Lines for the specifics. Usually, this does not allow for a complete answer and dilutes the impact of the oracle's advice. Read the hexagram and the Moving Line(s) carefully. If you feel you need help, a friend can aid with the interpretation.

As with any occult system, *never rationalize*. The *I Ching* is not a vague oracle; it does not drop philosophical placebos which could apply to anything under the sun. On the contrary, it goes right to the point. If you feel an answer was too vague, write it down for future reference, rephrase your question, and toss again. Often an answer may not be understandable immediately because it refers to an event coming up in the near future. If you keep a record of the question asked and the answer drawn, the meaning may become clearer soon.

Some people have been put off by the "sexism" in the text, especially when the answer refers to "the superior man" — that always applies to you, the questioner, even if you are a woman! If this is the only problem arising from a dual translation of material which is several thousand years old, I am willing to forgive it. For "superior man," simply read "superior *person*."

You may find references to traditional institutions and relationships: rulers and a hierarchy of subjects, family relationships, husbands, wives, sons and daughters, etc. These are not always meant to be taken

170

literally. Sometimes a man will draw an answer which refers to his role as that of a traditional wife, daughter or concubine. In such cases the answer is symbolic, and the quality rather than the form of his role is to be dealt with.

Often, too, you will find references to specific periods of time — days, months, seasons. There is no general rule about how literally to take these references. Often they are symbolic, and usually the symbolism is quite clear. Sometimes the references are accurate to the point of turning into puns. Do not be surprised if the *I Ching* does seem to make puns or joke with you. This has to be experienced to be understood; you will know if it happens. But jokes or word plays never happen at the expense of your answer. The mood of the answer, in fact, often indicates how seriously you should be considering the question within the context of your life.

Some people are put off by the more graphic "negative" images in some of the hexagrams. Again, take the quality of the answer into consideration rather than the literal image. For example, some hexagrams refer to punishments of criminals, imprisonment, or "dangerous" circumstances. Some of these images are not appropriate, if taken literally, in terms of contemporary Western society. Also, such images may appear to be overstatements of your situation. Since all human experience has been broken down into sixty-four basic situations, often the phrasing of a negative situation is described in the extreme. This does not necessarily mean that you are in danger — and even if you are in a dangerous circumstance, the *I Ching* is designed to make you aware of it and to lead you out of it. Like any good divination system, the *I Ching* often gives warnings so that you may avoid problem situations and danger. The warning itself is not to be feared; it is to be heeded in a practical manner. Remember too that your perception of the answer can color the situation, so try not to bring preconceived fears to your reading.

Intercession

As with any occult system, if you wish to intercede, you may use a Words of Power Statement to release all negative power from your situation. The Words of Power Statement helps mostly by preventing your possible fear from becoming a causation (or self-fulfilling prophecy) for further trouble. Your clear affirmation of your own control becomes a causation for positive action and positive good.

For example, you may say the following:
> "I release all negative power out of this situation, and replace it with my own appropriate wisdom to turn it to good."

If you prefer a more detailed Statement, see Chapter VIII for instructions. Here is an example:

WORDS OF POWER FOR AN *I CHING*-INDICATED PROBLEM
There is One Power,
Which is perfect safety;
And I (your name here), a perfect manifestation of this Power,
Am in complete control of my own life.
I am now perfectly safe, specifically in relation to the situation
   described in (state your hexagram and line(s), if any).
I release all negativity out of my life.
   And reaffirm my own safety and protection,
   Knowing that I will act in accordance with my greatest good,
   According to free will,
   For the good of all.
   And so it must be.

And remember — *It's best not to follow the I Ching's advice blindly.*
The *I Ching* is not meant to be used passively. Do not view yourself as a
humble supplicant at the foot of the oracle. You will not be struck down
by a cruel fate if you do not "listen" to the *I Ching's* advice. It is not
meant to replace your own thought processes — but to enrich them.
There may be times you do not agree with — do not even like — your
answer. If it feels wrong to you, if you don't feel comfortable taking the
suggested course of action, I suggest that you make a note of it, but do
not stop there. At such a juncture, some people might toss again and
again on the same question, hoping that a more comfortable solution
will come up. I do not recommend this. Often the *I Ching* will just find
other ways of repeating itself. (It is not unheard of for the same
hexagram to reappear, against "all odds".) Or the *I Ching* may give you
one of those lines which indicate that you've asked enough. Or you may
draw a series of answers which seem to grow increasingly vague until
your mind seems to grow equally vague and confused. I think that
asking the same question over and over is just the flip side of doing
whatever the *I Ching* "tells" you to do, no matter what. In other words,
it is giving more power to the oracle than to your own mind — and this is
not the intention of the *I Ching's* usage. The book is not an occult
authority-figure. Its function is not to "OK" your actions nor to give you
permission to do what you want to do — any more than its function is to
lay down a mystical law for you to follow against your own feelings or
ideas.

What should you do if you don't feel right about the answer you
draw? I suggest that you use such an occasion as an opportunity for
valuable personal insight. Find out why the answer feels wrong to you.
Be prepared to investigate honestly your behavior patterns and general
approach to life — areas which may stretch beyond the confines of

your original question. I suggest that you toss again, but with this new focus: "That particular course of action feels wrong to me. What do I need to know about this feeling of discomfort?" This is one way to discover how the use of the oracle can be multidimensional, and how the wisdom you achieve extends far beyond your immediate situation.

A primary reason for using the *I Ching* is to achieve self-understanding — not only in relation to the issue at hand, but to your entire life.

If the oracle is used in a creative way, you may find myriad side-benefits, including a sharpening of all your thought processes. You may notice these effects in many areas, not only those involving problems and decisions. In fact, you may also find your problems diminishing, and your decisions becoming generally less difficult to make. The *I Ching* exercises all parts of the brain.

How Does The I Ching Work, Really?

1. Some people consider the book a practical philosophical tool for mental focus; a compilation of brilliantly insightful thoughts and ideas all put in an orderly sequence. Confronted with such clarity and wisdom, a thoughtful person becomes better able to concentrate on any specific issue.

If this were true, wouldn't any book of wisdom serve the same purpose — if one turned to it at moments of decision and contemplated it seriously enough? Couldn't one use, say, the Bible, the Talmud, Plato, or even a collection of great quotations? Not really, the *I Ching's* unique value, beyond all such other books of wisdom, is that the style of its material has been intentionally slanted towards decision-making, action, and practicality. Thus it speaks more clearly to the modern person. Well, that's one way of look at it.

But this theory still does not explain how the fall of the coins or stalks leads directly to one's specific answer. According to this theory, any page you turn to at any time, would have to be as appropriate as the hexagram drawn by following the instructions. And some people use the *I Ching* in exactly this random way; when they have a question, they just open the book and read whatever passage happens to turn up. Often this seems to work. In fact, did you ever read the wrong hexagram by mistake, discover your error, and then read the correct one? Maybe you noticed that the "wrong" hexagram also gave you some helpful hints. I have seen this happen — but never with the same incredible accuracy which takes place when the oracle is used correctly. To me, that is the dazzler — your hexagram, your lines are always the most relevant and appropriate ones.

2. The next popular theory deals with this last point by explaining that the *I Ching* does two things:

(a) It puts in orderly sequence all the accumulated wisdom of human civilization over the ages. This is the collective unconscious — information which everybody knows on some level deep inside ourselves, but which most of us rarely reach. (b) The *I Ching* helps us to reach that information, specifically the part of it which applies to our question, by activating our psychokinetic powers. Psychokinesis — also called PK or telekinesis — is the ability to move objects with one's mind.

This ability was once considered to be mere superstitious legend. But now psychokinesis is being studied seriously in parapsychology laboratories from Russia to the U.S., because so many people have demonstrated their ability to cause objects to move by exerting a special kind of mental concentration. Parapsychologists now suspect that this talent it inherent in everyone, but how to exercise it intentionally still seems to be a mystery. In any case, it is possible that psychokinesis was well known in the Mystery Schools of ancient China, and that some triggering device (to unlock our inherent powers to influence the coins or stalks) is built into the *I Ching*. Thus we ourselves subconsciously cause the appropriate hexagram and lines to come up each time.

Many modern scientific students of the *I Ching* subscribe to this theory, including Lyall Watson in *Supernature:*

> *"There is nothing in the fall of the coins or in the text of the book that is not already in you; all the I Ching does with its beautifully* organized patterns is to draw the necessary information and decisions out..."*[11]

3. A theory, held by some totally "rational" people, goes a bit further: The *I Ching* seems to have a *personality* of its own. I am not referring to illiterate, superstitious people such as the peasants described in *The Golden Bough* — those fearful folk tossing beans and nuts over their shoulders to learn their fates. I am referring to a well-educated, intelligent, big-city types: including my friends and radio audience. Even Jung found himself addressing the oracle as if it were a person, "I have questioned the *I Ching* as one questions a person whom one is about to introduce to friends: one asks whether or not it will be agreeable to him."[12] Adam Smith, that thoroughly hip denizen of Wall Street, in his exploration into *Powers of Mind* speculates that the *I Ching* could be viewed as "an old and courteous friend — I supposed a Ben Franklin, who would talk to you in axioms. Asked about the stock market, the old and courteous friend got vague and could not find his

glasses."[13]

It is an inevitable reaction for some, to begin to feel that the I Ching is indeed a friend, even though it happens to be a book. It is always available to answer your questions. It speaks to you personally, often in terms only you can understand, with personal allusions which even border on in-jokes — between you and the book! It gives you its full attention, as a true friend does. It always takes you seriously. But beyond these characteristics, after one has used the book over a long period of time, the inevitable impression of personality begins to emerge. Is this projection? So many people have reported the same personality attributes: "gentle"…"kind"…"considerate"…"witty." Does everyone project the same characteristics onto the I Ching, or does it really have a distinct personality? I think that it does.

Part of the I Ching tradition recognizes that certain invisible spiritual powers work through the book, making it into "a sort of animated being," as Jung describes in his Foreword (pp. xxv xxvi). Further, it is part of all occult tradition, East and West, to recognize sentience (perception, feeling, understanding) and life-force in forms other than people, animals and plants. Thought-forms are examples of such other invisible occult beings. Thought-forms can be of a positive nature, imbued by their adept creators with specific characteristics — even personalities — and kept alive and intact by the acknowledgement of generations of believers. (Some of the ancient pagan gods and goddesses may have been thought-forms. As we have seen in Chapter III, the Devil is an example of a negative thought-form).

At this time, I cannot say for certain whether the I Ching was created as an equivalent to a Western occult thought-form. But I am quite sure that the I Ching is a sentient entity unto itself, and that — like a thought-form — it is nourished and reinforced by the positive energy exchange it has shared with its millions of users.

The thought-form theory does not negate the first two theories: In fact, I think that all three theories fit well together. What do you think? Choose any or all of the above — or perhaps you will come up with a theory of your own. In any case, I hope that you enjoy your I Ching, and that it enriches your life as much as it has mine.

Tarot Cards, A Visual Oracle

"It's in the cards."

—Popular folk saying

Tarot cards are a more accessible, personal and revealing oracle than many people seem to realize. Several decks of various designs are on the market today, some of them quite beautiful. The one I recommend, until something "better" comes along, is the *Rider* — also known as the *Waite* — deck. It costs approximately $8, and although once found only in occult stores, is now available in many bookstores, novelty shops, and even toy stores.

The tarot is such a helpful tool for self-understanding, personal growth and problem-solving, that I used to wonder why everyone wasn't enjoying its benefits. Over the years, I have realized that people can *misunderstand* the tarot in the following ways:

1. They may think it is a "fake" (i.e. they have probably gone to an irresponsible or inaccurate reader).
2. They may think you "have" to consult someone else to have your cards read, that you can't do readings for yourself.
3. They may think that you have to follow — or memorize — the instructions from a book, which can be a lot of trouble and/or boring.
4. They may think that the tarot is "scary," the old destiny (fate) misunderstanding.

None of this is true.

1. Any oracle or system of divination can be a "fake" in the hands of an ill-equipped or dishonest person.
2. You *can* do a reading for yourself. Of course, it's also fine to have someone else read for you, but this does not necessarily mean a professional card-reader. Anyone who understands and respects the Occult Principles in general and divination techniques in particular can do a reading. I feel that it's helpful to have at least one good friend who can do readings for you, and for whom you can do readings. If you find a responsible professional tarot reader, that is a bonus.
3. No valid official instructions exist for the tarot. The cards are an infinitely rich source of personal imagery. If you were to pin down the interpretation of a card, expecting it to mean the same thing every time it comes up, you would be missing out on the riches of the tarot. Unfortunately most of the books are too rigid. They are usually based on somebody's particular method, which at best may be a starting point

176

for you.

4.   As for the old "scariness" business, I hope that by now I've made my point about destiny or fate. The whole idea of dealing with the future is to see the trends before the future manifests as tangible form. You may then intercede and cause significant changes for yourself. The tarot offers an excellent way to visualize your future in order to plan it, rearrange it, and work towards its perfection. It is also excellent for perceiving various sides of any present situation, with clues for effective action. However, one aspect peculiar to the tarot sometimes shakes people up — the intense graphic imagery of a few of the cards. These seem to depict scenes of violence, disaster, suffering, swords and flames. It's important to understand that each card also has its positive side, which usually becomes apparent if you study the card carefully. There is a parallel here with the simplistic medïeval interpretations of "malefic" planets and aspects in astrology (p. 132). Tarot illustration grew directly out of a strong medieval tradition in which the polarities of Light and Dark in human experience seemed more graphic than today. This is another reason I recommend the Rider pack: It's a more "civilized" (i.e., culturally evolved) design, representing a more modern viewpoint than most of the earlier decks.

What Is The Tarot? Some Clues:

This deck of cards is the great-grandparent of all modern playing cards. Tantalizing legends surround the tarot. Some say the tarot is actually *a book* disguised as a deck of cards, or the remnants of such a book with portions of the original material lost in antiquity. Perhaps this legend refers to the burning of the great library at Alexandria in the first century, a disaster which destroyed so much ancient occult lore. Other legends claim that the individual cards are replicas (or reinterpretations of replicas) of *doors* — perhaps doors leading to secret chambers beneath the pyramids or to initiates' chambers in the Eleusynian Mystery Schools. These theories relate the tarot to a forgotten mystery tradition of *architectural magic,* similar to the hidden powers and messages said to be built into certain Gothic cathedrals.

Another theory holds that all the tarot cards derive from the diagrammatic spokes of a giant *wheel,* possibly once used for complex divination.

Yet other legends speculate that the tarot represents the surviving remains of some *entirely forgotten occult system,* and that these remnants — the cards we have today — provide such universal symbols that they have easily lent themselves to layers of cultural additions. Each Age adds something to the original meaning and design of each card.

177

In any case, the tarot works by means of *mnemonics* — a system which triggers the memory and the resources of one's subconscious mind by the use of visual imagery. That's why you'd be missing a great deal if you tried to interpret the cards literally, according to any specific, predetermined meanings. The cards were designed to have a life of their own, reflecting the life of the person for whom they are working. Ideally, the images will seem to move and change from reading to reading, or sometimes even within one specific reading. The symbols of the tarot came from the world of dreams, the collective unconscious, the depths of the Universe itself — from all of life. They speak to us — to both the reader and the *querent* (person being read for) — in intimate and personal ways.

Your own deck will take on your own vibrations. When you are using it, the deck may seem to throb with life and energy. Mine sometimes seems to pulsate just before I lay out a spread. Respect your deck. Try to keep it wrapped in a scarf, or somehow enclosed in a quiet place such as a drawer, rather than in the open. As with all occult objects, the deck tends to absorb surrounding vibrations, and you had best let it "rest" in seclusion between readings.

History

Occultists consider the tarot a Western oracle because it has been used in the West for so long, and because it seems so specific in its graphic imagery (as literal as a medieval pageant). The tarot lends itself to sequential time perception very well, but we can't really be sure that it originated in the West. I think that the deck transcends geography, so universal are its applications. I wouldn't be surprised if the tarot originated on another planet. (This happens to be my favorite theory about the origin of most advanced occult systems).

The first decks were seen in Europe in the fourteenth century carried by gypsies — who also appeared in Europe at that time. By the end of the century, the tarot had surfaced in the popular culture. But according to the gypsies, the cards had been in usage as early as the twelfth century. The tarot was commonly believed to have originated in Egypt, mainly because the gypsies themselves were believed to have come from there ("gypsy" is a version of "Egyptian".) This might account for the Egyptian-myth symbolism in the cards, but does not explain all of the Hebrew and Western biblical motifs. These could have been added during the Middle Ages, or could have been inherent in the deck. Other theories place the deck's origin as Greek, Spanish, Moroccan, Chinese, Indian, Korean, and Arabian.

Tarot cards caught on during the fifteenth and sixteenth centuries, mainly in the European courts, both as a system for fortunetelling and as a game. (Remember, these were the first playing cards). By the Renaissance, many of the Italian and French courts commissioned designs of their own decks. Some rare one-of-a-kind cards from this time still exist in museums and private art collections around the world today. The fifteenth century *Grimaud Tarot of Marseilles* deck is still available for popular use, and may be found in occult supply stores.

The first serious tarot scholar on record was the eighteenth century writer Antoine Court de Gebelin, who spent twenty years of research in mythology, ancient religions, and language. He wrote nine volumes correlating his work, called *Le Monde Primitif (The Primitive World)*. Volume I, published in 1775, dealt with the tarot in great detail, pronouncing it Egyptian in origin. Gebelin probably used the *Burdel Tarot Classic* deck, based on a series of Swiss woodcuts from the early eighteenth century, and he designed new versions of some of the cards. One of his followers, Alliete or Eteilla, redesigned the deck, popularized Gebelin's theories, and then proceeded to fame and fortune via the tarot. Eteilla, an ex-wigmaker and mathematician, had a flair for publicity and his new deck served him well. With much hoopla, he easily predicted various events in Paris during the cataclysmic year of 1789. The deck he used is still available today *(The Grand Eteilla* deck, readily available in occult stores).

Now we come to the nineteenth century and the wave of European secret societies, particularly those of the 1880s. These societies were dedicated to the pursuit of mystical and occult wisdom, patterning themselves after the Egyptian and Eleusynian Mystery schools as best they could. (Remember them from Chapter III, p. 49) Needless to say, the tarot fascinated the members of these societies, and most of the tarot books available today date from this time. In addition, many of the decks currently available were designed by these people, or are based upon their designs and theories.

What were their theories? Their work centred on the Cabbalah, mainly in its Christian interpretations; it was heavily laced with numerology, alchemy, astrology, and their favorite ceremonial/ritual magic forms. When you read books from this time, please bear in mind the old nineteenth century laws of initiation, secrecy and purposely disguised information, often arranged according to secret codes. Some books of this period actually admit to "secretly" rearranging numerical values and symbolic interpretations for the cards.

The most famous tarot authorities dating from this period include Eliphas Levi, Gerard Papus, S.L. MacGregor Mathers, and Arthur Edward Waite. This brings us to the Waite Deck, or Rider Pack, which I recommend. It was designed by Waite and Pamela Coleman Smith in 1910, in affiliation with The Golden Dawn, the famous secret magic society. Several versions of this deck are available, differing mainly in color (also in size: a tiny "unauthorized" thumb-sized version exists). Some versions are simply printed in black and white; you're supposed to color them yourself.

It seems that in the world of tarot publishing, retranslation, adaptation and even outright plagiarism abound. I won't go into which version of the Rider deck you should buy; suffice it to say that Rider was the name of the original London publisher. It's enough that I'm recommending a specific deck, because the choice of your deck's design, color gradations and all — should really be up to you. Look over several designs in the stores, and see which deck "feels" right. That will be the one to work with.

I prefer the Rider pack for several reasons. The designs were essentially clairvoyantly conceived by the artist, Ms. Smith. I like the art-nouveau style with its intense detail. This is the most contemporary "classic" deck, closest in mood to our own culture. Numerous other decks are available, from a French Napoleonic design, to decks depicting American World War I soldiers, to German animals, or copies of the medieval and Renaissance decks mentioned above. In addition, there is Aleister Crowley's pseudo-Egyptian "Thoth" design. One or several of these may speak to you. They do not speak to me. I think it's high time for a new deck, but I have not felt drawn to the more recent designs I've seen. (Please take this statement with a grain of salt — in case a great new deck comes out after this book is published.)[14] The point is, whatever deck calls to you, speaks to you, and works for you, is your deck; and that's that.

Many decks come with a little booklet of instructions for reading the cards; I put these booklets in the same category as the tarot books: unnecessary! Some books are fine for background, and I will include some recommended works (p. 259). They will provide a detailed history, suggested spreads, traditional meanings (which I consider limiting) and possibly some valid numerological — Cabbalistic information. I suggest that you approach any tarot instructions with healthy skepticism and intellectual discrimination. In fact, if you really want to work with books, I think it would be best to create your own study of the tarot with research into the subjects upon which the books have been based: the Caballah (Quabalah, Kabalah, and other alternate spellings); astrology, numerology, Egyptian hieroglyphs; Egyptian, Greek and Roman mythology; comparative religion; ceremonial magic (positive, of course); witchcraft; Jungian psychology; and the Hebrew language. Or you may simply bypass formal research, and get to know your deck. Look at it often, lay out spreads, meditate upon it, and correlate it to your own personal imagery — the symbolism of your thoughts and dreams. Work easily with your deck in a personal way, and follow your own instincts as to how to use the cards. Your

180

deck itself and your own Inner Bell will guide you.

Content

Let us now examine the tarot deck. (I am using the Rider, or Waite, deck as reference).

We see first of all, that the deck contains 78 cards, as opposed to the 52 in a deck of modern playing cards. Most of the tarot cards depict people in various situations, using symbols to act out whatever it is they are doing. Look closely and you will see that most of the people are androgynous in appearance: They could be men, women, boys, girls, men costumed as women, women costumed and bearded as men — anything's possible. The purpose of this is that they can represent anyone: you, aspects of yourself, the person you are reading for, the people in your life, facets of people's personalities. They become the people you need them to be. They may represent different characters in each reading. *They are the players* — and like the traveling troupe of players in *Hamlet*, they assume different roles to suit your needs each time they perform for you.

The tarot deck is illustrated in much more detail than modern playing cards, but we can see how the old designs were adapted into simpler playing cards over the centuries. The tarot has four suits of 14 cards each, 56 cards in all; an additional body of 22 cards, the *Major Arcana*, makes the total of 78 cards.

The symbols in these four suits give them their names — wands, cups, swords, and pentacles. Each suit has an ace, king, queen, knight, and page. When the tarot suits were adapted into the suits of modern playing cards, the wands became clubs, the cups became hearts, the swords became spades, and the pentacles became diamonds. The ace, king, and queen of each suit remained. The knight became the jack, and the page was dropped. Modern playing cards have a jester, or joker card. Where did this come from? From the Major Arcana only one card remains in the modern deck — *The Fool*, which was translated into the modern jester.

Modern playing cards have remained starkly unchanged once they became standardized. The tarot changed quite a bit over the centuries, but its basic elements and structure remain. The tarot is more detailed and more complex, and yet some people can read modern playing cards just as effectively. Why? I believe that this is because the original power (the mnemonic device, albeit watered-down) and the original magic remain.

As with the *I Ching*, possible explanations of the tarot's effectiveness may include a built-in triggering mechanism for psychokinesis or tapping the collective unconscious. Explain it any way you like, there is

181

STRENGTH.

ACE ♣ CUPS.

JUSTICE .

magic in the tarot, a magic so powerful that it's accessible to any
who taps it. You will see for yourself. The tarot is so powerful that it has
managed to remain workable for divination even after the vehicle (the
original deck itself) was changed radically into the modern playing-card
form and after 22 cards (the Major Arcana) were left out. Thus people
with a modicum of psychic ability are able to read today's playing cards
accurately — certainly a testimony to the power in the suits.

The Attributes Of The Suits

Each suit of the tarot contains layers of traditional meanings, and of
numerological and alphabetical symbolism as in the Caballah. I have
not yet found one tarot book with the level of accuracy which I think
would be necessary to decipher these layers. Only a true student of the
Caballah could do this, and it is not relevant to our purposes here. For
basic reading (divination) purposes, it is sufficient to be aware that the
tarot suits traditionally represent the four elements on this planet:
Pentacles=Earth, Swords=Air, Wands=Fire, and Cups=Water.

The other major meanings for the symbols in the suits:
• Pentacles: *finances, resources, and riches of all kinds (only one of*
which is money).
• Swords: *action, activity (sometimes violent in nature), manifest*
strength and energy.
• Wands: *direction, control, interactions, and interpersonal*
exchanges of energies.
• Cups: *emotions, love, resources of personal life-force and*
creativity.

These meanings are not inflexible. They do not always apply.
Remember that the cards keep changing. The above key is only a
guideline. You may find this guideline helpful once you've mastered the
tarot, and wish to tackle the challenge of reading ordinary modern
playing cards. However, I feel that for the novice it is much easier, and
more accurate, to read the tarot.

The Attributes Of The Major Arcana

These 22 richly illustrated cards might present a temptation to resort to
literal interpretations for two reasons: 1) they are numbered clearly in
Roman Numerals, I to XXI (The Fool does not have a number; he is
considered "O"), and 2) they each have a descriptive title. Thus the
reader might immediately want to figure out what each Roman
numeral and what each title "really means." But I feel that this can be a
pitfall, leading to too literal — and consequently irrelevant —

interpretations.

The value of the Major Arcana cards may be found in the intensity, the details, and the moods of the pictures. Traditionally the Major Arcana are all said to represent powerful universal forces, or forces of nature; the suits are believed to represent more personal trends and forces. I have found even these most general interpretations to be not necessarily true! The Major Arcana can become players to represent your circumstances just as easily as the suits. The richness of the Major Arcana designs will give your subconscious wisdom and your imagination a wealth of graphic symbolism to work with.

You may find personal meaning in the Roman numerals or you may choose to ignore them, as the reading seems to indicate. In the same way, you may find personal applications for the titles of these cards in a specific reading, and at other times the titles may seem superfluous. Please do not be literal in your interpretation of any Major Arcana card — or indeed of any tarot card!

Some Points To Remember Before Reading The Tarot

• Always remember that the interpretations of the cards and the traditional meanings of each card, as given in the books, may be used as springboards and starting points only. A responsible book will emphasize this up front:

> Persons reading the cards should bear in mind that the various meanings are suggestive and not meant to be conclusive. During a reading, the diviner of the cards should freely permit his own conscious and subconscious thought processes to assign expanded meanings to each card in a manner which feels most comfortable and responsive.[15]

• I have seen people read effectively after memorizing each card's meaning from a text or from a teacher. I have seen some people read effectively with a book close at hand for easy reference. But I strongly disagree with such practices. Some decks even have the "traditional divinatory meanings" printed right on each card! I think this is perhaps most limiting of all.

• You really do not need any external information which would hinder the free flow of your own mind, your own impressions, instincts, intuitions, and the communication of the cards to you. You will find that if you simply stare at the cards and describe what you see in each one, the mnemonic device within them will work automatically.

• Use good lighting! Save candlelight and semidarkness for other occasions. Wear your glasses, if you need them. It is more important to be able to see and study the cards clearly than to set a mood.

• Work in a quiet room, free from distractions. The vibrations of whatever else may be going on in the room might interfere with the reading. I recommend eliminating background music or television.

• If you are reading for yourself, try to be alone in the room. If you are reading for another person, or if someone else is reading for you, it would be best to have everyone else leave the room — no matter how loving or well-intentioned they may be. The presence of an onlooker could inhibit the freeflow of the reading in various ways. The reading could even address itself to the life situation of the onlooker! Also, surprisingly personal material may come up in the cards, material that you might prefer kept private. After you become adept at reading cards, this no-onlooker policy need not be rigid. There may be some occasions when the cards help with counseling two people, for instance — but this will be more advanced work.

• Use a clear flat surface such as a table top, desk, floor, or even a large bed. There should be enough room to spread the cards out easily. If you are reading for someone (traditionally known as "The Querent", or questioner), that person usually sits opposite you.

Take it easy! Never force anything. If you don't feel like reading, don't read. Never let anyone talk you, beg you, or coerce you into doing a reading. If you study this chapter and practice, it is likely that you will become a good reader. This may put you in some demand. Please be prepared for this; do not allow yourself to ego-trip on your new prowess or popularity as a soothsayer. Respect your mental energies and your Inner Bell, which will tell you when to read and when not to. If you have a feeling that you would prefer not to do a reading, there are myriad possible reasons not to. You may see something in the cards which either you or the querent are not ready to deal with. It's also possible that you may not be psychically in tune enough at that moment to do an accurate reading. Your conscious or subconscious mind may be concentrating on some other more compelling matter. A reading at this time might deplete your psychic energies. And of course, never attempt to read for anyone who doesn't clearly want it. A card reading always has to flow organically.

In fact if you do not wish to embark on any tarot readings at this time, let the matter wait. The tarot can be a powerful experience, and you can afford to wait until you feel totally ready to deal with it.

As with all responsible divination work, if a reading doesn't ring true, then do not try to stretch a point or rationalize to "make" it valid. When the cards are accurate, there is never any doubt about it. If the reading doesn't seem to be on target, simply put the cards away and wait until the time is right.

If you are reading for another person, be aware that any form of manipulation on your part is a ten-foot-pole negative occult activity! If you have any strong opinions on the matter at hand, if you feel you cannot be totally objective, best not to do the reading. In any case, never let the querent tell you his/her question aloud. Trust that the person will mentally "tell" the cards (see instructions below); this way there can be no chance of your unintentional manipulation.

Reversed cards: An old tarot tradition taught that if a card came up reversed (upside down), its more negative interpretation was said to apply. I feel it is high time tarot readers dispensed with this limiting belief. In my opinion, if a card comes up reversed, that may mean something in the visual interpretation, or it might simply mean there is some inherent resistance about the idea to which the card refers. However, I usually grant no particular significance to reversed cards, and I find it simpler to make sure that all the cards in the deck are placed right side up at the start.

Finally, always remember that nothing is inexorable; anything you see in the cards can be changed.

How to Read the Cards

The position of the cards in a spread is as important as the meanings each card takes on during a reading. Spreads are essentially the structures, the diagrams and the patterns you use for laying out the cards. There are many spreads. The books are full of them, and most of these are good. (I believe that learning a variety of spreads provides the main value of the books). You may eventually wish to make up some spreads of your own.

I shall present to you, as a suggested starting point, my variation on the popular *Celtic Cross* spread.

To begin, shuffle the cards until you feel a sense of completion. Place the deck *face down* in front of you.

Place your left hand (or both hands, if you prefer) on the deck, and hold it quietly for a little while. At this point, you may feel that the cards are somehow moving a bit. They may actually seem to throb with motion, or it may be a barely perceptible "breathing" sensation. Do not be disappointed if this doesn't occur; just be alert to the possibility. Meanwhile empty your mind as best you can of excess baggage — extraneous thoughts, worries, opinions, etc. Just feel the cards. This gives them a chance to (as I like to call it) "shuffle themselves."

Concentrate on the concepts of truth, clarity, and order. You may wish to set the psychic atmosphere with an appropriate Words of Power Statement. Here is a typical Statement, subject to your own changes and interpretations after you have read Chapter VIII:

WORDS OF POWER FOR A TAROT READING
There is One Power
Which is perfect truth, clarity, order, and mutual good;
This is all hereby manifest in this reading, with these cards,
Specifically for (name yourself and the querent, if any), perfect
   microcosm(s) of the Power,
According to free will.
And so it must be.

If you are reading for yourself, cut the deck in two sections, and replace the cut, with all the cards still face down.

If you are reading for someone else, ask the querent to hold the cards (still face down) for a short while, and to communicate a question *silently* into the cards while holding them. It is traditional to use the left hand for holding the cards, but I have found it just as effective to place both hands over the deck. (The left hand was believed to contain a channel which emanated directly from the heart. Today we may say that the left hand is motivated by the right side of the brain, which directs one's "relational" or intuitive activities). Now ask the querent to cut the deck and to replace the cut, still face down (preferably with the left hand).

Place the deck in front of you, face down and slightly towards your left. You are now ready to lay out the Celtic Cross spread. Even if you are reading for another person, the cards are always spread out so that they face the reader.

1.   Turn up the first card to begin the spread. This is the *significator,* which the cards themselves have picked. *The significator card defines the situation.* This is my main variation on the traditional Celtic Cross method. The significator, say the books, should be chosen by the reader or the querent by first looking through the deck and picking a card which seems to define the situation — or even looks like the person asking the question. I believe that such a technique is too limiting and superficial; also, it inhibits the first mnemonic insights. (Among the types of definitions and traditional meanings I avoid most are those such as: "This card represents a dark-haired older woman," or "This card represents a cold, blond, angry young man." Choosing a significator by its obvious physical appearance could define the situation from a limited, subjective point of view at the outset. But if you allow the cards to choose the significator for you, the question immediately becomes clearly defined from the point of view of working towards the solution with total objectivity).

187

Place the significator facing you, the reader, vertically face up in the center of your reading surface. *Look at the card carefully (each card you turn up will be studied in this way.)* Study the picture for first impressions. Describe what you see. You are not guessing, although at first it may seem that way — you are describing. Each time you do a reading the card may look different to you than it ever looked before. What do the characters seem to be doing, thinking or feeling? What is the mood of the card, of the characters? What do the symbols seem to represent? Keep looking and see if any detail seems to become more prominent than others; state the detail, describe it, free-associate. Do any of the images remind you of anything else? Does anything in the card seem to be moving or changing? Say whatever occurs to you — it could be an idea, an analogy, an anecdote, etc.

Everything you see in the first card represents the definition of the situation. This entire description process is repeated with each card. Each time the process is related to the meaning the card has in the spread (in this case, the significator, or definer of the situation).

NOTES

If you ever reach a "block" with any card and cannot describe it fully, leave it for the time being and return to it later. Sometimes a delayed reaction happens in interpreting a specific card.

If you are reading for someone else, the first few cards may require a minimum feedback. "Yes, that's accurate" or "No, that's off the beam" — such brief remarks are all that's needed. Do not let the querent "feed" you information, no matter how great the temptation is for either of you. (Sometimes a reading makes people feel open and enthusiastic). Ideally the querent should remain as quiet as possible.

2.   Turn up the second card and place it face up vertically, covering the signficator completely. This card describes whatever *covers* the situation or the question. The covering factor may be covering the situation in the sense of hiding it, or simply in the sense of influencing or coloring the subject in question. Look at this card and describe it in the same way as suggested above for the significator.

3.   Turn up the third card and place it face up, horizontally, covering the first two cards. This is the *cross* card; it represents whatever is "crossing' the situation, and also usually crosses the cover-card's meaning as well. This cross card may represent a difficulty or difficulties which may be obvious within the imagery of the card's illustration. It may depict a "negative" scene. If so, try not not to be upset; again simply describe what you see. You are now locating the problem and

WEINSTEIN'S CELTIC CROSS VARIATION

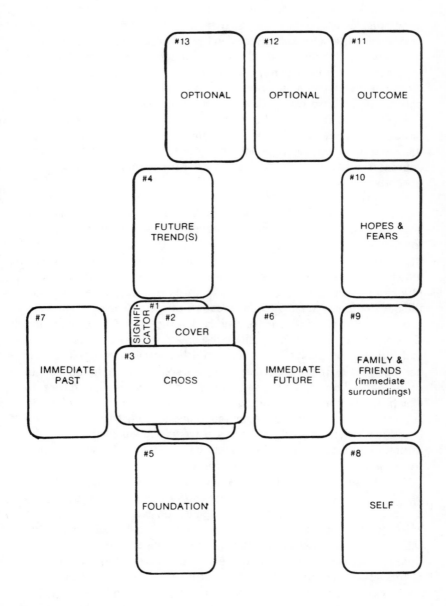

providing insights. On the other hand, the card may appear pleasant in its imagery. How could anything which looks so "good" be a problem? Keep looking — it will become apparent to you. Most common problems with "good" cross-cards are: the querent may not be able to accept the good in the situation, specifically some positive aspect of the good qualities which the cross-card depicts; the querent may not trust or believe in the power of the good in the situation; or the querent may not be aware of the positive value in the situation. Emphasize whatever seems important to you in the card. Note that it is the position of the cross-card which indicates that it is a problem — whether or not the content of the card seems to represent a problem to you.

4.   Turn up the fourth card and place it vertically, face up, and directly above the significator. This represents the direction in which the situation is heading. It depicts the *future* trends (unless the current course of action is changed). It is similar in meaning to the "future" hexagram of the *I Ching*.

5.   Turn up the fifth card and place it vertically, face up, immediately below the significator. This represents the *foundation* of the situation. This card indicates causation — the cause of the significator, the cover, the cross, and usually it directly leads to the future trend. Sometimes the cause may represent a pattern in the person's life. Sometimes it may be a karmic inheritance from another life, which has usually been repeated earlier in this life. The foundation card gives helpful clues as to the starting point leading to the creation of the problem.

6.   Turn up the sixth card and place it vertically, face up, and to the right of the significator. But pick up the cover and cross cards first and look again at the significator. *If the main character* on the significator is obviously facing to your left, then place the sixth card on the left instead of the right. This card represents the next step, *immediate future*, to which the situation is leading. The sixth card usually refers to something which is already beginning to happen, while the future trend card (the fourth) usually indicates a trend slightly further into the future. One could say that the querent has one foot (at least partly) into the situation which this sixth card represents.

7.   The seventh card (face up and vertical again) is placed to the left of the significator. But if the previous card was placed on the left — in accordance with the direction the significator was facing — then this seventh card goes on the right. In any case, this card now represents the situation just passed through and barely finished, *immediate past*. Symbolically we may say that the querent still has one foot stepping out of this situation (immediate past) and the other foot stepping into the sixth card's situation (immediate future). The influence of the immediate past is still strongly felt, and it leads directly into the situation which is just beginning.

NOTES

Cards number four (future trend) and number five (foundation) are usually closely related in a cause-and-effect pattern, the foundation being a strong cause for the future trend.

Cards number six (immediate future) and number seven (immediate past) are also directly related.

As I said, it's as if the querent were stepping directly out of the situation just passed through, and right into the situation just beginning. The significator, cover, and cross cards indicate all the feelings, ideas and experiences which are pertinent to being right in the middle of it all, at the moment of the reading.

8. Place the next card vertically, face up, in a line with the foundation card, to the right of the entire sequence so far. If the significator has been facing left, then this card, number eight, goes on the left of the sequence. This card indicates *the self* (the querent) or an aspect of the self (of the querent) which is important to acknowledge at this point.

9. Place the ninth card, vertically, face up, directly above number eight. This card is traditionally called *family and friends*. I extend that to mean *immediate surroundings* as well. Usually this card refers to the people surrounding the querent and the situation, but it could also mean the mood of the surroundings in general. The querent may not be aware of the particular aspect(s) of the mood around the entire situation. This card represents what exists in the surroundings — what should be taken into serious consideration and not overlooked.

10. Place the tenth card vertically, face up, directly in a vertical line above the previous two cards. This card represents *hope and fears*. How can these both be the same? Do you really want and hope the most for whatever you also fear the most? Some psychiatrists might say, "Absolutely"; I say, "*sometimes.*" Yes, sometimes you both hope for and fear the same thing, but not always. However, hopes and fears may still be linked. For example: sometimes you may hope for whatever this card is referring to — but you might also fear that it will not come about! Or, sometimes you may hope for one aspect of something and simultaneously fear another aspect of it (see "Form Contingencies", Chapter VIII, p. 247). In any case, be aware of both the hope and the fear attributes in this one card as you describe what you see.

11. The eleventh and traditionally final card is placed face up and vertical, at the top of the line you have just formed. This is known as the *outcome* of the situation. Actually, this card represents the way the situation will turn out — *if* the querent continues his/her current course

of action *or* according to whatever new insights (via the card reading) have already taken effect in the querent's mind. Most Celtic Cross spreads stop at this point. Usually the entire situation has been resolved.

However, sometimes the outcome card may seem inconclusive. If so....

12.   You may place an *optional* "bonus" card, directly to the left of the outcome card (unless you have been building the vertical line to the left; in this case the bonus card is placed to the right of the line). The idea is that the optional bonus card begins a horizontal path inward from the line. Still inconclusive?

13.   Place a *second* optional bonus card, number thirteen, to the left (or right, in accordance with the general direction cited above) of number twelve. I would advise stopping here. If the outcome still seems inconclusive, look for clues in the other cards in the spread to determine why things are still so fluid. In such a case, fluidity is probably an important aspect of the outcome. By now, though, the situation should be resolved; a story will have been told.

Intercession

What if you (or the querent) don't like the story — or more specifically, a particular card (perhaps one in a future or cross position)?

192

Remember, of course, that there is no need for either you or the querent to be upset over anything you see in the cards. Problem areas are pointed out so that they can be *solved* — not so anyone should go to pieces over them.

If anything in the reading disturbs you, place your hand on each "negative" card as you say a Words of Power Statement to strip it of negative power in your (or the querent's) life. Here is a sample Statement, subject of course to your own interpretation after you have studied Chapter VIII.

WORDS OF POWER FOR A TAROT READING

There is One Power,
Which is positive Power, for the good of all;
And this positive Power, working for and through (your name and
     querent's name),
Hereby dissolves and releases all negative power out of this card and
     what it represents (name each card by its "official" title),
And replaces it with the positive Power
Which belongs to (your and querent's name) by right of his/her/my
     consciousness,
So that everything which this card has been referring to,
Is hereby transformed to good,
In the most perfect, positive ways,
For the good of all,
And according to the free will of all.
And so it must be.

You have just changed some karma in a positive way.

Additional Notes for Tarot Reading

The cards which represent individual people — kings, queens, knights, etc., — do not always refer to specific people. They could mean aspects of people; that is, character traits. For example, if a king or any other card depicting a male turns up in the place of "self" for a woman querent, this does not mean that she is turning into a man, nor does it mean she is abnormally masculine. It could mean that something about that "male" character in the card represents an important element in the woman querent's psyche and life.

Similarly, the appearance in the cards of a male or female character in the querent's future does not automatically indicate a romantic involvement! The card could represent a friendship, a working relationship, or a significant influence (such as a teacher). Nor does such a card always represent a new (tall, dark, handsome stranger)

193

erson in the querent's life. If a person in the cards seems new — usually by showing up in a future position, the card could refer to someone the querent already knows reappearing in a new guise — or simply reappearing (in an old guise).

There are so many possibilities in the tarot which a limited or preconceived interpretation could not possibly uncover. For this reason it is extremely important to allow the cards to tell you what they mean each time. If an idea pops into your head while reading, say it. This is the psychic process. Do not edit or censor while you are reading. Do not dismiss a thought or an association as irrelevant, outrageous, impossible, crazy, or in any other judgmental way. If you are reading for another person and you think an idea is "too" strange, of course you may preface it by saying: "This may sound weird, but the card seems to be telling me such-and-such." If you go off the track, the querent should tell you. This does not mean that you should allow the querent to fill in details for you. You may simply ask from time to time, "Does this make sense to you, does this ring true *without* stretching the point?" A simple "yes" or "no" from the querent will suffice. You may need affirmation at the beginning of the reading, as I have indicated, and you may also need affirmations of the cards in the past positions, as well as the significator, cover, cross and possibly family and friends cards. If the querent insists that little or none of this rings true, perhaps you should discontinue the reading. Possibly the querent could be having trouble dealing with the facts (do not judge!), or this may not be the best time for you to read accurately (no blame!). Put your hands over the cards you have laid out so far, and say:

"The One Power, working for and through us, transforms this entire reading to positive good for all."

Then return the cards to the deck, shuffle them, and put them away.

Keep a dated record of each reading. If you have been reading for another, give a copy to the querent, and certainly always keep notes of your own readings for yourself. (Some people prefer to tape record their readings, and later refer to the tapes). Some readings may stretch over a period of many years. I recently found out about a reading I did for a friend seven years ago; the outcome card had just "come true." If he had not kept a record, the insights of all the other cards — revealed over the years — would have been lost.

The purpose of reading the tarot goes beyond simply "seeing the future." The tarot can also help us to understand the present — as well as the past. Insights often occur over long time periods, so keep your notes handy.

The question of charging money for card readings inevitably comes up. As a general rule, I would advise against it. If a reading is easily given, out of friendship, and with no strain or inconvenience to the reader, I see no reason to charge money for it. Most divination services, as I have indicated, work very well in a free give-and-take exchange between friends. (I read for my friend this week; she reads for me next week). If a reading feels like such a strain that you want to charge money for it, it would be better not to read at all. Of course, if you discover an unusual gift for the tarot, and would rather read cards than do anything else, and decide to make card reading your profession, that is probably a different story. Even then I would recommend that you check this decision out very carefully — preferably with both the cards and the *I Ching*. The karmic responsibility of doing psychic and occult work for others is never to be taken lightly.

Primarily, please be aware that you can read the cards for yourself, and that the insights and personal growth which can come from such work are immeasurable.

Phrase your questions with an awareness of what the future really means (trends rather than irrevocable fate). For example, instead of asking, "What is going to happen to me?" ask, "What should I know about such-and-such?" Note that the cards in the past and surrounding positions help explain why and how things got to where they are. Often such understanding is more relevant than where the future seems to be heading.

The popular spreads such as the Celtic Cross variation usually focus in time, in this way: The spreads start with an analysis of the present, provide some past background information and explanations, and proceed to the future trends. After a while, however, your readings need not be limited to this pattern. For example, you can ask the cards to show you all the significant sides of a current situation. They may then focus not in sequential time, but on many facets of the present. In such a case, the traditional meanings I delineated in the sample spread may no longer apply. You may use the same Celtic Cross pattern for convenience, but be aware that each position will then simply represent a different facet of the present.

You may also ask the cards to give you a karmic explanation of another lifetime. In such a case the significator may not represent this present-lifetime-moment of questioning, but instead this card may represent a significant moment in that other lifetime. All the cards' positions will then refer to that other lifetime — its immediate past, foundation, future and outcome (which could be the end of that life situation). This is advanced work, but you can do it if you are aware that the lifetime story you uncover is significant only in its symbolic meaning, and not to be taken literally. The cards will reveal to you whatever ideas you need to be aware of from that life experience. Do not get hung up on details. It can be misleading to focus on any lifetime other than this one. Keeping this in mind, you may also trace several lifetimes in one card reading, following a specific connecting thread such as a particular relationship. Or you may work this way for tracking down an "unexplained" problem such as a phobia or fixation.[16]

You may discover other uses for your cards. The tarot is an infinite source of insights and information. The more work you put into your cards, the more readings you do, the more you get to know your deck — the more your cards will help you develop in your own growth and self-understanding. If you have a friend (or friends) with whom you can share this process, that is a bonus. In any case, I hope that you enjoy the cards, and that they are as helpful and inspiring to you as they have been to me.

Throughout the book, every time a subject came up which could have benefited from an applied transformation process, I have suggested a sample Words of Power Statement to this effect — to cause change for the good. Now we shall embark upon a more detailed study of this process, to learn how to create your *own* Words of Power, and to understand how and why they work.

[1]Commenting in the *I Ching*, Book One, Hexagram 16, 6 in the second place.

[2]Colin Wilson, *The Occult*, Vintage Books, New York, 1973, p. 549. Wilson is recounting one of J.B. Priestley's anecdotes about precognition.

[3]Lyall Watson, *Supernature*, Bantam Paperback, New York, 1974, p. 271. This type of charlatanism seems to have led Watson and many others to conclude (erroneously, I believe) that all psychic readers are phony.

[4]Sir James George Frazer, *The Golden Bough*, Macmillan (paperback abridged edition), New York, 1969. *The Golden Bough* may also be found as an 8-volume detailed encyclopedia series, Macmillan, Great Britain, 1923.

[5]See Watson, *Supernature*, pp. 169-177 for scientific details.

[6]Numerologist Vicky Monbarren recommends Florence Campbell, *Your Days Are Numbered, a Manual of Numerology for Everybody*, The Gateway, Pleasant Valley, Bucks County, Pa., 1958.

[7]A Faber paperback, London. Out of print, but worth tracking down in occult bookstores or stores dealing in old books.

[8]Colin Wilson, *The Occult*, Random House Vintage Books, New York, 1971, p. 78.

[9]All my references to page numbers in the Bollingen have been drawn from my working copy, which is the eleventh printing, 1974. There seems to be some discrepancy between this printing and other printings of the identical text — a discrepancy only in page numbering. The difference involves only a page or so in either direction. If your own volume seems to be off by a page or two, I have tried to make all the references clear enough for you to locate.

[10]A computer need not be made of metal. "A computer can be any arrangement of objects representing a mapping of abstract numerical concepts," says William Fishman, my personal computer expert. Leibnitz, the seventeenth-century inventor of the binary system in the West (the basis of many modern computers) was astounded to learn of the *I Ching's* binary system from a Jesuit missionary to China. A detailed mathematical analysis of the *I Ching* may be found in "Scientific American," Vol. 230, Number 1, Scientific American, Inc., New York, Jan., 1974, pp. 108-113. Although this article is mathematically accurate, it seems biased and inaccurate in its analysis of the *I Ching's* practical method of use as an oracle.

[11]Watson, *Supernature*, p. 270

[12]See Jung's "Foreword," pp. xxv-xxxix. It was Jung's experiment to ask the *I Ching* how it felt about being translated into English

[13]Adam Smith, *Powers of Mind*, Ballantine Books, New York, 1975.

[14]Sure enough, since the first edition of this book, I have begun to use *the Aquarian Tarot* and have seen two fine feminist decks.

[15]Stuart R. Kaplan, *Tarot Classic*, Grosset & Dunlap, New York, 1972, p. 84.

[16]See Chapter V, "Karma and Reincarnation." If tracing incarnations is really your cup of tea, I suggest you read Jane Roberts' *The Nature of Personal Reality*. It can help you put other lifetimes into perspective with your current lifetime.

Chapter VIII

WORDS OF POWER, THE WORK OF SELF-TRANSFORMATION

Heat creates energy; this is signified by the wind stirred up by the fire and issuing forth from it. This represents influence working from within outward.

.....In order to be capable of producing such an influence, one's words must have power, and this they can have only if they are based on something real, just as flame depends on its fuel.

—The *I Ching*, Book One, Hexagram 37

Introduction

I have defined magic as transformation, and this chapter will deal with specific positive transformation techniques. Following the ideas in previous chapters, if you have transcended your perceptions of time and space...begun to accept responsibility for your own karma...made the distinctions between positive and negative occult work...perceived your link with the rest of the Cosmos...and embarked upon the techniques of divination — you have probably already experienced some degree of transformation in your life. By now, I hope it is clear that we are capable of directing and controlling our own lives...that the "outer reality" (the World of Form) need not dominate us...that there is no power greater than that of the self when the self is perceived in harmony with the rest of the Cosmos. The potential of transformation to be wrought *by the self* probably is now apparent, and the work in this chapter is simply the next step.

Transformation can manifest in many ways. There is an entire field of entertainment, also called "magic," which is actually a simulation, an imitation, of the kind of transformation which can be effected by occult work. Such simulated magic includes prestidigitation, or sleight-of-

199

hand, a technique causing material objects to seem to appear, disappear, or change. In the occult, these same phenomena can occur — not by trickery, but by actual changes in the molecular structures of the objects. Science prefers to call this "the paranormal," "psychokinesis," "parapsychology," and other technical-sounding terms. We are discovering that such phenomena can be measurable.[1] Scientific experiments have proven that the World of Form is flexible — far more flexible than it may have seemed to be.

When Uri Geller, the Israeli psychic, came on my show he bent silverware, keys, and other familiar "inflexible" objects. He did not apply intense physical pressure; he did not flex his muscles, strain, or force these objects to bend. He barely stroked them as he "willed" them to bend, and they literally curled up, seemingly by themselves. Actually he *asked* them to bend. I still treasure a stainless steel butter knife of my mother's which Uri bent in half without any obvious physical force. For me, this was a dramatic illustration of how flexible the World of Form can be.

But there were people in the studio whose perceptions did not allow them to accept or believe what was happening, even though they saw this with their own eyes. These people insisted, "It must be a trick!" I know that for Uri (and others with similar gifts, such skepticism has been a common reaction. Of course sometimes — in stage "magic" — it is a trick; that is, there are tricks which make a metal object look as if it is bending. But in the occult, we know that such phenomena can also be real, that actual change can manifest physically. Within the occult frame of reference, we can say that those people who categorically refuse to believe that this is possible are people who have chosen not to let their own World of Form be flexible (and of course, that choice is according to their own free will).

According to my own witchcraft beliefs, bending a fork or a key is only a symbol. *Changing a life* — for the better — is probably more relevant. But a symbol is important for what it represents; bending a fork or changing a life are the same thing — both work in the same way. Both are transformation.

The transformation of physical matter as a symbol of a psychological and spiritual transformation was a task of *alchemy*. The "Great Work" of alchemy was not meant *primarily* to transform base metal into gold, as is so frequently misunderstood. The goal was to transform the alchemist's psyche in profound ways. As Pauwels and Bergier state in *The Morning of the Magicians:*

> For the alchemist it must never be forgotten that power over matter and energy is only a secondary reality. The real aim of the alchemist's activities, which are perhaps the remains of a very old

200

science belonging to a civilization now extinct, is the transformation of the alchemist himself, his accession to a higher state of consciousness. The material results are only a pledge of the final result, which is spiritual.[2]

Jung has devoted an enormous body of study to this idea. As he puts it:

> Certainly goldmaking, as also chemical research in general was of great concern to alchemy. But a still greater, more impassioned concern appears to have been — one cannot very well say that the "investigation" — but rather, the *experience* of the unconscious.[3]

The important point is: *The World of Form is flexible — if we let it be.* It may seem paradoxical that an essential starting point to remember, when we set out to change the World of Form in any way, is that the Invisible World must be granted equal validity. As the *I Ching* says:

> All that is visible must grow beyond itself, extend into the realm of the invisible. Thereby it receives its true consecration and clarity and takes firm root in the cosmic order.
> —Book One, Hexagram 50

The work of magic involves both Worlds, and involves them equally: the World of Form and the Invisible World. It is only natural that our initial focus should be on the World of Form, because we are living in it, in physical bodies, on the the Earth Plane, here (as the Caballah terms it) in Malkuth. It is desirable that we work magic to change (improve) the forms of our lives — if we are aware that such work both *symbolizes* and begins a much larger work, as in alchemy. All magic (transformation) by its very nature involves the entire Cosmos; one of the working Principles is that we are all microcosms of the infinitely larger Whole. Thus it is important to bear in mind that the work of magic — even when applied to the individual — extends beyond our immediate perceptions and our initial goals. (We will explore this idea, as a process of holistic perception, in Chapter IX).

It may seem as if my emphasis in this chapter is more on the Invisible than on the Visible. But I shall merely be emphasizing the Invisible now in order to achieve a balance. Unfortunately, our culture has gone so far in emphasizing the importance of the World of Form that many of us may have forgotten entirely about the importance of the Invisible. Or we may acknowledge the Invisible, but not know how to relate to it nor how to work with it. We may be caught in the Western thought-mode of relating to the Invisible by the same set of guidelines and definitions which we use for the World of Form. If you have perceived the World of Form as inflexible and operative within certain limits, you might automatically have carried these definitions over to your perceptions of the Invisible World. This view of the Invisible World has led to many limited dealings with it, specifically in the West. Such a view has led to the concept of supervision by an external god or gods, and to "deductions" about the ways the god or gods may work. It has led to a sense of resignation to the concept of fate, luck, and destiny, and to the belief in various kinds of outer-directed powers which seem to rule our lives. Such a view has also led to fear and superstition, and a desire to *placate* these Invisible forces — especially when confronted by anything which does not fit into our limited perceptions and definitions of the Invisible.

According to occult belief, one of the attributes of the Invisible World is that *as we define it, so it seems to manifest in accordance with our definitions.* In other words, the Invisible World reflects an image back to us according to whatever we project onto it. (If we believe and project that "fate" is arbitrary, so the Invisible World will appear to consist of an arbitrary fate. If we believe that the Invisble World is harmonious and orderly, so will it demonstrate to us harmony and order). Actually, the Invisible World cannot be defined in familiar terms.

The first thing to acknowledge is that any definitions, any rules, any delineations we may use for the Invisible World are our own *choices.* Our choice here will be to view the Invisible World as the place of *Cause,* and the World of Form as the place of *Effect.* Our choice will then be to begin with our ideas, which are Invisible. We will perceive that our ideas can manifest into forms, which are Visible. "Ideas" in this context include emotions, thoughts, beliefs, and other mental processes. I have chosen to use "ideas" as a catch-all term mainly because the word seems to connote "change." In Jane Roberts' *The Nature of Personal Reality,* which embodies techniques similar to Words of Power, the term "beliefs" is used.

We will perceive that many of our past ideas have occurred on a subconscious level. When the ideas have manifested as the forms (or circumstances) in our lives, this process of cause and effect has also been subconscious. We will now bring into conscious awareness this process of ideas into forms. We will direct the cause-and-effect process in our lives to effect changes.

According to this method, we can view the entire World of Form, and everything in it, as *manifestations* of Invisible ideas. The Earth Plane, Malkuth, is the place where ideas manifest into form, and this is where we have chosen to live. Here we may see around us evidence of ideas manifest into forms — animals, trees, flowers, stars, oceans — all of nature. Each form is a perfect living idea. And so are we — perfect living ideas *in form*, of our Invisible selves (our souls). And so *every aspect of our lives is an idea*, which we have caused to manifest into a form. If we change an idea, therefore, the correlating form consequently will change!

This technique may be viewed as sequential: We will use the Invisible World "first," by employing a sequence of ideas spoken in words. The changes will manifest "later," in the World of Form, in our lives. We will use words as the causes, and note the changes in our lives as the effects. Most Western magic works with the Law of Cause and Effect in this way. It is in accordance with the Threefold Law of the witches, and with many positive Ceremonial magic traditions. If we understand that we exist in *simultaneous time* ("All time is now"), we can then make the conscious choice to work in sequential or linear time. But we are aware that linear time is not the only time-mode available to us. If we understand that we live in multidimensional space ("All space is here"), then we can choose consciously to work with a system which manifests in tangible form, on the Earth Plane.

It is also important to understand that the system of using *words* to trigger these changes is just one of many possible systems. We could use images, diagrams, thought-forms, rituals, meditation, shifts in emotions, or other techniques. The use of words is particularly appropriate for dealing with daily life on the Earth Plane, at this point in Western culture.

Words are symbols. They represent ideas, which are invisible; yet words themselves can be visible as written on a page, or otherwise perceived tangibly by our immediate senses. Even unsighted people can use words via hearing, or by the use of braille. Deaf people can use a sign language or think the words. Anyone accustomed to working with his/her immediate senses can build a bridge to the Invisible Realm by way of words; they help us to span both Worlds. Words are tools; they work in invisible ways to create visible results.

It is vital when using words for working magic to use the language you understand best. You can most accurately express the clarity and subtlety of your ideas in this way. Your work will be more effective and safer than if you use unfamiliar words. It is true that a psychic "build-up" has occurred in the traditional magic words of some languages; indeed, people believe some languages to have been especially devised for use in magic (for example, Hebrew). But since it is important to acknowledge your total responsibility and control from the outset, make sure you use the language you speak and read most easily in your own Words of Power. It is vital to strip away any mystery or confusion from the work, which might subtly give power away from the self.

Remember, the power in doing magic comes from *you*, and your words direct the Power. Your own words will serve you better than someone else's most eloquent incantations.

History

The use of words in magic and religion is as old as language itself. Verbal techniques of dealing with the Invisible may be divided into two categories: *supplication* and *affirmation*.

Supplication may be defined as any technique of dealing with a Higher Power (or Powers) which is believed to be greater than human, and existing on a more elevated plane, outside of human experience. Often the Power seems to be viewed as a sort of "mighty parent" (or parents) and in contrast, humans are but children. The Higher Power may seem to move in mysterious ways, may seem awesome, frightening, and impossible for a mere human to comprehend. Or in contrast, it can be merciful, compassionate, protective, and the giver of all life. In any case, such a Power seems to be basically *separate from* the human entity. A primitive response to such a Power has been trying to *please,* and to get the "God on our side." Or to decide that the "God *is* on our side." This conviction can lead to the justification of barbaric behavior, such as holy war or the persecution of other religions and races. Generally, anything which seems outside of human understanding is ascribed to that Deity's of Power's "will" — including death, birth, intense emotion, and dramatic manifestations of nature.

Supplication involves an acknowledgement of the human self as below the Higher Power. The process can involve entreaty for the Deity to "take care of" the humans who are worshipping. This worship may be expressed in a number of ways:

- Sacrifices — either symbolic sacrifices of an animal, or placing money or food in prescribed holy place.
- Self-sacrifice — avoidance of certain foods or fasting, avoidance of sex, or even self-flagellation or other forms of physical discomfort.
- Symbolic self-abasement — kneeling, grovelling, bowing down.
- Verbal self-abasement — acknowledgement of the self as "impure," humble, unimportant, etc. *in relation to* the Higher Power.
- Many forms of prayer — begging God to be merciful and kind in general, or to grant a specific favor. This kind of prayer can vary from the loftiest request (such as to save a life or protect a country) to the most gross ("please kill the enemy") to the most childlike ("please don't let me fail this exam").

A practice which has arisen out of prayer-as-supplication in the West has been to "make a deal" with God. One often hears of people who promised God in a moment of danger that if only He would rescue them, they would be "good" from then on, generally or in specific ways. Some people who make deals with God even without any immediate threat of danger assume if they perform in a certain way, God may also perform in a certain way. Supplication often provides a framework for people to act in a righteous way only because it is calculated to guarantee the Power's favors.

Some forms of prayer, however, have an element of *affirmation*, because they affirm a connection to the Deity on some level. The affirmation technique assumes the human entity's existence *as part of the Higher Power*. Affirmation acknowledges the unity of all life, the Oneness of all life, and consequently affirms the concept that the Higher Power is as much inside the self as outside.

Some religions have begun by advocating affirmation, and have then turned to condoning or encouraging supplication. It was believed that affirmation was a technique which only the priests and other religious leaders were capable of understanding; the populace wasn't "enlightened" enough. Many holy people who understood affirmation tried to teach it to their followers, and the followers simply ended up worshipping whoever was trying to teach it to them.

Another problem surrounding this work is that one may find various organizations claiming "ownership" of affirmation techniques. Actually, the basic technique is a heritage available to all of us. Affirmation comes from the collective unconscious; the technique may even be arrived at by a process of deduction from basic occult and metaphysical principles. Throughout the history of magic and religion, there have been numerous versions of affirmation and one hears of many names and descriptions for it. I have chosen to call it "Words of Power" — mainly because I traced the process historically back to the ancient Egyptian Goddess, Isis, and this is the term *She* used.

> Come to me, for my speech hath in it the power to protect, and it possesseth life....for I am Isis the goddess, and I am the lady of words of power, and I know how to work with words of power, and most mighty are (my) words.[4]

Isis was worshipped as a Goddess in ancient Egypt, but some of the legends surrounding Her may have been based upon the life of an actual person. She is described as having used Words of Power to cause miracles, primarily healing, and bringing the (apparently) dead and dying back to life. Isis restored Her "murdered" husband/brother Osiris to such a state of vitality that they conceived a child Horus.

Ra

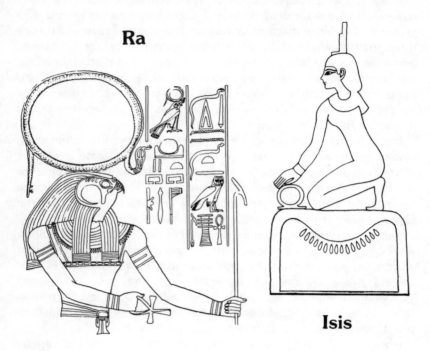

Isis

It seems that the ancient Egyptians who worshipped Isis did not know how to use Words of Power themselves; instead they revered as deities the legendary figures who had this knowledge. Isis was said to have learned Words of Power from Her father, the Sun God, Ra. Ra was believed to be the "One" God, or primal essence, and all the other gods and goddesses were considered to be manifestations (forms) of Him.[5] My theory is that when Isis learned that She was part of the Divine Power, Her own words took on Power as well.

In ancient and "classical" civilizations (beginning with Vth dynasty in Egypt, circa 2900 BC, and continuing through Greek and Roman periods to the first century CE), it seems that the popular religions led by priests and priestesses worshipped a pantheon of gods and goddesses, all primarily in the mode of supplication. However, the traditions surviving from these times through occult sources indicate a continuous thread of at least three main mystery schools that handed down affirmation techniques in secret to a select group of initiates. These occult groups are the Mysteries of Isis, the Eleusynian Mysteries of Greece (including the Dianic branches related to Celtic witchcraft), and the Roman Mysteries.

There is only one ancient civilization in which affirmation seems to

206

have been practiced by most of the population, and it is a legendary civilization at that: Atlantis. Legends about Atlantis agree on one main point: Many people had access to the use of some great, mysterious (mental) Power, and its misuse caused the entire civilization of Atlantis to self-destruct.[6]

Witchcraft is an ancient religion which traces its roots back to these early magic traditions; in fact, I believe that it goes even further back in time. Despite the fact that some of the Craft sects today worship the Goddess and the God as externalized deities, witchcraft works primarily by affirmation — the Power is believed to emanate from within. Witchcraft often employs combinations of ritual, sympathetic magic, and rhymed and/or chanted Words of Power. These are symbolic techniques, intended to aid in the concentration and focus of the use of the Power. Thus, spells, chants, charms, and "magic words," in witchcraft terms, are affirmation techniques. Folk magic, on the other hand, is primarily supplication based as it is on superstition. One might say that folk magic technically is not "magic" at all, but a *placating* system based on fear of external power.

In ancient Judaism, the original High Priests of the First Temple seem to have had a knowledge of affirmation; it is said that they knew (and could pronounce) the secret "Name of God." However, the majority of the ancient Hebrews seem to have prayed mainly by supplication. After the destruction of the Temple, a succession of conquering groups, primarily the Romans, eliminated the hereditary position of High Priests, so that the Priesthood became a political rather than a spiritual office.[7] Consequently the people serving as High Priests eventually became corrupt until the office of High Priest disappeared. The exact sequence of events surrounding this time seem to be buried in a mist of legends (recounted from the nonadept's point of view). In any case, after this period the knowledge of affirmation techniques in Judaism seems to have been left mainly to those few scholars immersed in the lifetime study of the Caballah. The goal of this study, stated simplistically, is to reach a heightened state of spiritual consciousness which is manifest in knowing and pronouncing the secret Name of God.

The Old Testament provides clues that affirmation may have been practiced by a few holy people. The stories about the miracles surrounding the life of Moses indicate that he may have learned something of Egyptian magic, specifically the Words of Power tradition.[8] Since the Bible seems to have been translated and handed down primarily by nonadepts, it is difficult to figure out what the mode of communication with the Higher Power may have been. Was it affirmation or supplication? I believe that the holy people and religious leaders made use of affirmation, and the common folk practiced supplication.

In any case, it seems clear that since Biblical times, the major emphasis in popular Judaism has been to worship and pray via supplication. The *minor* emphasis has followed a lesser-known spiritual tradition in which advanced levels of study and prayer lead to a form of affirmation, a Oneness with the God-force. There are numerous legends — from the non-adept's point of view — about the "wonder-rabbis" who could perform miracles because they had learned the Name. These rabbis were said to have been able to fly, bi-locate, create the *golem* (humanoid man of clay), heal, exorcise evil spirits, and perform other superhuman deeds.

In the New Testament, the miracles and healings of Jesus indicate the use of affirmation techniques; in fact, it is possible that Jesus attempted to teach affirmation to his followers. If this is the case, within a short period of time the original intent may have been distorted into a veneration of the teacher to the exclusion of understanding the teachings. Note Mark 12:23:

> For verily I say unto you, That whosoever shall say unto this mountain, Be thou removed, and be thou cast into the sea; and shall not doubt in his heart, but shall believe that those things which he saith shall come to pass; he shall have whatsoever he saith.

Styles

In the past century, several religious/philosophical organizations have emerged which teach affirmation techniques within the Judeo-Christian tradition. For example, Religious Science terms the method "treatment"; in Unity, it is called "affirmative prayer" and "affirmative meditation."[9] These techniques are particularly helpful to people who wish to pursue affirmation in a way which is compatible with Western Judeo-Christian concepts of prayer. Essentially, these groups work with the idea that "God is within," and they place a metaphysical interpretation upon traditional prayers and Biblical passages. Thus, it is not necessary to depart from more traditional monotheistic religious tradition in order to work with some form of affirmation.

You may also come across organizations which teach affirmation in a number of other styles: occult, metaphysical, psychological, even Eastern. Some are eclectic, and borrow from various styles. These groups may use such key terms as "mind-expanding," "consciousness-raising," "sensitivity training," "dynamic," "mind-power," "awareness" or "control." Whatever course of study you may undertake, I would like to remind you of my compendium of "modern dangers" in Chapter

III! Please watch out, and be careful not to hand over any of your own power, or control of your life to *anyone*. This has been a problem for many people — to inadvertently transfer their reverence, fear, awe and responsibility (previously assigned to God, fate or any outside force) over to a group leader. And some group leaders, either intentionally or subconsciously, might well accept such a role. This can happen even in the midst of teaching self-responsibility, self-determined karma, and the concept of the God-within. This contradiction, as I have said earlier, is a Cusp phenomenon. In the Aquarian Age, I believe it will no longer pose a problem; but please watch out for it now.

Ideally, the style of affirmation you choose to work with should not contradict anything you deeply believe. Affirmation should feel harmonious with your way of thinking and your way of life, and it should fulfill your needs. The most appropriate style for you can emerge organically out of your understanding of the content. I have attempted to keep the instructions for Words of Power in this book as nonsectarian as possible. Thus I hope you will be able to translate them into whatever style you wish — perhaps even evolve a style all your own. But please be aware that I am drawing upon a personal style of affirmation (in case you hadn't noticed!). Yes, it is witchcraft — specifically the style of the *witchcraft blessing*.

So now, before we get into the nonsectarian instructions for working Words of Power, I offer you — in my own style — a witchcraft blessing to guide the way.

It only applies to you if you want it to.

> The One Power that moves the Moon
> Moves through you.
> The Power that lights the Sun
> Lights your life.
> It is female and it is male,
> It is clouds and rain,
> It lives in the damp earth,
> In root and in bud.
> It moves the wind.
> It is all life, born and unborn,
> On this Plane and in the next,
> Visible and Invisible,
> In planet and star.
> It is Infinite, it blesses and protects,
> Heals and creates;
> It moves backwards and forwards in Time,
> Through all of Space —
> In this life, and in myriad others yet to come

And in the past as well.
This Power is yours,
As it is mine;
It is Goddess and it is God.
Use it, for the good of all,
And according to the free will of all,
With ease and with joy —
To bless your life.
And so mote it be.

Summary

The work of Words of Power is based on the traditional witchcraft concept that we live simultaneously in two Worlds: the World of Form and the Invisible Realm.

The World of Form is that which seems to exist outside ourselves. It may seem that we have no control over it. We do have control over it. The World of Form is more flexible than our current culture may have led us to believe. The Invisible Realm is the area in which ideas are born. These ideas later manifest as form. If we wish to direct and control the forms of our lives, we begin by working in the Invisible Realm. Here, we need guidelines.

A misunderstanding of the Invisible Realm has led to such misconceptions as "destiny," "fate," and popular superstitions. These are all ideas which relate to the concept of an "outer Power." In the Invisible Realm, there is no outer Power or force more powerful than the Power of the self.

Here are the guidelines. These are basic Universal Principles, born out of traditional witchcraft beliefs. These guide the work according to the stance between the Two Worlds — the World of Form and the Invisible World.

We work between the Worlds.

Words of Power: Basic Principles for Positive Occult Work

1. *For the Good of All:* All the work of magic must be done for the good of all only. Within the context of our current culture, this Principle may seem hard to comprehend. It may be necessary to simply state it at first, even before our conscious minds have grasped the Principle. It literally means that every magic work we do, works for the good of

everyone. This includes you, the worker, everyone involved in the situation, and ultimately every living being. The Universe works in perfect harmony, and we on the human level also fit into this ideal, infinitely perfect harmony. Our needs do not oppose this Principle; they are in harmony with it. If we work to fulfill our needs, this work by definition hurts no one and helps everyone. No "if's," no "but's," no "plus's" — it includes *all*. This does not mean manipulation. (So-and-so must suffer or give in or lose even a little for this thing to come about.") *No*. It does not mean compromise. ("*I* must give in a little, suffer, or compromise a bit for this to work for everyone's good.") *No*. It does not mean deprivation, nor does it mean rationalization. ("'You can't have everything.") *No so*. You, the worker, will be fulfilled and the people involved will be fulfilled *according to their needs*. This does not mean according to your definition of their needs. It means *according to the free will and receptivity of all*. And everything will literally turn out for the best. This is based on the concept of natural Universal harmony, which also means....

2. *The Universe as Macrocosm:* The Universe is comprised of harmony, the infinite and complete *unity* of all life. The Power is the life-force of the Universe, and in a sense synonymous with it. We are all inheritors of the Power, and the Power holds no favorites. It exists equally in everything and everyone; when we are in tune with it, we are in tune with the perfect balance of the Universe.

3. *The Microcosm:* That's each of us — that's the self. We are each individualizations of the Power, and anything the Power can do, we can do. The Power can create — worlds, stars, planets, babies — and we can create. The Universe is complete (it has everything it needs), and we are complete (we potentially have everything we need). We have the infinite resources of the Power to bring about the work of positive magic, to make our potential into reality. The way I like to perceive the self as microcosm is: we are each Goddess; we are each God. All of the power is ours to draw upon, by acknowledging this infinite perfection of the Power in each and every being. We, as microcosms, are each the centers of our own universes, of our own lives. Thus we may benefit from conscious use of the natural Law which keeps everything in the Universe running smoothly....

4. *The Law of Cause and Effect:* All you physicists out there already know about this. Well, physics and magic work in the same way. The Law of Cause and Effect is the basis of all life on this Plane, and of this work. Please keep in mind that at this level, we are working with the concept of linear — sequential — time, in which the cause comes before the effect. Modern physics has begun to work with the idea of effects coming before causes, as may be proven by the existence of *tachyons*, particles believed to move faster than the speed of light.

211

In this work the Words of Power are the *Cause,* and the results, or manifestations, are the *Effect.* The Cause often takes place in the Unseen Realm, and the Effect usually manifests in the World of Form. Much of the most powerful positive magic we may work happens through conscious directive use of the Law of Cause and Effect. We achieve our desired effects by setting up carefully the appropriate causes. Consequently, any negative work is also subject to this Law. Thus, if anyone is foolish or irresponsible enough to work in a manipulative or harmful way, then manipulation and harm automatically come back *to the worker* (and sometimes this happens where least expected). Remember, the witches believe that everything comes back "threefold." I cannot guarantee the *number* of times something comes back to you, but I can assure you that everything does come back. When you are working with Words of Power, and you are very specific — specific things come back. This is the simple, inevitable use of the Power. In negative magic, cursing comes back, wishing harm comes back, inflicting pain or death comes back. Yes, eventually it all comes back to the worker — the individual who set up the negative Cause in the first place. Negative magic does not inevitably affect the target — because of that person's conscious or subconscious self-protection — but negative magic inevitably affects the magician.[10] Remember that this is the idea behind the symbolic resignation of Satanists "selling their souls to the Devil." Negative use of the Law is not necessary. Just think of all the bounty of blessing, healing, and love coming back. Hence, remember *always* to stipulate in all of your work: *"for the good of all."*

5. *Free Will:* Since positive magic is nonmanipulative, it is important to include in your work *"according to free will"* or *"according to the free will of all."* Such a statement will eliminate the possibility of even unintentional manipulative ideas entering the work — either manipulation of another person or of yourself.

6. *Infinity:* By "infinity," I mean the concept of non-limitation. I see two main obvious applications of this and they both are infinitely comforting.

(a) *Anything* can be solved by working magic. There are *no limitations* on the potential applications of Words of Power. If you can just get yourself to the point where you can remember that no matter what problems seem to arise, they are potentially solvable within this frame of reference — then you have instantly eliminated being overwhelmed, in despair, or out of control. You just say, "As weird, as terrifying, as confusing as this situation may seem to be, I will now handle it with Words of Power, my own use of positive magic." Then you automatically have the problem half solved.

(b) Always remember that no matter what the problem may be, there is an *Infinity of Solution.* If you've ever had that old familiar feeling of seeming to be in a double bind, of having only choice 1,2, or 3, or whatever you can think of as solutions — and none of them feel completely comfortable — then you understand the saying, "having to choose the lesser of two (or three) evils." Well, within the Infinity of Solution there are *myriad,* infinite, other solutions you might not yet have dreamed of, and they all fit in with these Principles. Notice "for the good of all," for example. Right from the start you can work for a solution (even if you haven't thought about what it is specifically yet) which is totally for your good, with no pain, no compromise, and which hurts no one — in fact which helps everyone. And it isn't necessarily choice 1, 2, or 3.

How will the solution come about? It will come most quickly if you allow yourself to believe that your subconscious mind will deliver the solution to you (i.e., the Universe will deliver it to you through your subconcious mind). In cases like this, it is often best to "leave it up to the Goddess," or the God, or the Power, or your eternal soul, or your subconscious mind — all being the same. To clarify this type of application — using the Infinity of Solution — it helps to bear in mind....

7.   *The Concept of Form and Essence:* Even if you don't know exactly what you want, you know the feeling or *essence* of what you want. This feeling can be a key for you. You direct the work by specifying the essence, and you allow the Universe to pick the form. Remember that the World of Form is more flexible than we may think! Forms come out of the Invisible Realm and manifest in the "tangible" world. Sometimes we know exactly what forms we need. But when working with Words of Power, it is wise to stipulate always that the effect need not be limited to any particular form alone. It is always possible that something better might manifest. So be open to the flexibility of form — not for compromise, but for fulfillment.

8.   *Transformation:* Yes, change. This is the part that at its most dramatic looks like a bonafide miracle. In the use of positive magic for self-help, no less important are the quiet miracles of turning negatives into positives, or of establishing new Causes and getting new Effects. A problem may originally be seen as the effect of an "older" negative cause. When perception changes, the problem may be transformed into a positive cause for a new effect. Presto, chango!

And don't forget transformation of the *self,* the ultimate goal of positive magic. As you do the work, so you yourself change in positive ways. One might say that the very act of viewing life in this way is a new starting point, or causation, for a more rewarding life. The shift of perception to "anything is possible!" is a direct response to the concept of nonlimitation; this becomes the first transformation. The work itself is transformation, and the changed person living in this way is ever-transforming himself/herself.

9.   *Love:* This starts with self-love. Self-love is not to be confused with an "ego-trip;" which in my opinion, is not self-love at all, but overcompensation for not loving oneself enough. A primary function of self-love is an unequivocal acceptance of the validity of getting what one wants — of respecting one's needs. It's an acceptance of the validity of getting what one wants — of respecting one's needs. It's an acceptance of the total responsibility for one's own life, karma, and future — and the past as well. *Love always includes responsibility.* And after self-love is acknowledged, love for others flows more freely.

10.   *The Now:* Occult work is done in the present tense. Remember that we are working with the occult concept of simultaneous time; that "All time is now," that all time — past, present and future — is "happening" at once. Remember that magic transcends our Earthly (linear, sequential) perception of time.

It is helpful to keep in mind that "the future is made up of all the nows."[11] If you get the now in order, the future will follow accordingly. So when you use Words of Power, try to think in terms of the present tense, rather than projecting into the future.

All these Principles work in harmony with one another in nature. In our work, we connect with the laws of nature on a deep level. One might say that our work is truly *supernatural;* it is not "un"-natural, but natural in the profoundest sense. Witchcraft is a nature religion. If we wish to draw upon its imagery, we may view ourselves as most effective in the workings of positive magic when we are at one with natural law.

Instructions For Composing Words of Power

Words of Power work with a sequence of ideas, which is stated according to the Basic Principles we have just delineated. Here is a simple example of a complete Words of Power Statement. For purposes of this example, we will work for the goal of *fulfillment.*

1.   There Is One Power
2.   And this Power is *perfect fulfillment.*
3.   And I (your name here), am a perfect manifestation of this Power.
4.   Therefore, *perfect fulfillment* is mine, here and now,
5.   For the good of all,
6.   And according to free will.
7.   And so it must be.

Instead of *perfect fulfillment,* we may have chosen to state: *perfect abundance, prosperity, love, health, harmony* — any specific quality or qualities, goal or goals we wish to experience. The use of the word "perfect" may be antithetical to the beliefs of some who feel that "perfect" represents a state of unattainable by mortals. Semantics again. For those who cannot use "perfect" comfortably, let me qualify it by saying that "perfect" is used here in the personal sense — i.e., *perfect for you,* the worker, in harmony with the Universe. If the word "perfect" still feels uncomfortable, then "appropriate' or "right" will do just fine.

You may wish to make variations of your own. Any personal variations in style are appropriate, as long as you follow the basic structure of the Words of Power Statement. This structure is:

1. An affirmation of the One, all-inclusive, mind-life-Power-energy-force.

2. A definition of the specific quality, or goal, for which you are working; defining it as an integral part of that One over-all Power.

3. An affirmation, by name, of yourself as a manifestation (in microcosm) of the over-all Power.

4. An affirmation of the quality (goal) which you have named as *already existing within you.* This quality is already yours, by right of your consciousness, by means of the definition of yourself as part of the Power. You, by definition, have all of the attributes of that original Power, because you are an individualization. a manifestation, of It. Everything the Power has, you have already. The Words of Power are a way of putting yourself more directly in touch with the Power, and in control of It.

5. The specific declaration that this work is *for the good of all.*

6. The statement that this work is *according to free will.*

7. An affirmation that you have concluded the work. (Variations: "And so it is" or "And so is it" or "And this is so.") "And so mote it be" is the traditional witchcraft phrase which literally means, in older English, "and so it must be." Incidentally, "Amen" means the same. Just don't choose a concluding statement that implies doubt, such as "I hope it is so." It *is so; that's the whole idea.*

The Words are the cause. They go out into the Law of Cause and Effect. They "come back" (they manifest), as the *effect.* Even though the Words of Power process may be thus described in this "rational" sequence, please bear in mind that it is based upon "relational" concepts. (See Chapter I and Chapter IX for definitions of "rational" and "relational" concepts.) In this case, the effect is perfect fulfillment.

If you wish to define the One Power, the over-all energy force as

"God," of course you may do so. To many people, this idea defines God in any case. For Step 1, you may use the phrase: "There is One God-Force," or "There is One God-Power," or "There is One God."

This, however, is a matter of your own individual style. I personally have chosen to define the over-all concept as The Power, because when I think of "God," I mean the masculine individualization of The Power, and when I think of "Goddess," I mean the feminine individualization of The Power. I refer to The Power as all-inclusive. This is in keeping with my own witchcraft beliefs. If you too feel an affinity for this tradition, you may use it.

Basic Words of Power, Witchcraft-Style:[12]
1. There is One Power, which is Goddess and God,
2. And which is perfect fulfillment.
3. And I (your name here), am Goddess (or God) Incarnate.
4. Therefore, perfect fulfillment is mine, here and now.
5. For the good of all,
6. According to the free will of all.
7. And so mote it be.

If you prefer a more contemporary variation:

Basic Words of Power, "Scientific" Style:
1. There is One Creative-Life-Force in the Universe,
2. Which includes perfect fulfillment.
3. And I (your name here), hereby instruct my subconscious mind
4. To use this Power to create my own perfect fulfillment,
5. For the good of all,
6. And according to free will.
7. I now release these Words into the Law of Cause and Effect.

Working Words of Power in Behalf of Another Person

To work Words of Power for another person, first it is necessary to understand the concept of nonmanipulation, and of everyone's free will (See p. 212 for specifics), and to have that person's *permission*. I recommended that you ask permission openly and honestly. If the person says to go ahead or, if the person asks you to work, unsolicited, bear in mind the following concepts: We are all equal inheritors of the One Power. You have no more of the Power than anyone else, and the other person has no less. Our subconscious minds (or our souls) are all part of the same Power. Therefore even if *you* say the Words, you are not "really" doing the work; you are helping the other person to do it for himself/herself. You are contacting the other person's subconscious in order to help point the way; it is the other person's subconscious that begins to do the work and makes it manifest. As Mel Brooks says, "We are all singing; I have the mouth."[13] So please understand that even if *your* mouth says the Words, the other person is "singing." (In fact, the entire Universe is singing.) And *it will not work if the other person does not want it to.* Therefore, it is not up to you to decide what the other person "needs" or "should have." So always ask first. Ask whether to initiate the work at all, and ask the person *what* he or she wants. Then, simply insert the other person's name in Step 3. Thus, to work for another person:

Words of Power for Another Person

1. There is One Power,
2. And this Power is *perfect fulfillment.*
3. And (other person's name here) is a perfect manifestation of this Power.
4. Therefore *perfect fulfillment* is his (hers) here and now,
5. For the good of all,
6. And according to the free will and receptivity of all.
7. And so it must be.

Of course, you may use any style or variation on the basic Statement. Note that when working for another person, Step 6 is expanded: *"And according to the free will and receptivity of all."*

Needless to say, when the results of the work manifest for the other person, do not expect praise. It's not an appropriate motivation to work for another in order to prove what a wizard you are. Remember that traditionally no one claims "credit" for positive magic. The other person's subconscious mind worked at least as hard as you did, in the Unseen Realm. And the entire Universe joined in. Beware the ego-trip!

It is always important to be extremely careful of your intentions when you work Words of Power for another person. Do not force your work on another, ever. Do not coerce, or argue, or try to convince the person in any way. If the other person wants your help, he or she will tell you. And conversely, do not let another person talk you into doing the work if *you* do not feel like it. *Non manipulation* is a primary facet of the work. Ultimately, of course, it would be best for everyone to work for himself/herself. The work one person does for another is what I call "back-up" work. We will deal more specifically with these concepts in the "Additional Ideas" section at the end of this chapter.

The Release of Negatives

This is an optional step which is recommended but not always necessary. This step is used when you specifically know of something, some negative quality or idea, which you wish to "get rid of." For example, to return to our original Words of Power Statement, when working for fulfillment as a goal: let us say that we know *exactly* what the problem is that we wish to eliminate. Let us say that it is worry; then we insert a statement that we are releasing the worry. Remember that when you release something, you are releasing the *cause* of that negative, as well as the *effect*. We do not have to know consciously what caused the worry in the first place. But we have to acknowledge that something in the Unseen Realm must have caused the worry (remember the Law of Cause and Effect), or it wouldn't be there. We would not want to release the worry and then be left with a headache, or a backache, or any other negative *effect* in the place of worry. So we insert a release statement, releasing both cause and effect of the problem. Then we reaffirm the original goal (always conclude the Statement with a positive idea). Thus:

1. There is One Power.
2. And the Power is *perfect fulfillment*.
3. And (name) is/am a perfect manifestation of the Power.
4. Therefore, *perfect fulfillment* is mine (his, hers) here and now.
5. *I, (he, she) hereby release(s) all negative causes, effects, manifestations, forms and the essence of worry.*
6. And *perfect fulfillment* is mine, (his, hers)
7. For the good of all,
8. According to the free will of all.
9. And so it must be.

Of course, you may release any negative ailment, symptom, discomfort or problem in this way.

Notice how you always follow the release of the negative with a restatement of the positive goal. Remember, as a general rule, when releasing a negative, never leave a "gap." Always fill the "space" that the negative left when it exited. Fill that "space" with the positive you are working for. Most often your goal will be the opposite of the negative you released.

Notice, too, how I used Words to *qualify* that negative on all sides: "all causes, effects, manifestations, forms, and essences of — —." I feel that negatives must be dealt with in very firm and in no uncertain terms! You may find it helpful to add, when defining a negative, "I release any

218

channel within me which gave this negative Cause power; I release any negative resignation (to the problem), and any unhealthy need to have this problem."

Negatives may seem tricky at first. Notice how you feel after you say a Words of Power Statement. Do you feel the slightest twinge of doubt or disbelief? If so, repeat your Words of Power and release *any* negative: "I hereby release any distrust in this work, any feelings of guilt over my own good results, of my 'right' to do this work, any sense of limitation, doubt, fear or disbelief in this work." *Release anything that seems to be negatively holding you back.*

At first, this may seem paradoxical. For example, if you doubt that the Words of Power will work in the first place (a common cultural problem for beginners), what good will it do to say that you release the doubt? Well, you might try saying the release in this way, or at least understand this concept: "Even if my *conscious* mind seems to be having some trouble believing in these Words of Power, my *subconscious* mind knows that they are working."

Another way to state the release is to say, "I *dissolve* and release: (state the negative)." Some people can actually picture the release taking place in this way: Pain can dissolve, so can worry, fear, unhappiness, tension, anxiety, disease, colds, coughs, etc.

Acting in Accordance

> If words and conduct are not in accord and not consistent, they will have no effect.
> *The I Ching*, Book One, Hexagram 37

The use of Words of Power is not a passive technique. Your self is what sets the Words in motion, and it is your own responsibility to follow through. This does not mean thoughtlessly running around trying to solve a problem. It does not mean worrying over something by re-thinking it over and over. It means *acting in accordance;* it literally means *behaving in harmony* with the Words you have put forth. For example, if you have said the Words of Power invoking perfect health, you may have set up a cause which will manifest (as effect) the appropriate doctors, medicines and treatments. Watch for the signs and be open to them. *Acting in accordance* works in this way: The Words of Power set up an "alchemical" process for you. Your own personal energy force connects and merges with the Universal energy forces. This creates a whole new vital flow of energy which is now yours. Another way of explaining this is that your own personal power "plugs in" with the Infinite Power and is thereby transformed into something new and special. When this occurs, this Power, this new

219

energy "needs" to become active. At this point, it is very important to let it work in the World of Form — you simply go with it. You need not force yourself to act. If you're not ready, you're not ready. Also, sometimes acting in accordance simply means opening up to your good in new ways. But if and when you feel active, it is a natural process to simply let the action happen organically. This means creative action; follow what feels right. It may seem the same as acting before you got into this work, but more likely it will feel different. You may even establish totally new patterns of action. You may be breaking old habits, but now you will be acting in tune with your Words of Power.

Remember that this form of magic works completely in accordance with natural laws. Consequently the results often seem to happen "naturally" — so naturally, in fact, that some people do not even notice how one step leads to another. Then, by the time the problem is entirely solved, the solution may seem like the most logical and un-miraculous occurrence in the world. And nonbelievers may scoff: "Your magic didn't heal you, Dr. So-and-so did, or that new miracle drug they just discovered, is what did it." Fine. We're not aiming for applause or adulation; we are after results. It doesn't matter how results seem to manifest, it doesn't matter what form they take. The proof of the pudding is in the perfect deliciousness of the results. In my opinion, if you work Words of Power for perfect health, it doesn't matter whether the sick person leaps right out of bed, instantly healed, or whether the right doctor helps with the right diagnosis, the right treatment, and *then* the sick person recovers. What does matter is that the person is healed. The results of your work don't have to look dramatic. Sometimes they may look extremely dramatic, but that again is all a matter of style or form.

Sometimes acting in accordance means some active physical participation on your part (looking for the right apartment, the right lover, etc). Sometimes acting in accordance means only being open to your own good, when it comes to you. Sometimes it means watching for signs, for manifestations. What acting in accordance does *not* mean is rethinking and reworrying the problem over and over, or doubting that your Words of Power are working. Acting in accordance means learning to trust in the effectiveness of your own power to direct your own life.

Emotional Atmosphere

Concentrate on the *feeling* you want. The emotional atmosphere may be the actual start of the work itself. Begin by focusing on the mood that you want to have, as a reality, after the work is accomplished. If your life is too hectic, you may concentrate on the mood of peace; if your life is too frustrated, you may concentrate on the mood of fulfillment; if your life is lonely, you may concentrate on the mood of what it would ideally feel like to love and be loved.

Qualifiers

You may add the following phrases to your Words of Power Statements, according to your needs:

> "With perfect ease"
> "At the most perfect time" or "with perfect timing"
> "Painlessly" or "with no pain"
> "Joyfully" or "happily."

These qualifiers further provide the mood in which the work takes place. I suggest that you insert a qualifier *after* you state "For the good of all." Or if you prefer, you may add it right *before* the concluding phrase, "And so it must be."

Applications

Words of Power may be used for virtually any positive goal: healing, money, love, creative fulfillment, a job, an apartment, a house, a husband, a wife, a lover, good friends, a good night's sleep, a diet, a harmonious relationship. (When working for relationships, no names are used, as is explained later in this chapter).

You may also use Words of Power for such conceptual goals as safety, protection, clarity, focus, inspiration, energy, wisdom, or self-realization. And Words of Power may be used to release any negatives: smoking habits, drug habits, insecurity, neurotic needs, phobias, fears — even "evil" spirits (this is the basis of exorcism). Just remember that when you release a negative quality out of your life:

> 1. You are releasing both the cause and the effect of the negative quality;
> 2. You always replace the negative with a positive quality. And this is usually the direct opposite of the negative. For example, release "insecurity," replace it with "security"; release "poverty," and replace it with "prosperity."

Form and Essence

When you work with Words of Power, you use very specific means to set up specific causes, and get back specific results (effects). That is why it is so important to think carefully before you actually begin to work for something. It might be helpful at first, to write things down. I suggest a list of primary problems (to be released) and primary goals (to be set in motion). I suggest two columns, side by side: "The Release" column and "The Goals" column. Now you can see quite clearly what you want to get rid of and what you want to achieve. I suggest that you keep your goals rather broad at first. Begin by listing the *qualities* of life that you desire, such as health, happiness, love, or prosperity. These are *essences*. The *forms* in which they will come have not yet been specified.

Now determine any *specific* things that you want or need to make your life more comfortable (or even bearable). These things might seem mundane, material, or practical; but do not judge them. Acknowledge them and put them in "The Goals" column. Do not deny a need, however, earthly it may be. Write down each one: a toaster-oven, a car, a dishwasher, a color television, a new suit, whatever. These are *forms*. It is perfectly valid to work Words of Power for forms — for specific objects — to draw them into our lives. However, often we may see that several forms fall into a single category, that of *one essence*. For example, such forms as the money for the rent, the money for the telephone bill, a new wardrobe, and a trip to Europe all fall into the *essence* category of "abundance," or "prosperity." If you work your Words of Power for the goal of prosperity or abundance, you will receive all the money necessary to pay your bills and purchase what you need. You may take care of this by working for the essence. You do not have to list all those other things (forms), because they would automatically be taken care of by achieving the over-all essence first.

Working For Form

Perhaps you have the money you need to purchase something, but want to make sure that you spend your money wisely. For example, say you want to buy a car, have saved for it, and now you want to make sure that you get the right one, but that you don't know much about cars. Then it's not the essence (the money) for which you work your Words of Power; it's literally the *form* of the car itself.

Even when working for a specific form, it is helpful to think about the category (in terms of essence) under which you could "classify" that particular form. When my friend R. phrased her Words of Power Statement for a car, she asked herself: "What do I need (in terms of essence) in order to draw into my life the right car for me?" She decided that the form of the car would be considered a manifestation of two main essences — wisdom and abundance. She then phrased her work in this manner:

> There is One Power,
> Which is perfect *abundance* and *wisdom*.
> And I (name), a perfect manifestation of this Power,
> Hereby know my own *abundance* and *wisdom*
> Specifically by drawing into my life and my possession
> *The perfect car for me which fulfills all my needs,*
> And for the good of all,
> According to free will.
> And so it must be.

She then acted in accordance (shopped around, asked questions) and found the perfect car for her: a reasonably priced, newly painted yellow VW. The car was used, but in perfect working condition, with a friendly owner who years later was still available for questioning, and with a friendly garage where the repair people were familiar with that car.

Once when I didn't have the money for a particular item, I didn't work my Words of Power for the money; I worked for the form itself. What I needed was a reel-to-reel tape recorder. It seemed as if all the money in the world wouldn't have helped me to pick out the right one, or begin to know how to attach it to my wall. So I worked for the goal of "the right reel-to-reel tape recorder for my life, according to free will and for the good of all." And I received one as a gift from my sister (who, it turns out, knows quite a bit about tape recorders); then a close friend, an engineer, appeared and set it up for me. This is another example of working for a specific form. So there are many occasions when it is appropriate to work for forms. *However, sometimes working for a form is a limitation.* Remember that old adage, "Be careful what you wish for; it might come true"? There is a whole body of folklore on this subject, about people being granted magic wishes, having them come true, and then not liking what they got (See Chapter I, p. 4). These result from the misunderstanding of Form and Essence. If you wish to work specifically for a form, it's always best to add a qualifying phrase which releases any limitations of form. Thus I would add to my statement for the tape recorder:

> I hereby draw into my life
> The right reel-to-reel tape recorder for my needs,
> *or its equivalent or better.*

Working for Essence

Examples of "empty" form fulfillment abound both in popular literature and in real life: the millionaire who makes all the money he wanted and then is unsatisfied because it did not buy him happiness or love; the glamorous movie star who wins fame and fortune, but ends up lonely, exploited, misunderstood....you know, all the old cliches. These are examples of form fulfillment, when essence fulfillment was the true need.

How can you tell the difference? How do you know whether you want an essence or a form? First of all, ask yourself some essential questions: 1. *What is the feeling I want from achieving my goal?* If your answer to this question is specific, then you know it is appropriate to work for a form. For example, if your goal was to have a toaster, and the feeling you want from that is knowing you can make toast whenever you wish, then you can be fairly certain that you need a form. The same principle applies for a car (when you want to drive), a coat (when you want to be warm outside), a new stove (if your old one is broken and you want to cook), etc.

But what if the answer to this first question was "I want security," or "I want to be loved," or "I want to feel contented"? Then ask yourself.... 2. *Can that same feeling come to me in any other way (or ways) than the specific goal I first thought I wanted?* You do not have to be able to think of any other specific ways. Simply try to imagine if it is conceivable to have the same feeling from another form — *any* other form, no matter how "impossible" it may seem (remember the Infinity of Solution). If the feeling is your goal, then what you want is essence. And it can come to you in many ways. Further examples of questions you can ask yourself, next:

- Do I really want "a million dollars," or do I want the "happiness" I think it will bring?
- Do I really want "a trip to Spain" or do I want "the perfect vacation for me"?
- Do I really want "a husband," or do I want "financial security," or "emotional security," or just plain all-encompassing "security"?
- Do I really want "a certain person to fall in love with me," or do I want "the perfect relationship for my life"?
- Do I really want "to be a movie star" or do I want "creative fulfillment," or "recognition of my talents"?
- Do I really want "to be president of the company," or do I want "a feeling of self-importance"?

224

Remember, do not judge your goals. Sometimes a specific form is so socially acceptable that it might prevent us from acknowledging the true essence of our needs. And sometimes we may not have wanted to acknowledge an essence, because we have judged its validity. But any need is valid, as long as it doesn't hurt anyone, as long as it is in keeping with all the Principles. And any need may be fulfilled by your work once you have honestly acknowledged the need to yourself. It is perfectly acceptable to acknowledge that you want a feeling of emotional security, financial security, or a feeling of self-importance. These are all essences.

When in doubt, remember, *the essence is that feeling, that quality which you think that a specific form will bring to you.*

Here are some examples of people who worked for essence:

A. wants to release from his life the feeling that he "never has enough money." He specifically chooses as his goal "the sum of $35,000" to see his family and himself through a certain period of time and to pay old debts. Then he stops and thinks, "No, this is a form. What is the essence I really want?" He then chooses and states the goal, "the essence of financial security for myself and my loved ones." He includes in his Words of Power statement the release of "any feeling of deprivation or insecurity." Soon the results of his work manifest in many ways: a raise of salary, then an opportunity to open a small part-time business of his own. The small part-time business grows into a large full-time business, and after two years' time he has $65,000. In this case, working for a specific form, a specific amount of money, would have been a limitation.

B. was not happy in his job, making sound recordings for commercials. He decided that what he wanted to release from his life was the quality, the feeling, of drudgery and lack of fulfillment. He thought at first that what he wanted was "a new job." But then he thought, "No, a new job is a form." He liked his boss and his coworkers, he enjoyed working with film, he would in fact have liked to do more with film than merely recording sound — but he was not sure what form this might take. He worked his Words of Power for the essence goal of "fulfillment in work." And soon he found himself branching out from sound recording, to editing, to directing. Although he remained with the same company and the same people, soon he was assigned complete creative control of some documentary films to be used for charitable institutions. B. now feels creatively fulfilled and has also discovered that he enjoys directing film. He didn't literally get "a new job," but now has a new role in his old job — and yes, he was surprised by the form in which is fulfillment came. B. didn't even know how much he would enjoy directing, nor how good he would be at it. In this case, working for essence delivered the side benefit of a new focus for his entire life and his future. A form "new job" might not have done that at all.

E. needed to make some changes in her life, made a list, and saw that conditions looked quite complicated. She was a dance teacher with a new baby. E. and her husband had been living in an apartment which doubled as a dance studio, but now the baby needed a room too. The apartment was too small. They didn't want to pay much more rent, she didn't want to leave the neighborhood where she had local students, and her husband found their home convenient for commuting. Should she phrase her Words of Power for the goal of "a separate dance studio"? Or "a new place of work for her husband"? Or a "full-time baby nurse"? Or "the right day-care center"? Or "a new group of students"? Or "a job teaching dance somewhere else"? Forms. The essences, E. and her husband finally decided, were "the most appropriate living and working conditions for the whole family."

They worked their Words of Power with this goal. The results were as complex as the needs, and absolutely "perfect" for everyone. E. and her husband found an apartment in the same neighbourhood, reasonably priced, which had an extra living room and dining room. The landlord allowed them to break down a dividing wall, and E. then had a perfectly sized dance studio. The apartment had room for the baby, plus an extra bedroom. The couple rented this out to a young woman student, who gladly became the resident baby sitter. E's students found the location perfect. E's husband still commuted with ease, the student had a friendly home, the baby had a new "older sister" — and the entire solution was resolved for the good of all.

Who chooses the forms, when you work for the essence? Your subconscious mind, also known as the Universal Power, the God, the Goddess, the eternal souls of everyone involved. Remember, the world of Form is more flexible than we may think! We need not direct it how to move, inch by inch, in order for it to deliver into our lives that which we need. We need not allow it to "seem" to limit us. The World of Form is as unlimited as the Invisible Realm.

So we have seen that sometimes it is appropriate to work Words of Power for forms, and that sometimes working for forms is limiting so we work for essence. Also, sometimes working for form is unethical and dangerous. This is when the form you want involves other people — or even one other living being. Now it is time to emphasize two other Principles: for the good of all and free will. Of course all the work you do has the phrases "for the good of all" and "according to free will" built right into it. But let us examine more closely how this applies in two classic situations involving other people — a love relationship and a job situation.

226

A Love Relationship

Unfortunately, most negative magic in this emotional area is based on two misconceptions: harming the "rival" or manipulating the "beloved" by name. Neither of these dangerous practices will get you what you want. When you work with Words of Power, remember that you are setting up a Cause. If you set up a Cause of harm to anyone (for example, a rival for the loved one's affections), that harm can come back to you. And the Universe will choose the form in which it comes back, too. It could come from anywhere, any area in your life. That is bad karma, to put it mildly. And as for manipulating the loved one: Manipulation then becomes the Cause, and by that old trustworthy Law of Cause and Effect, that's just what comes back to you, the sender — manipulation. And again, the Universe will choose the form, which can then come back to you where and how you least expect it.

No matter what pop-"witchcraft" or "magic" spells you may have seen or heard about — and some of these may be quite imaginative, involving images, dolls, candles, string, photographs, articles of clothing — these are all dangerous. Avoid them with a ten-foot-pole. (Remember Chapter III!) Control yourself. Using Words of Power to cause harm, or to cause manipulation (which is actually a form of harm) is not only dangerous — it is not effective. Negative techniques work against the laws of nature.

Of course, if you work Words of Power for the essence of love in your life, you are working with the laws of nature. And by not specifying the form (the person), you get the love which is right for you. But somehow, in our culture this very idea may be difficult to grasp emotionally. I think that this is partly because we are still influenced (conditioned) by the medieval-chivalry-Hollywood-love myth. Another way of saying this is that we are an "oedipal" society, fixated on the concept of one perfect mate, unlike some more "primitive" cultures in which everybody loves everybody, or at least everybody knows he/she is potentially capable of loving everybody. In addition, we are also influenced (conditioned) by a deceptive cultural "winners/losers" syndrome: "I can't have what I want unless the other person loses out," or conversely, "If the other person gets Melba, I lose out."

But remember all the Principles: There is enough in the Universe for everyone, there is an infinity of possible solutions, and yes, there is an infinity of love. So the more love, the more consideration that goes into your Words of Power, the more love and consideration you get back. This does not mean sacrifice or compromise! Throw away any concept of manipulation, throw away any concept of resignation, compromise, deprivation — and work for love, for real love. You can have it.

227

Work first, if you must, just to *believe* that this is possible. And finally, because this is such an important (and potentially dangerous) area, here is a prestructured Statement, a typical example of how to do this work. Of course you may adapt the style, but be careful not to change the ideas. And remember: *Never mention another person's name!* You are not working to "get" another person to love you; you are working to "get" yourself totally fulfilled in love. The focus is on *you*, not on another. This may be difficult to believe, in the heat of passion, lust, fixation, frustration, romance, or any other state which may be less than total clarity. But consider the side benefits: Not only are you going to have the perfect love relationship for you with no compromise, but you are also going to find yourself sane and open enough to enjoy the love relationship on a meaningful level.

Words of Power for a Love Relationship[14]

There is One Power,
Which is *perfect love*.
And I (your name here), a complete individualization of the Power,
Hereby draw to myself the most appropriate, fulfilling, *perfect love relationship*, which is right for me.
This takes place in a perfect exchange of love with the right person,
And for the good of all,
According to the free will of all,
And so it must be.

You might insert as a release: "I hereby release all loneliness, despair, negative emotional patterns, etc."

If you have been truly fixated on a specific person, then be careful to insert a statement such as "I release all feelings of manipulation out of this work, and out of my life." Another way of dealing with the ideas of *free will* and *for the good of all:* If you find yourself thinking (as, alas, so many of us have done) that you "couldn't be happy unless it was so-and-so," then think clearly to yourself before you start, "The love relationship I am going to work these Words of Power for will give me *as much happiness as* (or more than) I've pictured coming through having so-and-so reciprocate my feelings." I suggest that you deal with this idea as the emotional atmosphere for setting up the work, rather than risk the use of another person's name in the Words of Power themselves. The use of a name, until you are adept at this kind of work, is dangerous! You might let some manipulative thought leak in that could boomerang back on you.

Simply understand as best you can that your own perfect love relationship will indeed be for the good of all. It may very well turn out to be so-and-so. But then you will know for sure that so-and-so chose you entirely out of his or her free will. But please understand that even if it turns out to be someone else, *this does not mean that you have to compromise.* Just keep on saying your Words of Power every day (and act in accordance) until you are totally, completely, perfectly satisfied in love.

Any situation involving another person may come up against the same cultural "winners/losers" problem. Some examples: If you are one of two or more people being considered for a certain job.....if your team is playing another team.....if your horse is racing another person's horse.....if you're an actor up for a part (remember *Rosemary's Baby?*) .....if you're the understudy to the star (remember *All About Eve?*)..... if you want anyone to do anything for you.....if you want anyone to do anything for anybody.....if you want something from someone.....if you want something to happen, which it seems someone can "make" happen.....if you want your boss to give you a raise.....if you want Santa Claus to give you a toy — it's all the same thing. You cannot manipulate anyone and get away with it, ever. You can ask for what you want, clearly, openly and honestly, either in a direct conversation, in a letter, or on the phone. But you cannot ethically or safely use Words of Power and the Unseen Realm for any purpose of manipulation at all.

A Job Situation

This can often seem to be a competitive situation. Personally, I would not work the Words for a specific job, even if I were being considered for one, because that again involves individuals. I would work for the essence of the right job, even preceeding a scheduled interview for a job I really wanted. The Universal Power will choose the form (i.e., the specific job). Think about what you would want from the ideal job: If you could have any job in the whole world, not "what would that job be?" but "what are the *feelings* that I would like to get out of it?" These will be the essences to work for. I personally would choose fulfillment, abundance and security.....

Words of Power for a Job

There is One Power,
Which is *fulfillment, abundance, and security.*
And I (name), am a perfect manifestation of this Power.
So I hereby draw to me *fulfillment, abundance and security* in my life,

Specifically as the *perfect job for me,*
And for the good of all,
According to the free will of all.
And so it must be.

Again, if you have a specific job in mind, think first as you are setting up the emotional atmosphere: "The right job will come to me which will give me at least as much (if not more) contentment, money, happiness, as I pictured coming through being Secretary of State (or whatever)." And, if you find yourself thinking manipulatively about an individual ("if only Mr. Big would hire me" or "if only Jack Spratt would be fired"), insert a release of this as a negative: "I release all feelings of manipulation out of my life and out of these Words of Power." Remember, don't feel guilty, either. You are not harming your competitor. This is for the good of all. And again, trust and believe that you won't have to compromise. Keep working the Words and acting in accordance until the right situation manifests.

You can see that when there's any doubt, keeping the concept of Form and Essence in mind, use your Words of Power naming the essence. And if you are not sure what the essence is of what you want, simply say "My subconscious mind knows what it is I need from this situation, my conscious mind will know it at the right time, and I draw it to me now, according to free will and for the good of all."

The same principles apply when you are working for any *exchange of services.* If you wish to *draw* someone to you, whether it is for professional help (doctor, dentist, astrologer, whatever) or for friendship or even to create a study group or other organization — remember that there must be an equal exchange between you and the other(s), according to the needs of all and the free will of all.

Words of Power for an Exchange of Services

There is One Power,
Which is a *perfect flow of energy and mutual help.*
And I (your name), a complete manifestation of this Power,
Experience this perfect flow of energy and mutual help in a perfectly appropriate equal exchange of services with the right person (people),
Specifically, I draw to me the right (fill in: doctor, astrologer, helpers, etc.)
For a relationship which is for the good of all
And according to everyone's free will
And so it must be.

230

Of course, act in accordance following this work. This does not necessarily mean that the first person you encounter will be the right one. But it will be very clear to you when you do find the appropriate person with whom to have this exchange. A big clue will be the revelation of the way you can fulfill the other's needs, in ways you may not yet be aware of.

When you are dealing with a complex situation involving large groups of people, divergent aims and morals, and when you don't have sufficient information about the issues.....when you can't ethically (in good conscience) say what the outcome of a situation should be, then simply direct your Words of Power *"for the good of all."* Work specifically for the good of all with, for example, politics, elections, wars — yes, even sporting events. Remember, there need be no winners or losers! The other people might not understand this yet, but you do. I further recommend that when involved with larger groups of people you always add, "This work applies to all who wish to participate according to their free will and receptivity." There will be a lot of beautiful "fall-out" from working for the good of all — no matter what your preferences, no matter who you want to win the election, the battle, the race. Try to work in such a way that nobody loses and everybody wins. If you can't do this yet, I advise you *not* to work with Words of Power for any group or competitive occasion. Manipulating a baseball team, a tennis match, or a war — no matter which is the "better" side — is dangerous, and comes back of course on the worker as *manipulation.*

When you work with these Universal laws, you are tuning in to Universal harmony at the deepest, most creative and most effective level, where there are no winners or losers. This may also be hard to believe or accept, at first, in the context of a (cultural) "step-on-the-other-person-to-get-ahead" atmosphere.

Money (and Material Abundance)

Money has been a much misunderstood subject in our culture. Some people feel that it is immoral to use magic in order to materialize money in their lives; such people seem to feel that it places them at an unfair advantage over others. On the opposite side of the spectrum are people who want to use magic (or any form of affirmation) *mainly* for material goods, and seem to forget that money is simply a form manifestation of other (Invisible) riches. I feel that both extremes are misunderstandings of the balance of resources in the Universe.

There are famous stories about Indian adepts who can materialize coins out of thin air. An interesting point to note is that usually these are

231

people for whom money is practically meaningless. This trick is used as a demonstration of other principles such as the control we all have, in potential, over material possessions rather than their apparent control over us.

In any case, I believe it is perfectly fine to work Words of Power for money, (1) if you do not specify the amount, and (2) if you work simply for the fulfillment of your needs — even if you are not yet consciously aware of what those needs are. But you know that you probably need a place to live and enough food and clothing to keep you healthy and warm. If there are others, such as children, who are financially dependent on you at this point, your Words of Power work may include these fundamentals for them also. If you have any specific needs — such as tools of your trade or any particularly meaningful material objects (books, records, whatever) — do not judge these as nasty materialistic desires. Your needs are valid, as long as they do not deprive or harm any other being.

When witches work magic for money, they often use the phrase "just enough," meaning just enough to feel satisfied. Sometimes the forms they need come along in ways other than the money to purchase them. So when you work for money, be aware that your material abundance may also come as gifts, prizes, etc. Money, after all, is a form. Abundance is an essence.

As you work, try to be aware of any residual judgments or guilt feelings attached to your needs. Do you feel that you are taking money out of the hands of starving people? Do you feel that you are not worthy of being satisfied? Do you feel that money is a crass part of our culture?

Also note if you have any problems on the other side of the coin, so to speak: Do you feel that you want to be incredibly rich? Do you feel that you must have some specific sum to feel secure? Do you believe that money will buy you happiness, power, or any other essence? In other words, watch out for any form contingencies, (see p. 247) and carefully release them. Remember that there is enough of everything in the Universe for you to have your share. And what is your share? "Just enough," as the witches say. Also be on your guard for any negative causations — such as feelings of deprivation or loss in other *areas* of your life — which may have been manifesting as not enough money for your needs. Be aware that when you are balanced out and feel fulfilled in every (essence) area of your life, money will automatically balance out for you and fulfill your needs also. Here is a Words of Power Statement for abundance and fulfillment (you may also use the word "prosperity"):

232

Words of Power for Money (and Material Abundance)

There is One Power,
Which is *perfect abundance and fulfillment.*
And I (your name), am a perfect manifestation of this Power.
The Power, working for me and through me, provides for me all
the abundance and fulfillment which is rightfully mine.
I draw to me and create in my life all that I need in the World of
Form to fulfill my needs,
This may come specifically in the form of money.
I hereby release all cause, effect, manifestation, form and essence
and any channel within me,
Which may have been preventing the appropriate flow of
abundance in my life.
I draw upon the balance of resources in the Universe,
For the good of all,
According to the free will of all,
And I affirm my own wisdom in understanding my needs, and how
to fulfill them.
I call to me *just enough* resources,
Knowing I deprive none,
And am not deprived myself,
I have just enough.
And so must it be.

Sometimes it all comes at once. Sometimes the abundance comes gradually. Very often we must act in accordance. Acting in accordance often means mainly being open to "accelerating gifts" from the Cosmos. These gifts, while fulfilling real needs, help us to adjust to the idea of "just enough" — not too much and not too little. For example, I know one witch who had never worked magic for money before. After her first self-blessing Words of Power Statement for money, it took several months for the full abundance in her life to manifest. First, someone gave her $10 in exchange for a favor she had performed. The person was wealthy, and insisted on this gesture; it meant no loss to him. Next, someone presented her with a dozen jars of pickled herring (her favorite delicacy). Next, someone provided free veterinary care for her cats. By now, she was becoming accustomed to the concept of what "just enough" meant in relation to her personal needs. Next, someone gave her an expensive quilt for her bed. Next, she got a raise at her job. By this point she had "just enough" and has continued to experience her personally fulfilling abundance ever since.

You may have to experience the results a few times (or maybe even once) to prove to yourself how exquisitely the Universal harmony works when you are in tune with it — like the intricate workings of jewelled clockwork.

Ma'Kheru, or The Word of Truth

> The superior man abides in his room. If his words are well spoken, he meets with assent at a distance of more than a thousand miles. How much more then from near by! If the superior man abides in his room and his words are not well spoken, he meets with contradiction at a distance of more than a thousand miles. How much more then from near by! Words go forth from one's own person and exert their influence on men.....Must one not, then, be cautious?
>
> The *I Ching*[15]

The concept of Ma'Kheru, or Maat, was a highly regarded state of being in ancient Egypt. In fact, it was always hoped that by the time a person died, he/she would have reached this state of personal evolution. The word itself is difficult to translate. In hieroglyphs, it looks like:[16]

Witches who trace their own traditions back to the early Egyptian Mysteries still integrate the concept of Ma'Kheru, Maat, or The World of Truth into their work. Once one has attained Ma'Kheru, *every* word that is spoken literally comes true. This state is reached by speaking only those words which *are* true. The greater Gods and Goddesses were in this state, and you too may strive for it — as the witches do, *in essence* — for yourself. This state is attained by being very careful to say exactly only what one means. Consequently, "idle chatter, or lying"[17] serves only to dissipate the truth and the Power. In our own lives, this means: *Watch what you say! Say what you mean, and mean what you say.* You don't even have to use the specific technique of Words of Power to achieve Ma'Kheru, for your words always to speak truth and come true. But in my opinion the principle of this important idea applies specifically to us today, if we are involved in the use of Words of Power in our daily lives. One might say that the use of Words of Power could conceivably get a person today to a state of Ma'Kheru, where literally every word comes true. But even if this lofty ideal is not your immediate goal, please remember the principle behind it.

That principle, as I see it, is that *all words are incipient Words of Power.* All words contribute to setting up causations (Causes) and bringing back Effects on the speaker — or on the spoken-about. Perhaps (when one is just idly conversing) the effects are not as swift or as obvious as when one has consciously worked a Words of Power Statement — but the results eventually show up. Also, if even part of the time you are involved in working actively with Words of Power, you are more consciously and directly "plugged in" with the Law of Cause and Effect. Therefore even at the times when you are not formulating specific Words of Power Statements, not thinking directly in the terms of this work, even when you are just chatting with your friends — *your words still have Power!* This is not as overwhelming an idea as it first may sound. You do not have to automatically button your lip and take a vow of silence in order to avoid dire consequences. I simply recommend a series of helpful hints, or guidelines, which my friends and I have all learned and helped each other to remember. After a while, these guidelines become second nature (or perhaps they were "first nature" to begin with?) In any case, if you have friends who are interested in this work, you will find it easier to remember your own Ma'Kheru if you all help by reminding each other. Even if you are the only one on your block doing this work, you will still be able to master these guidelines for yourself. Then not only will your Words of Power be more effective, you will also notice that the rest of your life will be more completely under your own control.

Hints and Guidelines for Ma'Kheru

1. Notice, with a sense of personal responsibility, what you are saying. Specifically, watch yourself for negative statements, such as "I'm dropping dead.....I'm crazy.....I'm sick and tired.....I'm fed up.....I give up.....I'm a nervous wreck....." etc. These are *self*-directed negatives. Now watch and see whether you've ever in moments of rage, frustration, worry or other (valid) emotions, pronounced, about other people that he/she/they, is (are) no good.....crazy.....stupid.....sick .....moronic.....heading for a fall.....looking for trouble.....going to get hurt....." etc. These are *other*-directed negatives. The use of negative pronouncements — whether directed towards the self or towards another — is a minor form of *cursing*. It is indeed the setting up, by means of words, of negative Causes. By the Law of Cause and Effect, they can automatically come back to the speaker. Negative statements cloud and dissipate the work of Words of Power. And in the lives of people who do not consciously use Words of Power, such negative

words can unconsciously continue to set up causes, which come back by the Law of Cause and Effect. Any negative statement is a spoken subconscious directive. Remember, negative statements can harm not only the person who is spoken about; they always potentially harm the speaker. Everything comes back.

2. Learn to *modify* your statements. Once you're used to watching for negative remarks, you'll find it's easier than you think to change your phrasing almost immediately. I am not advocating an "everything-is-wonderful" approach. I feel this is often not appropriate; why deny real, negative feelings if you are actually experiencing them? Of course these feelings will be changed; that's the purpose of this work. But, meanwhile, why grin and bear it? So modify those negative statements that just seem to pop right out, and thereby remove any power from them, which could set up negative causes. Instead make modified statements such as "I feel as if.....it appears to be.....it feels like.....it seems to me that.....in my opinion....." Learn to express yourself in this way with no harsh pronouncements. It is also helpful to state negatives, if you must, in the *past* tense: "I was discouraged....I was unhappy.....there were problems....."

3. The most powerful way to literally strip a negative statement of all "bad" power is to say out loud (or quietly inside yourself), "I take it out of the Law," or "I don't put this into the Law," (meaning the Law of Cause and Effect). You say this immediately *after* you say a negative statement, or *before*, if you can catch yourself in time. You can also say this after you hear another person pronouncing a negative statement. If it is a person who understands the work, you may, of course, say this out loud. If it is someone who wouldn't know what you were talking about, to save embarrassment or lengthy explanations you may simply silently think it. Taking a negative statement out of the Law in this way immediately prevents it from causing a negative effect (if, of course, it is according to free will and for the good of all that the negative effect be prevented). My friends and I spent years overcoming our respective negative speech habits of the past. We agreed to remind each other consistently (in abbreviated form) "take that out!" Some examples of mastering one's own Ma'Kheru:

"What a terrible day; everything's going wrong."
"Take that out of the Law!" (And now, just watch the day get better.....)

Or, in an argument:

"You're full of hot air!"
"I take that out of the Law."

"Well, er.....um.....it *seems* to me that you *might* be full of hot air. (Note how this takes the steam out of arguments).

Or, some true examples: I blush to admit that I used to refer "playfully" to my dog as "little fleabag." And soon not only did my dog get fleas, but so did my entire apartment. I took that out of the Law pretty fast, and worked the right Words of Power (releasing fleas) and sped over to the vet (acting in accordance), drew into our lives the world's fastest-acting flea powder, and have never insulted my dog since. This was a dramatically literal example, cited for purposes of illustration. There are possible, less literal effects of the careless use of words.

Whenever I hear a gloom-and-doom character on the radio or television predicting terrible things for anyone or anything, I take it out of the Law.

> *Radio voice:* "The United States is turning into a military fascistic demogogy....."
> Me: "I take that out of the Law."

Of course you have to consider the other person's free will (no manipulation, remember?) even with Ma'Kheru. For example, recently, I overheard a woman in a restaurant: "I'm so sick.....my doctor is no help at all.....I just get infection after infection.....my blood is no good.....my hormones aren't working....." The woman appeared to be in perfect health. I know that many hypochondriacs can quite effectively *create* illnesses by setting up a stream of negative Causes like this. Eventually the Effect can manifest as actual disease. But did I take it upon myself to prevent this? No. I mumbled into my scrambled eggs, "That doesn't go into the Law, unless she wants it to, according to her own free will and receptivity."

When in doubt, when things look complicated, better not interfere. Take your own negative statements out of the Law. Take the negative statements of others out of the Law when they are directed either at you or viciously at someone else. *(Gossip columnist:* "Lorna Lovely is working herself into an early grave." *Me:* "I take that out of the Law.") But don't interfere if it is obviously someone else's karma, as difficult as that may be for you. For example, *Person at a party:* "This party stinks; I hate parties, I can't dance....." This is none of my business, and none of yours. Leave the person to his/her own cause and effects, knowing that you remain untouched. As for the borderline cases, invoke "for the good of all," and "according to the free will and receptivity of all," just as in using Words of Power. For example:

> *Clergyman in a TV sermonette:* "And so mankind is doomed to suffering and travail....."

237

Me: "I take that out of the Law for myself, and according to free will, for the good of all." Those who want to participate in suffering and travail should be free to do so; those who wish to omit these aspects from their lives may participate in taking it out of the Law, according to their free will and receptivity.

What about lying? Please try not to. What about those "kind little white lies"? This is really up to your own conscience. But always take all the negativity out of a lie of the Law or it can perpetuate and come back as some form of dishonesty in your own life. An added tip to actors, singers, typists, writers, or anyone in a position to *quote* a negative statement, in the line of work: Yes, take it out of the Law, according to the guidelines above.

Singer (aloud): "You've got me in between the devil and the deep blue sea." (Silently) "I take this out of the Law."

Actor (before going on stage as Hamlet): "I do not put any negativity into the Law."
Same Actor (later, on stage): "Ah, that this too, too solid flesh would melt....."

Comedian: "Take my wife — please."
Wife: "I take that out of the Law."

Technically, Ma'Kheru fits in with the concept of "acting in accordance." And need I add: Never, never "undo" your Words of Power by saying anything afterwards which denies their effectiveness, such as "I don't really believe in that nonsense," or the more subtle, "Gee, I wonder if this stuff really works?" Also, don't perpetuate a problem by repeating it over and over, after you have said your Words of Power. Let the Words go out into the Law, release your doubt as best you can, and trust in the Law's good workings and the positive Power of your work.

Finally, remember that the reverse of negative words is *positive* words. Any words of kindness, of love, encouragement and caring, amount to blessings. These are *good* to put into the Law (when you mean them) even in daily speech:

"You look terrific."
"I really feel good today."
"I want to remember this wonderful moment."
"Good doggie."
"I really want to understand you."

238

Positive words will come back to you.

> Things look swell
> Things look great
> Gonna have the whole world on a plate
> Starting here
> Starting now
> Honey, everything's coming up roses...[18]

> Grab your coat
> Don't forget your hat
> Leave your worries on the doorstep
> Just direct your feet
> To the sunny side of the street.[19]

Lyrics like these may go into the Law as essence.

Additional Ideas for Using Words of Power for Self-Blessing and Blessing of Others

• Essentially, *one* Statement of Words of Power is enough to create a new Cause and Effect (manifestation) for each situation you wish to work on. Most people find it easier to work by saying the Statement once a day or a few times a week. It may be repeated until the results manifest. More often than once a day may connote doubt which can slow down the manifestations.

• The Statement may be said aloud or it may be thought in silence.

• The Statement may seem to need changes or revisions over a period of time. If so, change it accordingly, until your Inner Bell is satisfied.

• *Back-up work:* It can be helpful to enlist the support of another person who may state Words of Power "for" you only if you can truly accept the idea that you don't need that other person's (or other people's) help. Please understand that even if you were on a desert island, working all alone, your work would be just as effective as if an entire coven of experts were all blessing along with you. It may be comforting to know that another person is working along with you; it may even speed up the manifestations — because often another person has an objectivity which you yourself may not consciously perceive when in the midst of a problem. But remember that you are always the one who is doing the work for yourself, and nobody can do it better than you, instead of you, or for you!

• Ideally, this work is comfortable and energizing. So, if you perceive any discomfort when working with Words of Power...

1. Try to identify the discomfort; then you may label it as a quality to be released. *Example:* Doubt or worry might pop up in your thoughts as you work, and be perceived as a source of fatigue if you are suppressing or working against these feelings without acknowledging them. So you state, "I hereby release all doubt (or worry) from this work."

2. You may simply solve the problem of fatigue by adding the qualifier "with ease." This serves to negate any misconceptions about Words of Power being difficult to do.

3. If you have tried either or both of the above suggestions, and still perceive any feelings of hard work, fatigue or discomfort of any kind surrounding the work, perhaps you ought to reexamine your goals. Stop the work for a while, and think about what you really want.

• If you feel too confused, too upset to know exactly what goal(s) to work your Words of Power for, work in stages. Try any or all of these methods:

1. Work your Words of Power specifically for an atmosphere of calm, clarity and comfort.

2. Release any negative quality you perceive in yourself (confusion, depression, whatever) and replace it with an affirmation of its opposite (clarity, happiness, etc.). You will find that being able to define the negatives and the positives surrounding your problem is a big step towards being able to clarify the problem itself, and consequently release it.

• How long does it "take" for Words of Power to manifest? It could take a split-second; it could take years — or any time in between. It often can be a limitation to stipulate any specific time period in your work, however compelling such an idea may seem. In fact, the idea that "this problem must be solved by such-and-such a date" may in itself be a problem! Remember, sequential time is a limiting perception. So if you are concerned about timing: (a) state as a *release*, "I release any worry or concern about timing." and/or (b) insert as a qualifying phrase, "This work manifests at the perfect (or most appropriate) time."

"Perfect timing" does not mean frustration in waiting, compromise, or rationalization. The manifestation comes when we are organically ready for it. It may come in stages. If there is a significant delay, it may be an indication that a more important problem or limiting idea (Cause) may need work first. If so, work for the goal of "wisdom and understanding of my needs." The important point to understand is that once you have said these, your Words of Power are working in the Invisible World — even before they manifest in the World of Form.

Advanced Work: Problem-Solving with Words of Power

When a problem seems overwhelming, that usually means that you have been giving it a great deal of power in your life. But this is not necessarily a negative phenomenon, as long as you do not try to ignore or avoid the problem. It can be your subconscious mind's way of telling you that you are now ready to look at something important that you might not have been able to see before; and the time has come to see the problem because you are now ready to deal with it, and equiped to solve it.

Most of us have some negative tendencies, habits, patterns which might have been operating as Causes on a deep subconscious level, creating negative Effects in our lives. When we understand the principles of karma (Chapter V), and the work of Words of Power, we are then equipped to deal with problems on these deep levels, and literally to change our karma in huge ways. Some problems which might ordinarily have taken years of this lifetime to work out can be dealt with through responsible karmic understanding and careful Words of Power work; and the process now can become a remarkably short one. Some problems which might even take several lifetimes to work through can also be solved with this same approach — within a short period of time, and within this one lifetime.

1. *Tracking down causations:* If you wish to work in a sequential (linear, step-by-step) way, you can attempt to trace the problem back to its original causation, or Cause. Sometimes simply being aware of the Cause is enough to automatically solve the problem. Sometimes it is necessary to work Words of Power to change the Cause (as well as the Effect).

Please remember that within this view all problems may be seen as Effects of some personal Cause(s) for which you are somehow responsible.

2. *Accepting responsibility:* The first step is to accept responsibility for the causation — even if you do not yet know what the causation actually has been. If the problem has manifested in your life, then it is *your causation,* no matter how things appear to be. It is vital to accept responsibility for the causation up front, because this is the first step towards acknowledging your ability to change it.

Often, deep problems have been caused subconsciously. But this does not mean you are exempt from responsibility. Karmically speaking, you are responsible for your subconscious as well as your conscious activity.

Now, it may be a temptation at first to attach some form of self-judgment, blame, guilt or anger to the act of accepting responsibility. In

241

fact, in some cases this erroneous idea can be the problem! That is, the problem can simply be having been unable to accept responsibility for something, because it is too painful to live with the self-abasing feelings which may seem to be part of accepting responsibility — especially accepting responsibility for some past "mistake." As was pointed out in the chapter on karma (V), accepting responsibility is a simple act. No self-judgment, no guilt, no blame, no anything goes along with it. Try to get into the habit of accepting responsibility for the causations in your life — even in the abstract sense — in a pure and simple way.

This is not, however, mean accepting responsibility for other people's lives. Just *yours*. If another person is involved in the problem, you accept your part of the responsibility, and leave the rest up to the other person's free will. It is entirely up to the other whether or not he/she wishes to work with the problem in this way. If you solve your part, you will have solved the problem for yourself.

If you have equated accepting responsibility with self-judgment, this could have made it too awful a process to deal with. Consequently, you might have developed a habit of blaming others, feeling helpless, blaming fate, and generally not feeling in control of your own life. Things may then seem to happen from outside the self. But this entire attitude can be a causation for new problems! Such a causation can be solved by working Words of Power for the goal of "complete acceptance of my own responsibility for my own life, without any blame, guilt, anger or judgment."

> Only when we realize that our mistakes are of our own making will such disagreeable experiences free us of errors.
> The *I Ching*, Book One, Hexagram 60, Six in the Third Place

3. *Negative Perceptions:* Sometimes the problem can be obscured by one's perception of it. In fact, sometimes the process of negative perception in itself can be the problem. A problem is one thing; but *how you perceive it* can vary in myriad ways. The most common form of negative perception is allowing a problem to seem so important that it "blocks out" all other aspects of one's life. For example, an ancient Greek legend tells of a talented poetess who threw herself off a cliff because her lover had rejected her. In other areas of her life, she was creatively fulfilled, successful, and much appreciated. She had lost perspective on every positive area of her life by concentrating on (giving too much power to) the pain she perceived as rejection.

There are many possible explanations for losing perspective, having to do with early childhood experiences in this life, or even experiences in other lifetimes. If you perceive any problem with in appropriate

242

perspective, such a perception could be more of a problem than the alleged "original" problem which triggered the response. In occult terms, the negative perception could become a negative causation for future negative Effects (experiences) in one's life, creating a chain of negative Cause and Effect.

I am not recommending repression of emotions; I am recommending that one's perceptions of a problem be appropriate to the role of the problem in one's life.

Watch out for any tendency to allow the perceptions of another person to color your own perceptions. For example, if my friend believes that the worst fate in the whole world is to live alone — this does not necessarily have to be true to me, even if she thinks it is true for me. It is simply her perception.

This same principle applies to the area of *perception of another person's karmic choice.* If another person chooses (and in occult terms, these are all karmic choices), to leave you, to become sick, to leave this Earth Plane, to do anything which you perceive as painful for you — it is valid for you to experience the pain up to a point. Beyond that point, it can become an unwillingness on your part to accept the other's free will. I am not advocating selfishness, heartlessness, coldness, or the denial of genuine emotional responses. I am suggesting that another person's karmic choice be seen within the context of the other person's life, more appropriately than solely within the context of your own life.

In any case, if you catch yourself experiencing a problem with a perception which seems to fill your horizons with pain, despair, worry, or suffering — stop and ask yourself: "Is this problem as 'bad' as it seems? *Or is my perception of it 'worse' than the problem itself?"* If the answer appears to be that your perception is inappropriate, say Words of Power for the goal of correcting your perception first. For example: "Even though this problem may seem to fill my horizons, this is only because I have perceived it in this way. I now perceive it in perfect (appropriate) perspective for my own life, as a problem which I can solve."

After you have taken care of the perception aspects of the problem, you may direct your Words of Power, with more objectivity, directly to the goal of solving the "original" problem itself, whatever that may be (if there still is a problem left to solve).

4. *Direct Causations:* Sometimes we have directly and completely created problems for ourselves, albeit suconsciously. This is often easier to spot for other people ("He/she is *asking* for trouble"), and sometimes difficult to spot for ourselves — even after the fact.

Whatever your problem is, ask yourself: "In what way could I conceivably have created this problem?" If you have directly created a problem, this question is usually not too difficult to answer (if you approach it objectively). For example, if you leave the water running in your sink while you go off on a vacation, and come back to find a flooded floor, this is a problem that you have directly created.

However, it may not always be that clear. So next, ask yourself: "in what way could I have *drawn this problem to me?*" Often we can draw a problem into our lives by creating a negative *emotional atmosphere* which is literally a breeding ground for such a problem. For example:

- If a person has been emotionally experiencing a feeling of *loss* in his/her life (often unacknowledged or not appropriately acknowledged), this can create an emotional atmosphere which can manifest symbolically in tangible ways. The person may literally lose a material possession, or even be robbed.
- If a person feels *vulnerable* (and this vulnerability needs appropriate acknowledgement), he/she might thereby create an atmosphere in which he/she becomes "victimized" in some way, or even directly attacked.
- If a person feels *guilty* about something and has not appropriately dealt with this guilt, he/she might draw into his/her life some "punishment" — which at first glance may seem unrelated to the source of guilt.

In general, if one has created a negative emotional atmosphere through which a "new" problem has manifested as an Effect, it is important to acknowledge the existence of the negative emotional atmosphere and to investigate its Cause. In the above cases:

- The person who may have lost something or been robbed should figure out *why* he/she felt the emotional sense of loss — and deal with that (and do Words of Power in that area).
- The person who became victimized should figure out why he/she felt vulnerable in the first place, and reaffirm his/her own personal power.
- And the person who felt guilty should figure out where the guilt came from and release the guilt.

In all cases, one solves the problem by tracking down the emotional atmosphere — rather than being deflected by the forms in which the Effects seemed to come, often "out of the blue." In all cases, one may work Words of Power on both the Causes (including the emotional atmosphere and the Causes behind that), and the Effects.

5. *Participation:* When a problem involves more than one person, it may appear as if someone else caused the problem and you become an

"innocent" victim. In such a case, you may now see that you participated — by *allowing yourself* to take on the victim role. Silent suffering is just as much participation as noisy fighting. It is not always so clearcut, but in general, problems of participation are usually the result of a misunderstanding of one's personal power — in relation to other people's power.

The key is that *everyone has equal power.* If you view another person as having authority over your life and free will in *any* way (if you feel threatened, afraid, or subservient) — then you are giving the other person too much power. If you take advantage of someone in any way (if you bully the other person, feel condescending, pitying, or believe that you must do something for the other's "own good"), then you are giving *yourself* too much power in relation to the other. Giving another too much power or taking too much power yourself are both sides of the same coin: misunderstanding personal power. "The tyranny of the weak" is the term applied to a whole list of manipulative behavior which a person can employ to "get" power over another person. People who try to make others feel guilty, who act manipulatively, who assume the victim role to "make the other look like a villain," are actually trying to exercise extra power by the technique of appearing to possess less power themselves. Conversely, if you feel sorry for someone — if you view the other in a subservient role and then condescend — you can be, in effect, saying "I feel threatened by the other person's apparent power, so I will manipulate the situation to make it look as if I am stronger." This can become quite complex, and get into all sorts of games.

"It takes two to tango," as the old song goes.

If you are experiencing a problem in relation to anyone (or any group), ask yourself, "In what way could I have participated in this problem?"

Again, you accept responsibility for your own role only, and do not dwell on the other's responsibility. Leave that up to free will. Of course if it is someone you can talk to openly, you might explain these principles. Many relationships can be helped in this way. And then leave it up to the other, whether or not he/she wishes to work in this way.

If you discover that you do have problems in this area, work Words of Power to release your own "negative participation" — Causes and Effects — and work towards the goal of your "positive participation in all future interactions." I also recommend that you work for this goal: "perfect (appropriate) understanding — and expression — of my own personal power."

6. *Perpetuation and Negative Resignation:* These two attitudes usually go hand in hand, and may be conscious or subconscious.

245

Perpetuating a problem is literally "keeping it going." Whether or not the problem was originally of your own making within this lifetime — if you continue to live with that problem, you are responsible for perpetuating its existence in your life up to this point.

For example: If a person entered into a relationship a long time ago, and if over the years the partners grew away from each other until the relationship became a negative situation, if all attempts at repairing and restructuring the relationship have been unsuccessful — then the seemingly passive act of simply staying within that relationship probably is perpetuating the problem. Sometimes perpetuating a problem can be disguised to look as if one is "dealing with it" or "sticking with it." But "dealing with" or "sticking with" a situation is a constructive act, which becomes evident when there are positive results. On the other hand, perpetuating a problem is demonstrably nonproductive; thus, in fact, it becomes self-destructive.

Sometimes perpetuating a problem is a subconscious activity. Sometimes perpetuating a problem comes from not recognizing (acknowledging) that there even is a problem! Another way one can perpetuate a problem is by ignoring the principles of other people's free will and their karmic right to remain unchanged. For example, there are people who may claim that "if only so-and-so would behave differently, I would be happy."

It is not necessary for one to have created a problem in order to accept responsibility for it — but one makes the problem one's own by perpetuating one's existence within it.

Negative resignation to a problem may manifest generally as a vague feeling of helplessness, hopelessness, or inertia, of having already given up. Or negative resignation may manifest specifically in thoughts such as "why bother.....what's the use.....there's nothing I can do about it anyway," etc. Thus it is a manifestation of (conscious or subconscious) feelings of lack of one's own personal power.

Often an attitude of negative resignation presupposes one's "inevitable" future to achieve one's goals. One may feel negatively resigned to the few limited alternatives which one perceives as being the only available solutions. This is, in effect, a total lack of awareness of the Occult Principles, of the myriad other alternatives which can become possible and potential once you acknowledge and activate your personal power.

In any case, *perpetuation of a problem* and *negative resignation to a problem* may be corrected by concentrating back on the self, and on one's own personal power and ability to cause change in one's own life — no matter what anyone else seems to be doing, saying, or decreeing. The thing to do is ask yourself: "Am I perpetuating a problem?" And if you have been doing so, accept the responsibility.

Some problems literally disappear when you stop perpetuating them. Others are considerably diminished and more easily solved. If the "available" solutions seem impossible, if the odds seem against you — carefully structure your Words of Power Statement towards these goals: (a) to acknowledge your own Power, (b) to find your own center and Inner Bell, (c) to achieve the *essence* of the fulfillment of your needs, and (d) draw upon the Infinity of Solution as suggested in "Form Contingencies" below. Of course, state in the *release* section that you do not perpetuate the problem any longer, nor do you perpetuate any other problems. If it seems applicable, release "all negative resignation" as well.

7. *Form Contingencies:* A form contingency is a limiting idea — usually manifest in a form — which seems somehow connected to another idea, seems to be a part of the package. Usually a form contingency seems directly linked to (or even part of) a positive idea, a goal, or something you want. Often the culture supports popular form contingencies, which may then seem to be "facts of life": "If you have (or are) *this,* then you can't have (or be) *that."* In the past, most people buckled under and accepted form contingencies, but lately people are realizing that they need not accept them. Actually form contingencies need not be accepted by anyone — whether the forms are culturally enforced, decreed by some "authority," or privately deduced. A form contingency is always an illusion, and a limiting one at that.

One of the main problems with this phenomenon is that if you believe in a form contingency deeply enough (often subconsciously and unnoticed), you can continue to draw to yourself "evidence" of its seeming validity, by means of Cause and Effect (the Cause being your own belief in it). Be especially watchful for form contingencies lurking within the *goal* of a Words of Power Statement, because they can build in a negative situation (or perpetuate one), right along with the achievement of your positive goal. Form contingencies can lurk in the most surprising places. The key for discovering them is to notice any *limitation* or even any feeling of limitation.

In general, a form contingency may be seen as some manifestation of negative resignation. A form contingency says: "You have to compromise, you can't have everything...so if I do this, I can't do that; if I have this, I can't have that; if I get this (positive thing), it means that (negative thing) must inevitably come along with it." Thus you can see that if you inadvertently build a form contengency into the process of solving some problem, you can thereby create a new problem by building its causation right into your solution for the old problem.

The solution for dealing with form contingencies is simple: Remember the Infinity of Solution; and remember that given essence may be fulfilled in myriad forms. If you have noticed any hint of negative association or limitation when doing a Words of Power Statement, state in your release: "I release all form contingencies, and I replace them with the Infinity of Solution, and with perfect fulfillment of essence." If you discover a specific form contingency, of course, you may name it specifically as you release it. And you may categorically release "all form contingencies" within your Words of Power work — as "preventive medicine."

And of course remember Ma'Kheru; if anyone tries to apply a form contingency to you, take it out of the Law!

8. *Indirect Causations:*

> Therefore, it is important to begin at home, to be on guard in our own persons against the faults we have branded.
> The *I Ching,* Book One,
> Hexagram 43

If you have taken care of all areas of personal responsibility, and if a problem still persists in your life, then you are probably dealing with an indirect causation. If something seems to "happen to you" in any area of your life, and none of the above methods for discovering direct causations seems to apply, here is a way to track down indirect Causes. Ask yourself, "What is the quality of this negative event or problem?" Once you have answered that, then ask, "Have I *enacted* this same quality in *any other area* of my life — either towards another person or towards myself?" This may take some thinking at first, but after a while it becomes obvious and easy.

Here is a true example: F. was crossing the street when a car suddenly swerved; the driver, angrily yelling at F., almost hit her. She thought, "What did I do to draw that to me?" She searched. She hadn't created it, she wasn't "looking" for an angry accident, she had not created an emotional atmosphere for abuse, she was not negatively resigned to it, she was not participating in it in any way. In other words, she honestly ruled out all the above causations. But she knew that *something* coming from her own consciousness was trying to give her a message by means of this near-accident. Then F. asked herself what the *quality* was, and the answer was clear: *"anger."*

Now, she asked, where had she been feeling angry — either towards someone else or towards herself? And she found the causation there. That morning F. had been furious at her boyfriend. She had also been angry at herself for allowing him to borrow something he had not yet returned. F. had, earlier that day, already acknowledged her *participation* in the interaction with her boyfriend. But instead of simply acknowledging, F. had attached blame and anger to the acknowledgement — directed both towards herself and towards him.

Since she hadn't solved this emotional atmosphere of anger, she literally drew a stranger's anger towards her in a dramatic (and at first glance unrelated) episode, to point out to herself that there was an important emotional area in her life that needed "fixing." According to the Law of Cause and Effect, the quality of her own anger had come back to her indirectly.

First F. accepted responsibility for her participation in drawing the near-accident, with no blame. Then she accepted responsibility for her own anger towards herself and towards her boyfriend (no blame). Finally, she worked a Words of Power Statement to release anger and replace it with creative energy and self-determination. Thus, this was an indirect causation which was just as important as a direct causation, and just as helpful for indicating an important solution.

9. *Balancing the Dark and the Light:* As we have seen in Chapter IV, witches acknowledge both the Dark and Light aspects of all life. Neither Dark nor Light is to be ignored; neither Dark nor Light is to be given too much power. There is no judgment on either Dark or Light, even though it is in keeping with the witch philosophy to work towards the Light, as a choice in magic and in life. This is the essence of positive magic.

In general, one may apply witchcraft philosophy to problem-solving in this way: Problems may be seen as manifestations of the Dark while we are experiencing them, while they are giving us discomfort or pain. As long as these problems remain unsolved, they remain Dark (negative) aspects of our lives. But our own personal power and energy — aligned with all the positive and Light forces of the Cosmos — can transform these manifestations into light and positive aspects of our lives. This, of course, is the goal in problem-solving. Just as in nature, every Dark aspect in each of our lives has the potential to return to Light.

All the above causations for problems, both direct and indirect, are solved by acknowledging the Dark without judgment. This is the first step towards transforming it to Light. This may be a delicate process: A problem can seem overwhelming and even insoluble if one overemphasizes its darker, negative aspects — and gives the problem (and consequently the Dark) too much power. But neither is the Light to be overemphasized or given too much power either! This can be the other extreme — ignoring the Dark entirely, refusing to see it, or to acknowledge its existence; specifically, refusing to acknowledge the Dark within oneself.

This can occur for many reasons, as we have just seen in the above process of tracking down causations. Most often people may not be aware that they have any recourse to solving their problems by way of the Occult Principles, nor aware that they have a personal power to exercise for good, nor aware that the process of acknowledgement can be a nonjudgmental, neutral and effective step. Once people learn about the acknowledgement process, once they learn that they *can* work in positive ways, then they are able to accept responsibility for their own karma. Then problem-solving can become a clear process.

But there are some people who may still feel that the Dark is somehow "bad." And if they acknowledge its existence within them — even as potential — they may think that they too are somehow "bad." Hence they may not be able to see anything negative, even if it is most obviously manifesting in their lives. Because of our Piscean Age cultural heritage, there may be times when any of us might slip into this pattern. We may judge not only ourselves as "bad" (if we perceive error or negative behavior) but also judge Dark or negative aspects anywhere in life, as "bad" (i.e., death is bad, illness is bad, weakness is bad, old age is bad, anger, anxiety, worry, fear, insecurity, mistakes — all these and many other common occurrences may seem "bad"). But this is like saying the moon is bad when it wanes to crescent form, or that the sun is bad on a cloudy day. *There is no judgment on the Dark. It exists in potential, in every life form, and without the Dark there could be no Light.* And furthermore if one ignores the Dark completely, it can literally take over. We have seen in Chapter IV how this became a widespread problem in the Middle Ages.

Well, few people resort to blaming all their problems on the Devil or evil spirits these days (fortunately for us witches), but there are still people who may project their own negative aspects onto others. This can happen between individuals ("It's all your fault!") or between nations ("Wipe out the enemy"), or in social groups ("There goes the neighborhood").

Then, too, there are people who may simply lapse into some form of escapism — drugs, drink, overwhelming immersion in work or in the problems of others — anything to avoid facing the Dark within. There are even people who may force themselves to keep smiling and saying how wonderful everything is even in the face of some obvious pain. At certain times, any one of us could act in this way. But *ignoring pain is not a solution.*

The first step towards releasing pain is to recognize it.
—Spirit K.

If the Dark is ignored for too long, if problems within are denied, they may cry out to be heard (and solved), as various negative manifestations may develop in a person's life. Today, many of these manifestations are recognized as danger signals by the medical and psychiatric professions, so there is no need to discuss stress-related illness, depression, anxiety, psychosis, or neurosis here. There are numerous authorities today who are excellently equipped to deal on this level.

But there are still some manifestations which in occult terms are specifically related to ignored pain, to ignored problems, to ignored aspects of the Dark within. Some of theses manifestations may not seem to be directly related to anything in particular — but within the occult frame of reference, we can trace the causations clearly, and thus solve many a mysterious problem or event.

10. *The New Causation:* We have seen how helpful it can be to track down the original negative Cause of a problem, but it is not always necessary to do so in order to effect the appropriate solution. If none of the above methods has revealed a specific negative Cause for you, you may say a Words of Power Statement for the goal of "perfect revelation of the Cause of this problem according to free will and for the good of all." Now, if the Cause still does not reveal itself to your conscious mind, it may not be right for you to know the Cause at this time. But you still can solve the problem. The important thing to remember is that there has been a negative Cause and the problem has become a negative Effect of it. This can be diagrammed:

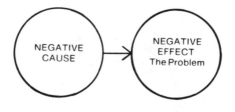

It is also important to bear in mind that if the problem has been left unacknowledged, or if for any reason it continues to remain unsolved, the problem itself can then become a Cause for further negative Effects (and consequently further problems).

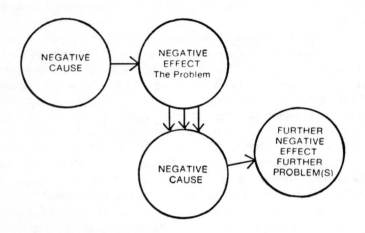

This process can go on and on (in linear time perception); a chain of conditioning can thus be set up in a person's life which can reinforce the seeming reality of the original problem. *But* Words of Power can intercede to transform the moment in which an Effect is about to become a new Cause. This moment of transformation changes the heretofore negative Effect into a positive Cause instead of a negative one.

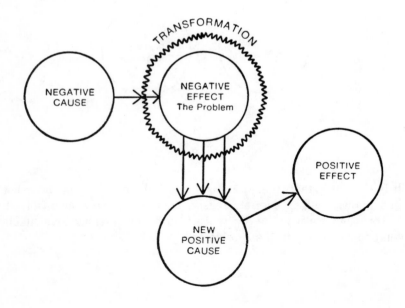

This transformation may also be accomplished simply by a swift s̲
of perception, a sudden deep awareness that "anything is possible!"
can be brought about by a long and specific Words of Power
Statement. Or it can be brought about by a short Words of Power
Statement which is based upon an understanding of the Principles and
ideas delineated thus far. That is, if you know that you are responsible
(no blame) for the Cause, and you know that you are consequently
responsible for and perfectly capable of causing change, then you
merely acknowledge this new moment as the beginning of *The New
Causation*. This means that you are now setting up a new chain of
Cause and Effect — this time a *positive* one.

You may simply state: "The New Causation somehow turns this
entire situation to good, for the good of all, and according to free will."

You may do this if a situation seems complicated, if you are in a
hurry, or if you have not been able to track down the original negative
Cause. As you do this, of course you are aware that the Infinity of
Solution may now reveal to you entirely new and "unthought-of"
solutions.

After a while, you may acknowledge that this process (The New
Causation) is actually always operating in your life, even on a
subconscious level. In other words, you may put The New Causation
on "automatic pilot."

Words of Power for Setting Up The New Causation
In Your Subconscious Mind

The One Power
Which includes The New Causation,
Is always operating for and through me, (your name here),
As I am a perfect manifestation of this Power.
Both consciously and subconsciously
I am always creating, drawing to myself, and participating in the
most perfect circumstances for my own fulfillment —
Including everything I need and want —
And for the good of all,
According to the free will of all.
And so it must be.

After you have established this process as operative in your life, you
may still work Words of Power Statements when the need arises, but
now you state specific goals as "*minimum effects* of The New
Causation, specifically such-and-such" (and release negative specifics
also as "minimum effects").

Many people prefer not to work on this level until they have spent long periods of time absorbing all of the basic Words of Power work. It is not ever necessary to set up The New Causation in this way; you may prefer simply to acknowledge its future existence in your life as potential. And certainly, it is not advisable to do this, or any work, until you have absorbed and understood it completely, until it rings your Inner Bell of truth.

One final point: The New Causation, and all Words of Power, can work backwards as well as forwards in time. Basically, this means that when you take responsibility for changing your future (and present) karma, you positively affect your past karma as well. The further implications of such work on past karma are vast, and it is not necessary to go into them here. They belong in a more advanced book (and are indeed excellently discussed in Jane Roberts' *The Nature of Personal Reality*). Suffice it to say for now that it is possible to "clean" one's karma — past, present, and future. Since there are infinite potential positive future circumstances to be found through the Infinity of Solution, there are also infinite potential positive *past* circumstances just waiting to be remembered and drawn upon.

Up until now, we have focused on the individual, on the self, in the process of working positive magic for transformation. Now it is time to widen the magic circle and to see how the use of positive can work for others — for our loved ones, our communities, our planet....and beyond.

[1]An excellent example of responsible documentation on this subject may be found in the report of the Stanford Research findings on Uri Geller. Russell Targ and Hal Puthoff, "Information Transmission Under Conditions of Sensory Shielding," *Nature Magazine*, Oct. 18, 1974, Macmillan Journal United, London. Further documentation on Geller, Charles Panati, Ed., *The Geller Papers*, Houghton Mifflin, New York, 1976.

[2]Jacques Bergier and Louis Pauwels, *The Morning of The Magicians*, Avon Books, New York, 1968, p. 118. Also, pp. 103-141.

[3]*The Collected Works of C.G. Jung*, Volume 13, *"Alchemical Studies,"* Bollingen Series XX, Princeton University Press, Princeton, New Jersey, 1970, p. 237.

[4]E.A. Wallis Budge, *The Gods of The Egyptians, Vol. II, Dover Publications, Inc., New York, p. 207.*

[5]*E.A. Wallis Budge, The Egyptian Book of the Dead*, Dover Publications Inc., New York, 1967, pp. xciii-xciv.

[6]Dmitri Maerezhkovsky, *Atlantis/Europe: The Secret of the West*, Rudolf Steiner Publications, New York, 1971.

[7]Hayyim Schauss, *Guide to Jewish Holy Days*, Schocken Books, New York, 1962, pp. 131-132.

[8]For example in Exodus, 8:13: "And the Lord did *according to the word of* Moses...(italics mine). Also, Doreen Valiente tells of various ceremonial magic books purporting to teach "the secret Words of Power which Moses used." *An ABC of Witchcraft Past and Present*, St. Martin's Press, New York, 1973, p. 273. Even though her research revealed these particular books to be medieval ramblings about manipulative magic, the idea that Moses understood and used Words of Power has been a popular subject in occult lore.

[9]For information about Religious Science techniques, I refer you to Ernest Holmes, *The Science of Mind*, Dodd, Mead, and Co., New York, 1938. Information about Unity may be obtained by contacting Unity School of Christianity, Unity Village, MI 64045.

[10]It is important to note that negative actions can also come back upon the person doing the action — even if such action isn't performed with magical intent. For example, some contemporary ritualistic acts performed in the name of science: experiments which involve inflicting pain or illness in laboratory animals...parapsychological experiments which involve "cursing" control groups of animals and plants....and psychiatric/psychological techniques which involve hitting pillows and other objects as effigies for people to express anger. As with verbal cursing and other forms of negative behavior, it is important to be *aware* of the potential consequences (see "Ma'Kheru" section in this Chapter, p. 234).

[11]"The future is made of all the nows" is a statement made by my friend the spirit K. Another "spirit," Seth, in *The Nature of Personal Reality*, says: "Your point of Power is in the present."

[12]For more advanced Words of Power work in a specific witchcraft tradition, see *Earth Magic, A Dianic Book of Shadows*, by the author.

[13]*The Incomplete Works of Carl Reiner and Mel Brooks*, 2000 Years with Carl Reiner and Mel Brooks, "Fabiola," Warner Brothers Records, Inc., 1973.

[14]This is also an ideal way to draw into your life the right pet for you. Specify "the right dog," "the right cat," etc.

[15]*The I Ching*, Bollingen Press, pp. 237-238, Book One, quote from Confucius, commenting on Hexagram 61, "Inner Truth," nine in the second place.

[16]Budge, *The Gods of The Egyptians, op. cit.*, p. 215.

[17]Justine Glass, *Witchcraft, The Sixth Sense*, Wilshire Book Co., N. Hollywood, California, 1970, p. 70.

[18]Lyric from *Gypsy* by Stephen Sondheim and Julie Stein, Chappell & Co. Inc.

[19]Lyric by Dorothy Fields and Jimmy McHugh, Shapiro, Bernstein & Co., Inc.

Chapter IX

WIDENING THE CIRCLE

A crane calling in the shade.
Its young answers it.
I have a good goblet.
I will share it with you.

This refers to the involuntary influence of a man's inner being upon persons of kindred spirit. The crane need not show itself on a high hill. It may be quite hidden when it sounds its call; yet its young will hear its note, will recognize it and give answer. Where there is a joyous mood, there a comrade will appear to share a glass of wine.
This is the echo awakened in men through spiritual attraction....
At first it acts on those who are inwardly receptive. But the circle grows larger and larger.
—The *I Ching,* Book One, Hexagram 61,
nine in the second place

It is important to note that by the very definition of this work, every time a being helps himself/herself through positive magic, the process of larger-scale help has already begun. The entire structure of life in the Universe is simultaneously helped, because built right into the "individual" work is an inherent connection of microcosm to Macrocosm — "for the good of all, and according to the free will of all."

Thus when you help yourself, you *do* help others; automatically you are positively influencing and positively affecting others in basic ways; you help yourself by a process which connects yourself with others and with positive forces in the Universe. There is indeed an "echo" effect awakened for those who wish to hear it, to feel it.

This process can be directly applied to broader social and cultural situations.

Group Work

It is not necessary to work magic in a group; but it can be enjoyable, supportive, and effective to be able to call upon others who are studying and working in similar ways. Group work does not necessarily mean establishing a formal coven, society, or club. In fact, the kind of group to which I refer may not even meet physically — at least not very often. Or it could meet at appropriate times, joining energies and working together. The kind of group I recommend may be less organized, more free-floating than any other groups to which you may have belonged before. I recommend a network of friends who can call upon one another at any time — to tackle a problem when it arises, to do back-up work for one another, or to lend individual objectivity, encouragement and mutual help. You can keep in touch by phone or even by mail (or by ESP!), as well as get together in person when it is appropriate.

You may form such a group by discussing the possibilities with people you already know. Or you may simply work Words of Power to draw into your life the right people (see Words of Power for "An Exchange of Services," p. 230).

Why a group? Specifically, when working on personal problems, if one is working all alone ("solitary," as we witches say), one may lose objectivity, give into to old patterns of despair, create or perpetuate a negative causation. A friend or group of friends who are as deeply committed to this kind of work as you can always be standing by to remind you that *anything is possible.* Such friends can help you remember *the infinity of solution,* help you track down causations, and generally help you do the work quickly and effectively. Also, there is much to be said for the old occult tradition of linking energies for mutual as well as individual goals.

There may still be various kinds of personal, social and cultural influences in your life which seem antithetical to your new occult vantage point. Let's face it, magic does not yet seem to be a socially accepted mode of life in many communities. Many of us may have other groups around us, ongoing from before we entered into occult work. And it may often seem that the other people in our lives can offer little or no help when we are working within the occult frame of reference. Of course there is no blame for this, and it is important to accept their own free will. It would be outlandish to drop all these other people and start all over again. But whom can we turn to?

A circle, network, or group of people with similar interests which may exist outside our other immediate relationships can then reinforce our own progress within the occult frame of reference. Such a group can provide a nourishing and encouraging exchange for all members, speeding up the development and the insights of each one. All the members can then grow and develop — separately and yet together.

It is not always practical to expect your family or close friends to choose to jump right into these occult waters in the same way that you may have done. In many cases this might happen, but the key phrase here is: *if they choose to.* The positive aspect of any group (new or old) which gets together by choice is that you are likely to have mutually harmonious goals and energies which organically mesh. The psychic support alone is worth it. And in practical terms, it is of inestimable value to be able to call up a friend in order to discuss any problem within a mutually understood frame of reference. If a group comes together to share the work, to live by the occult principles, to deal within the occult frame of reference — you can speak openly because everyone agrees to the same premises.

You may be delighted to find that at least several of your loved ones join, because people are usually in each other's lives due to similar karmic ties and interests in the first place. But equally delightful is the prospect of drawing to you new people who may become important to you and to them, in deep and meaningful and new ways. No matter who surrounds you, no matter who works with you — never, never push, proselytize, manipulate or try to convince anyone of anything! Free will and harmonious vibrations are the keys for group work.

So you don't have to join an organization, form an organization, recruit members, sign up, pay dues, take lessons, make rules, or even hold formal meetings. It you do decide to hold specific meetings, always pick the most mutually convenient times and places, and always respect the free will of any who do not show up (no blame!).

I have purposely chosen not to delineate any form for your group, because it is best if that happens organically and naturally, and if the form of the group itself grows directly out of who the members are.

If you wish to create an actual witchcraft coven, you may simply study Chapter IV and the recommended books, and then discuss and mutually agree upon your own group's traditions. (Detailed instructions for forming and working with a witchcraft coven are given in my book, *Earth Magic, A Dianic Book of Shadows,* pp. 22-30). For any group — witchcraft or other — it can be most propitious to do group work on the Eight Holidays (p. 75) if you believe in their importance. Perhaps there are other traditional holidays which are meaningful to you, or perhaps you may want to determine new ones.

You may discuss problems openly, in your own occult group therapy, or you may work silently for each person. You may work for specific goals already established by members of the group (and their loved ones). You may work for larger goals such as communal problems — naturally according to free will and the good of all.

The ideal group works (1) for its individuals, (2) for the group as a whole, (3) for its loved ones, and (4) for the larger global community and beyond. The importance of this kind of work seems obvious to numerous cultures other than our own, yet we consider many such cultures "primitive." I believe that when we extracted magic from our Western religions, we extracted a necessary ingredient for the health — and survival — of the planet. I also feel that we owe an acknowledgement of gratitude (perhaps reciprocal) to myriad other groups, whose religious convictions categorically impelled them to continue working their magic, positively, through the Invisible Realm — for all of us.

"The Americans want to stamp out our religion. Why can they not let us alone? What we do, we do not only for ourselves but for the Americans also. Yes, we do it for the whole world. Everyone benefits by it."

—Mountain Lake, a Pueblo Indian[1]

The Influence of Magic on Culture

Until quite recently, magical-religious practices were viewed as merely a source of psychological nourishment to the cultures that practiced them. Western dominant groups (such as the "Americans" to whom Mountain Lake referred in 1920) that wished to subordinate those cultures, for political or economic gain, simply tried to stamp out the religion along with the cultural group. Today the areas of psychic development with which such early cultures dealt have taken on a newly respected significance in the West. Data validated by science indicates that not all occult powers are mere superstition — that in fact, some occult techniques manifest genuine power.

Some members of the Western occult community may be alarmed by recent rumors of governmental agencies doing research and attempting to harness and use psychic and occult powers for their own purposes. But I am not alarmed. As soon as the majority of the population becomes aware of the positive nature of occult work, and understands how to practice it, there can be no danger to the community at large. In fact, the results will be surprisingly opposite. I believe that if positive occult practices and the Principles upon which they are based become common knowledge and part of our culture, everyone will benefit. The culture itself will undergo basic changes — for the good of all.

260

One of the joys of positive magic is that it need not be exclusive property. It does not apply or belong to any specific privileged, dominant group. The essential attributes of positive magic — the Principles by which it works — deny the need for privilege, dominance, power-plays or any inequality. For example, consider the redefinition of one word: "power". When applied to magic, "power" no longer means somebody is strong because somebody else is weak. The word means *equal personal power,* available to anyone who wants to draw upon it — anyone and everyone, at no one's expense.

As one modern author puts it:

> Power has generally meant the ability to advance oneself and, simultaneously, to control, limit, and if possible, destroy the power of others. That is, power, so far, has had at least two components: power *for* oneself and power *over* others. (There is an important distinction between the ability to influence others and the power to control and restrict them). The history of power struggles as we have known them has been on these grounds. The power of another person or group of people, was generally seen as dangerous. You had to control them or they would control you. But in the realm of human development, this is not a valid formulation. Quite the reverse. In a basic sense, the greater the development of each individual the more able, more effective, and less needy of limiting or restricting others she or he will be.[2]

Similarly, I believe that we will witness the exit, as obsolete terminology, of such words as "domination," "sacrifice," "oppression," "inequality," and "victimization," along with many such words and their concepts. The causes for their existence in our culture will be eliminated.

Another Look at the Two Sides of the Brain

Why has our particular culture placed the occult in such low regard? Because our culture still tends to perceive ideas and things in *opposites.* The occult perceives ideas and things as a whole. This precludes opposites.

As noted in Chapter I, it has been helpful to view the human brain as capable of being "divided" into two sides. In occult terms, we may use this idea as a metaphor; we may view the two sides of the brain as symbols of the functions they are said to represent.

The functions of the right side of the brain are known as "relational";

they include intuitive, simultaneous and holistic perception. These modes of perception are most helpful for the ideas of magic. They enable us to comprehend the occult ideas that all time and all space co-exist inextricable — and that all of life is intricately linked in a harmonious, all-inclusive Whole. The idea of the Invisible World is more easily grasped by the right side of the brain than by the left side. The idea of working in the now, the relationship of microcosm to Macrocosm — indeed all the Occult Principles — are accessible within the "relational" mode of consciousness.

But these concepts have not been utilized fully in the West.

Our culture has chosen to build upon another kind of perception, utilized by the left side of the brain. Its abilities are known as "rational" (although in this context the word "rational" is not necessarily synonymous with "sane," as it might be in everyday speech). Equating "rational" with "sanity" is an obvious semantic conclusion within the framework of a primarily "rational" culture! In this context, "rational" means the ability to differentiate; the ability to see things in sequence, in a linear way (i.e., such as time divisions). Also in this domain are the verbal, analytic, systematic, specialized and individualized functions of thinking and acting. An excellent example of the "rational" function is the story of Adam in the Garden of Eden, differentiating each species of flora and fauna and naming it. In occult terms, the "rational" mode of thought deals primarily with the World of Form.

Besides the ability to differentiate, another aspect of "rational" thought is that it is selective. It categorically screens out myriad psychic and other Invisible influences as irrelevant (to survival), and tends to deny the very existence of whatever it has screened out. This kind of perception, when utilized in its extreme, defines its reality in limited terms and then has difficulties in perceiving any other realities. Thus a primarily "rational" perception would have difficulty in dealing with the Invisible World, among other occult concepts.

Rational perception is also oriented to the survival of the fittest, a natural outgrowth of which is the "triumph" of the individual over the environment.

In any case, the concensus seems to be that by now too much rational perception has gone too far. Yes, it has led us to advanced technology, and the biological survival of the human species by dominance over its environment. But too much technology and too much dominance have begun to threaten the existence of the environment itself, as well as the human species (along with numerous other species).

Now, at the Cusp, people have noticed that the culture has been leaning in this "rational" perception direction for so long that the culture has gotten lopsided. The planet seems recognizably in danger on many levels. On the individual level, more and more people have been decrying a lack of "meaningfulness," "humanity," "spirituality," etc. in our accepted way of life. On the social level, the inequities seem staggering when we consider the hierarchies of power, finances, and living conditions which exist among humans. (Few of us humans have even begun to seriously consider the implications of the inequities we have perpetrated on other species, but the extinction of various animal races is just one example). And on the physical planetary level, systematic destruction of natural resources and potential threat to existing resources has become obvious. The people whom it has not yet become obvious or relevant may be said to be thinking along "rational" lines, because people who thus perceive time primarily in sequence usually feel that the future is too far away to be of concern.

Some people who have sensed a lack in our civilization have reacted by seeking a rapid, total transfer to a different mode of consciousness. But switching from one thought-mode directly to another will not create a balance! In fact, it is a reaction which is still perceived in terms of opposites.

Since the mid 'sixties, there have been all-too familiar stories of people who went too far, either with mind-altering drugs or pseudo-mystical and quasi-religious cults. Many such people could not return to society except within the confines of mental institutions or subculture organizations; the latter have arisen at the Cusp to encompass victims of such experiences. Further, some people may categorically deny the lingering existence of "rational" thought within their own psyches; so great may be their zeal to escape it, that they pretend it isn't there any more. They may think they are jumping directly out in the "relational" (or they may call it "an altered state of consciousness," or whatever) when they are simply jumping in place. They may change costumes, customs, even language. But if their orientation remains predominantly "rational" — and therefore limiting — they may not even be able to perceive that nothing has essentially changed for them.

This can be a confusion of *form* and essence. It is important to note that what we are referring to here as "relational" thought (including the spiritual, esoteric, mystical, or magical) does not necessarily have any particular form. It can come in any form, because it is an essence. "Rational" thought gives credence to forms, and this can sometimes lead to self-deception.

Numerous people have noticed that Eastern tradition is rich in spiritual paths, and many Westerners have sought such paths. In fact, some of these paths have wended their way to us and become franchised and packaged. These are *form*, and bear little or no resemblance to the spiritual *essences* upon which they purport to be

based.

Of course, the transfer from Western over to Eastern thought has also been conducted in more responsible and gradual ways. This movement has been extremely popular and effective for numerous reasons; and I am not advising against it, but I would like to point out that this not the only way to "relational," holistic, intuitive, spiritual consciousness. In fact, it may be difficult for some people to make a leap from one culture directly into the thought processes of another. This point has been noted by Western occultists since the first major influx of Eastern philosophy into Europe in the nineteenth century.[3]

I think it is important to bear in mind that there can be a process of distortion — of meaning, intent, and practice — when one culture is superimposed upon another. But what bothers me the most is when people turn to Eastern esoteric ways, denying the existence of Western esoteric ways entirely — or indeed denying the existence of any other esoteric ways.

I believe deeply in the enrichment of cross-fertilization and the sharing process of spiritual traditions, rather than total superimposition of one tradition on another. I have begun to glimpse the riches of certain African and Native American magical traditions — to name but two — which have nourished my own work and outlook. I suspect that these traditions would be helpful to many spiritually deprived, "rational" types in the West.

For me, "holistic" (which is as good a word as any for the thought-mode of occult work) means "all-inclusive"; to deny any aspect of one's own cultural heritage, or to deny the existence (in potential) of any other cultural heritage, is not holistic. It is a screening-out process — "rational," sequential, linear and limiting.

"Holistic" does not mean *either/or*, it does not mean *instead of*, or in *denial of*, or in *replacement of*. It means *all-together*.

Some Westerners still seem to get upset about occult beliefs. I have encountered a few people who have said to me, "Do you really believe in that stuff?" — in a surprisingly accusing, hostile tone of voice. Many witches, occultists and astrologers have had similar experiences. I am happy to say that I have had only a small number of such reactions.

But such reactions are understanable in this context: since this is indeed a basically "rational" culture, it is not surprising that somebody could feel genuinely threatened when confronted by a (seemingly) totally opposite belief-structure. This belief-structure would seem to contradict whatever the "rational" person truly trusts and believes in — science, philosophy, organized religion, or whatever. People in this mostly "rational" culture are encouraged to perceive things in opposites and to presume that opposites often connote threats, one idea vs. the other idea. So it might feel like, "Her belief in that "stuff" exists in defiance of my belief."[4]

Drawing the Circle

However, Confucius goes still further. He shows that opposition is actually the natural prerequisite for union. As a result of opposition, a need to bridge it arises.....This is the effect of the phase of opposition — a phase that must be transcended.

The *I Ching*, Book Three, Hexagram 38

I am acknowledging that our culture is now in this phase: the turning point from opposition into its naturally harmonious evolution — not from one opposite to another opposite, but to a state of harmony which transcends opposition. In occult terms, this is believed to be a part of the ensuing Aquarian Age.

I have chosen the two-sides-of-the-brain metaphor as an appropriate one of this point in time (sequential time!). Actually, there could be three sides of the brain, or twenty, or millions of sides (facets) — each with its own perceptions.[5]

If we are to continue with this metaphor a bit further, we can see how to transcend both rational and relational perception, utilizing the most helpful aspects of each and encompassing both in a whole which not only integrates the two, it takes them to a state where they can no longer be defined as two, but as One.

In the province of the mind, what one believes to be true either is true or becomes true. In the province of the mind there are no limits. In the province of the mind, what one believes to be true is true or becomes true. There are no limits.

John C. Lilly, M.D.[6]

But the problem with living in a "reality" which has *no limits* can be quite unnerving. It is one thing to talk about "relational" reality and to describe it as an intellectual possibility. It is another to experience *no limits* (as a reality). This may feel as if one has jumped out into the wild blue yonder, into a space where all guidelines are lost, and where the territory is not only unfamiliar — it is not even territory anymore.

But this happens when rational perception is left behind.

More specifically, this happens when you think the "rational" is left behind, but when it is still lurking (unacknowledged), manifest in making the two kinds of perceptions seem like such opposites, specifically making the "relational" look totally opposite to the "rational."

I feel that when you enclose the "rational" within the "relational," then you have a whole viewpoint. This is a way to draw the circle. In other words, I think that the two-sides-of-the-brain theory is a helpful stepping stone to get us to a really unlimited viewpoint — a viewpoint which includes both concepts together, and transcends their "separateness."

In a larger sense, there really aren't two sides of the brain. The whole theory is a "rational" step to help you to acknowledge the "relational" — which is in itself a step to help you to draw the circle.

Western magic starts with the "relational," and gives you "rational" systems for dealing within it. This book has dealt with several of those systems. They may be employed in a linear, sequential, "rational" fashion, dealing with daily life — as long as you are aware that they are encompassed within a broader reality which goes *beyond* daily life.

You do not have to leap into one side of your brain or another. You have both sides already functioning, only you may not have been aware of it yet.

You can build your own reality. You may do this by gradually and organically shifting your perception over to the area that has been termed the "relational." You may do this comfortably and easily, by accepting yourself and trusting yourself and starting with the now — whoever and wherever you happen to be. You may say to yourself "anything is possible." Then you can proceed to build a new, more positive reality for yourself — by choice — in what may be called a "rational" step-by-step way. You can "afford" to be "rational" once you

266

are aware that it isn't the only way to perceive reality.

Always try to keep the full realization that it is you who are building your reality, and that it can begin to become less limiting — *infinite in possibility* — gradually, as you choose to direct it, and as you grow. You do not have to abandon the World of Form; just please be aware that the Invisible World coexists. You never have to threaten your beliefs, nor perceive them to be threatened. Just encompass them within a wider circle!

The circle starts with the self.[7] The self is part of the Whole. Help of the self helps the Whole; help of the Whole helps the self. The circle is a traditional path of positive magic in the West.

Magic is not the only alternative open to you; it has simply been the focus of this book. In fact, this book has been a circle (in the Invisible World of ideas), even though its shape on the physical Earth Plane may seem more rectangular at first glance.

Many people may think that a circle is a closed shape. In the occult, a magic circle is capable of becoming wider and wider.

Now, if you would like to widen the circle, you may contemplate yourself in relation to:
- your loved ones
- the rest of your culture
- the rest of your planet
- the rest of the Universe

And you may ask yourself, "What do I want to contribute to:
- my loved ones?
- the rest of this life?
- this culture?

- the World of Form?
- and beyond?"

And know that whatever it is you want to do — you can do it; in a way that harms none, helps all, is always according to free will, can be infinitely full of delightful surprises — and also fulfills yourself.

And as each one of us begins to do so — *the circle widens.*

[1]Quoted by C.G. Jung in his autobiography, *Memories, Dreams, Reflections*, Vintage Books (Random House), New York, 1963, pp. 251-252.

[2]This is not a witch or a magician talking, this is a feminist psychiatrist, Jean Baker Miller, M.D., in *Toward a New Psychology of Women*, Beacon Press, Boston, 1976, p. 116. So we may note that there is more than one frame of reference in which new truths may be found for our culture.

[3]"The dharma of the West differs from that of the East; is it therefore desirable to try and implant Eastern ideals in a Westerner? Withdrawal from the earth-plane is not his line of progress...Development by meditation alone is a slow process in the West, because the mind-stuff upon which it has to work, and the mental atmosphere in which the work has to be done, are very resistant." Dion Fortune. *The Mystical Qabalah*. Ernest Benn Ltd., London. 1974. pp. 10-11. (This was written in 1935).
As Jung succinctly puts it (and Jung was a *great* advocate of Eastern philosophy, specifically Taoism): "It cannot be emphasized enough that we are not Orientals, and that we have an entirely different point of departure in these matters." *Alchemical Studies*, p. 14.

[4]If I had given power to the other person's belief that my "stuff" threatened him in any way, then I'd have set up an *emotional atmosphere* (see p. 220) for drawing into my life far more hostile reactions than I have. The more I hold on to my own reality that my belief does not threaten the other person's — and that his does not threaten mine — the fewer such episodes "come along."

[5]Actually, the "two sides of the brain" theory applies *only* to the area known as the *forebrain*, or cerebral cortex. There are indeed "other" areas of the brain, and we do not yet know how these affect thinking, behavior, or perceptions. As acknowledged by science, they are: 1- the *mid-brain* (which involves emotions), 2 the *cerebellum* (which involves balance), and 3- the *medulla oblongata* (which involves "vital functions" such as breathing).

[6]John C. Lilly, M.D., *The Center of the Cyclone, An Autobiography of Inner Space*, Bantam Books, New York, 1972, p. 139.

Supplementary Reading:

RECOMMENDED WITH YE WITCHCRAFT STAMP OF APPROVAL

FOR CHAPTER I

1. *The Morning Of The Magicians*, by Pauwels and Bergier. The first major work from the vantage point of *contemporary* validity of the occult. Excellent for skimming — which, in fact seems to be the authors' intentions.

2. *Something's There*, by Dan Greenburg.
A delightful *personal* journey into the occult by the contemporary humorist.

3. *Supernature*, by Lyall Watson.
A snappy *scientific* journey into the occult — especially recommended for those who want occult data from the World of Form.

4. *The Psychology of Consciousness*, by Robert E. Ornstein.
All about the two parts of the brain, the "rational" and the "relational."

FOR CHAPTER II

1. re: Time — *The Greening of America*, by Charles A. Reich.
An excellent description of this Cusp time, from a sociological vantage point.

2. re: Space — *The Betty Book*, by Stuart Edward White.
Written in the 1930's, data from the 1920's, as supplied by reputable Invisible entities, through the medium Betty. Subject matter includes much information about Time as well as Space — definitely "relational", and well-presented.

FOR CHAPTER III

1. *The Dictionary of Angels*, by Gustav Davidson.
Everything you need to know about the angels, demons, and the whole unearthly gang who were *believed* to reside in Heaven and Hell during the Middle Ages. *(Caution: Do not try any of the "instructions" at the back of the book).* This book is delightfully illustrated and excellently researched.

2. *The Mystical Qabalah*, by Dion Fortune.
Positive Ceremonial Magic (mostly Christian) at its best, explained by a leading expert. *Extremely* technical.

271

3. *Ritual Magic In England,* by Francis King.
If you are interested in the historical perspective.

4. *"Mind Training, ESP, Hypnosis, and Voluntary Control of Internal States",* by Elmer and Alyce Green.
This article may be tracked down in PSI, *The Other World Catalogue,* by June and Nicholas Regush, Putnam, N.Y., 1974.
It says it *all* re: the "Modern Dangers"! Highly recommended.

FOR CHAPTER IV.

1. *An ABC of Witchcraft Past and Present,* by Doreen Valiente.
If you want *one* all-inclusive book about witchcraft, this is *it.* Not only accurate, thorough, and well-researched — but wonderfully organized. And written by a witch.

2. *Witchcraft, The Sixth Sense,* by Justine Glass.
The best that I know of which has been written by a non-witch.

3. *The Circle Guide to Wicca and Pagan Resources,* by Circle, for those who want direct contacts and connections of a primarily witchcraft orientation. It would be impossible for me to list here all of the growing number of occult/witchcraft/pagan journals, organizations, shops, mail-order groups and yes — *covens* that are now surfacing. But the Circle people have done it for us! The Guide is available in (mostly occult) bookstores and can also be ordered directly from: *Circle,* P.O. Box 219, Mt. Horeb, Wisconsin 53572.

4. *Drawing Down The Moon: Witches, Pagans, Druids, and Goddess Worshippers In America Today, by Margot Adler.* A first-hand survey by a Gardnerian witch who is also a fine journalist. Paperback edition: Beacon, 1981.

5. *The Witches Almanac,* by Elizabeth Pepper and Jon Wilcox. This is a ten-year series which is now out of print, but they are collector's items, and worth reading if you can find them. (Still found in some occult stores). Yearly almanacs by and for witches — with lovely illustrations, a wealth of information, articles and instructions which are never out of date no matter what the year.

6. *EARTH MAGIC, A Dianic Book of Shadows,* by Marion Weinstein.
I wrote this book to answer the question Chapter IV in *Positive Magic* still leaves somewhat open: "How does one *become* a witch?" My Book of Shadows tells how I personally practice the Craft, and presents techniques and suggestions that you may either use directly or adapt to your own work. Written for beginners and adepts alike, a modern witch's workbook in the ancient Book of Shadows tradition.

Addenda: "The Witch's Cat" in *The Cat Catalogue,* Workman Publishing.
This article is also by the author and is for (familiar) cat-lovers.

FOR CHAPTER V

1. *Life After Life,* by Raymond A. Moody.
Scientific "case histories" of what it feels like to die and return to the Earth Plane. Totally corresponds to occult information (which the totally scientific author does not seem to know a great deal about).

2. *The Unobstructed Universe,* by Stuart White.
Follow-up to *The Betty Book* (see recommendations for Chapter II). Betty leaves this

Earth Plane, but keeps in touch with a superb flow of information and personal data.

3. *The Nature of Personal Reality, A Seth Book,* by Jane Roberts. It's hard to define who "really" wrote this book. It was dictated by the Invisible entity, Seth, to Jane Roberts (actually *through* Jane Roberts) and her husband, Robert Butts, who set it all down with admirable accuracy, down to the minutist details of the dictation process. Rated by my spirit friends as "an excellent treatise." (Actually, all the Jane Roberts/Seth books are excellent; this one happens to be most relevant to my work at this point).

FOR CHAPTER VI.

1. *Linda Goodman's Sun Signs.*
If you wish to explore astrology at the sun sign level, this is the most reputable book I have found thus far.

2. *The Astrologers And Their Creed,* by Christopher McIntosh.
Excellent for an historical/philosophical perspective.

3. *Astrology, How and Why It Works,* by Marc Edmund Jones.
A technical book: how-to!

4. *How To Learn Astrology,* by Marc Edmund Jones.
Also technical, although considered by some astrologers to be a "primer". Definitely how-to.

5. *The Astrology of Personality,* by Dane Rhudyar.
Technical, clear how-to. Natal charts — the works.

6. *The Case For Astrology,* by John Anthony West and Jan Gerhard Toonder.
Just like the title says; helpful for building confidence in the workings of the stars.

FOR CHAPTER VII

1. *Secrets of The I Ching,* by Joseph Murphy.
A Judeo-Christian *version* of the I Ching, correlating it to the Western Bible. Based on the Bollingen. Thoroughly reputable, and most helpful adjunct to I Ching work for people with traditional Jewish and Christian beliefs.

2. *Change, Eight Lectures on the I Ching,* by Helmut Willhelm.
Technical treatise by Richard Willhelm's son, Translated by Cary F. Baynes. (The lectures were delivered in Peking, in 1943).

3. *Tarot Classic,* by Stuart Kaplan.
A truly all-inclusive modern work, includes lots of historical data, and beautiful illustrations.

4. *The Tarot Revealed,* by Eden Gray.
My favorite traditional tarot writer. All her books are fine; I just lean towards this one.

5. *The Pictorial Key To The Tarot,* by A.E. Waite.
He co-designed the Waite deck, but in my opinion this book requires a grain of salt.

FOR CHAPTER VIII.

1. *My Story*, by Uri Geller.
Interesting for those who want to know first-hand what it *feels* like to transcend the World of Form regularly. Uri Geller is not technically an "occultist"; his accomplishments are of importance, however, to occult study.

2. *Self-Realization and Self-Defeat*, by Samuel Warner Ph D. It amazes me how close this "behaviorist" psychological approach is to our own work! Excellent for tracking down causations. Just add "Words of Power" at the point where this book leaves off.

FOR CHAPTER IX

These books do not seem to have been written yet. The closest I could find was anything by Buckminster Fuller. For witches and pagans: The Circle Network News and *The Circle Guide to Wicca & Pagan Resources*, Circle Publications, Madison, WI.

Bibliography

Adler, Margot, *Drawing Down The Moon: Witches, Pagans, Druids and Goddess Worshippers in America Today*, New York, Viking Press, 1979. Beacon (paperback), 1981.

Allen, Woody, *Without Feathers*, New York, Warner Books, 1975.

Ashlag, Rabbi Yehuda, *Kabbala Ten Luminous Emanations*, New York, Research Centre of Kabbalah, 1969.

Bach, Eleanor, *Ceres, Juno, Pallas, Vesta*, New York, Celestial Communications, 1973.

Barker, Raymond Charles, *Treat Yourself To Life*, New York, Dodd, Mead & Company, 1954.

Bergier, Jacques, and Pauwels, Lois, *The Morning Of The Magicians*, New York, Dover Books, 1968.

The Bible, King James Version, New York, Signet, New American Library, 1974.

Budge, E.A. Wallis, trans., *The Egyptian Book of the Dead*, New York, Dover Publications, Inc., 1967.

 , *Egyptian Magic*, New York, Dover Publications, Inc., 1971.

 , *The Gods of the Egyptians*, Vol. I & II, New York, Dover Publications, Inc., 1969.

Boyer, Paul, and Nissenbaum, Stephen, *Salem Possessed*, Cambridge, Mass, Harvard University Press, 1974.

Campbell, Florence, M.A., *Your Days Are Numbered, a Manual of Numerology for Everybody*, Pleasant Valley, Bucks County, Pa., The Gateway, 1958.

Castaneda, Carlos, *Journey To Ixtlan: The Lessons of Don Juan*, New York, Pocket Books, 1974.

The Cat Catalogue, ed. Judy Firestone, Workman Publishing, N.Y.

Cerminara, Gina, *Many Lives, Many Loves*, New York, Signet Books, 1963.

 , *Many Mansions*, New York, Signet Books, 1950.

Charles, R.H., *The Book of Enoch*, Oxford, Clarendon Press, 1912.

Circle Guide to Wicca and Pagan Resources, Circle, Wisconsin, 1979, 1981.

Crowther, Patricia and Arnold, *The Witches Speak*, Douglas, Isle of Man, Athol Publications, Ltd., 1965.

Custer, Edith, ed., *The Mercury Hour*, C-7, 3509 Waterlick Rd., Lynchburg, Va. 24502.

Davidson, Gustav, *A Dictionary of Angels*, New York, Macmillan Company, The Free Press, 1971.

de Laurence, L.W., ed., *The Lesser Key of Solomon, Goetia, the Book of Evil Spirits*, Chicago, de Laurence, Scott, & Co., 1916.

Doane, Doris Chase, and Keyes, King, *Tarot-Card Spread Reader*, West Nyack, New York, Parker Publishing Company, Inc., 1971.

Donnelly, Ignatius, *Atlantis, the Antediluvian World*, New York, Rudolf Steiner Publications, 1971.

Dubos, Rene, *So Human an Animal*, New York, Charles Scribner's Sons, 1968.

Dunne, J.W., *An Experiment With Time*, London, Faber Paperbacks.

Evans-Wentz, W.Y., ed., *The Tibetan Book of the Dead*, London, Oxford University Press, 1960.

Fortune, Dion, *The Mystical Qabalah*, London, England, Ernest Benn Limited, 1974.

   , *Psychic Self-Defense*, London, The Aquarian Press, 1967.

   , *Sane Occultism*, London, The Aquarian Press, 1967.

Frazer, James George, *The Golden Bough, A Study in Magic and Religion* (8 volumes), London, Macmillan and Company, Ltd., 1923.

   , *The Golden Bough*, Canada, Macmillan Paperbacks, Abridged Edition, 1969.

Fuller, Buckminster, *Synergetics*, New York, Macmillan Company, 1975.

Gardner, Gerald, *Witchcraft Today*, New Jersey, Citadel Press, 1970.

Gardner, Martin, "The Combinatorial basis of the "I Ching," the Chinese book of divination and Wisdom," *Scientific American*, Vol. 230, Number 1, January, 1974.

Geller, Uri, *My Story*, New York, Praeger Publishers, 1975.

Glass, Justine, *Witchcraft, the Sixth Sense*, California, Wilshire Book Company, 1970.

Goodman, Linda, *Sunsigns*, New York, Bantam, 1968.

Gordon, R.K., trans., *Anglo-Saxon Poetry*, London, J.M. Dent & Sons. Ltd., 1954.

Graves, Robert, *The White Goddess*, New York, Farrar, Strauss, & Giroux, Noonday Press, 1970.

Gray, Eden, *The Tarot Revealed*, New York, Signet Books, 1960.

Green, Alyce, and Green, Elmer, "Mind Training, ESP, Hypnosis, and Voluntary Control of Internal States," *PSI, The Other World Catalogue*, New York, Putnam, 1974.

Greenburg, Dan, *Something's There*, New York, Doubleday, 1976.

Hall, Manly, P., *Unseen Forces*, Los Angeles, Philosophical Research Society, Inc., 1973.

Harding, M. Esther, *Psychic Energy*, Princeton, N.J., Bollingen Series X, Princeton University Press, 1973.

   , *Women's Mysteries*, New York, Bantam Books, 1973.

Harris, Thomas, A., *I'm O.K.-You're O.K.*, New York, Avon Books, 1973.

Haskins, James, *Witchcraft, Mysticism, and Magic in The Black World*, New York, Dell Publishing Co., Inc. 1974.

Head, Joseph, and Cranston, S.L., editors, *Reincarnation in the World's Religions*, Wheaton, Illinois, Quest Paperbacks, the Theosophical Publishing House, 1970.

Heller, Joseph, *Catch-22*, New York, Simon and Schuster, Dell paperback edition, 1955.

Holmes, Ernest, *The Science of Mind*, New York, Dodd, Mead, and Co., 1938.

I Ching, Wilhelm/Baynes translation, Princeton, N.J., Bollingen Series, Princeton University Press, 1970.

Jones, Gladys V., *Reincarnation, Sex, and Love*, La Canada, California, New Age Press, 1971.

Jones, Marc Edmund, *Astrology, How and Why It Works*, Baltimore, Maryland, Penguin Books, 1971.

   , *How To Learn Astrology*, New York, Doubleday.

Jung, C.G., "ANION, Researches into the Phenomenology of the Self," *The Collected Works of C.G. Jung*, New York, Bollingen Series XX, Pantheon Books, Volume 9, part II, 1959.

   Alchemical Studies, Princeton, N.Y., Bollingen Series XX, Princeton

University Press, 1970.

, *Man and His Symbols*, Garden City, New York, Windfall Books, Doubleday and Company, Inc., 1964.

, *Memories, Dreams, Reflections*, New York, Random House, Vintage Books, 1965.

, *The Portable Jung*, J. Campbell, ed., New York, Viking Press, 1971.

Kaplan, Stuart R., *Tarot Classic*, New York, Grosset & Dunlap, 1972.

Kenton, Warren, *Astrology, The Celestial Mirror*, New York, Avon Books, 1974.

King, Francis, *Ritual Magic in England*, London, Neville Spearman, Ltd., 1970.

Knight, Gareth, *The Practice of Ritual Magic*, Dallas, Texas, The Sangreal Foundation, Inc., 1969.

Koch, Rudolf, *The Book of Signs*, New York, Dover Publications, Inc., 1930.

Krakovsky, Rabbi Levi Isaac, *Kabbalah, The Light of Redemption*, Jerusalem, Israel, The Press of the Yeshivat Kol Yehudah for the Dissemination of the Study of Kabbalah, and New York Research Centre of Kabbalah, 1970.

Laurent, Emile, and Nagour, Paul, *Magica Sexualis*, trans. by Raymond Sabitier, New York, Falstaff Press, 1934.

Lee, Dal, *Dictionary of Astrology*, New York, Paperback Library, 1968.

Leek, Sybil, *Diary of a Witch*, New York, Signet Books, New American Library, 1968.

Le Guin, Ursula K., *The Left Hand of Darkness*, New York, Ace Books, 1969.

Leland, Charles Godfrey, *Aradia, The Gospel of the Witches*, New York, Buckland Museum, 1968.

Lilly, John C., M.D., *The Center of the Cyclone, An Autobiography of Inner Space*, New York, Bantam Books, 1972.

Maerezhkovsky, Dmitri, *Atlantis/Europe: The Secret of the West*, New York, Rudolf Steiner Publications, 1971.

McIntosh, Christopher, *The Astrologers and their Creed*, New York, Praeger, Inc., 1969.

Merriam Webster Dictionary, New York, Pocket Books, 1974.

Michelet, Jules, *Satanism and Witchcraft*, New York, The Citadel Press, 1939, 1965 edition.

Michell, John, *The Earth Spirit, Its Ways, Shrines, and Mysteries*, New York, Avon Publishers, 1975.

Miller, Jean Baker, M.D., *Toward a New Psychology of Women*, Boston, Beacon Press, 1976.

Moody, Raymond, A., Jr., *Life After Life*, New York, Bantam Books, 1975.

Morfill, W.R., *Secrets of Enoch*, Oxford, Clarendon Press, 1896.

Murphy, Joseph, *Secrets of The I Ching*, West Nyack, N.Y., Parker Publishing Co., Inc., 1970.

Murray, Margaret, *The God of the Witches*, New York, Oxford University Press, 1970.

The Mysteries of the Qabalah, Chicago, Yogi Publication Society, 1922.

"On a Pacific Island, They Wait for the G.I. Who Became a God," *The New York Times*, New York, April 19, 1970.

Ornstein, Robert E., *The Mind Field*, New York, Viking Press, 1976.

, *The Psychology of Consciousness*, New York, Viking Press, 1973.

Ostrander, Sheila, and Shroeder, Lynn, *Psychic Discoveries Behind The Iron Curtain*, New York, Bantam Books, 1971.

Panati, Charles, ed. *The Geller Papers*, New York, Houghton, Mifflin,

Pepper, Elizabeth, ed. *The Witches' Almanac*. New York, Grosset & Dunlap, Annually 1970-1980.

Pepper, Elizabeth and Wilcock, John, *Witches All*, New York, Grosset & Dunlap, 1977.

, *Magical & Mystical Sites, Europe and the British Isles*, New York, Harper and Row, 1977. London, Weidenfield & Nicholson, 1977.

Plato, *Timaeus and Critias*, H.D.P. Lee, trans., Middlesex, England, Penguin Books,

1971.

Puthoff, Hal, and Targ, Russell, "Information Transmission Under Conditions of Sensory Shielding," *Nature Magazine*, England, Oct. 18, 1974.

Reich, Charles A., *The Greening of America*, New York, Random House, Bantam Books, 1971.

Reik, Theodor, *Pagan Rites in Judaism*, New York, Farrar, Strauss and Company, 1964.

Robbins, Russell Hope, *Encyclopedia of Witchcraft and Demonology*, New York, Crown Publishers Inc., 1959.

Roberts, Jane, *The Nature of Personal Reality, A Seth Book*, New Jersey, Prentice-Hall, 1974.

Roberts, Susan, *Witches, U.S.A.*, New York, Dell Publishing Co., Inc. 1971.

Rudyhar, Dane, *The Astrology of Personality*, New York, Lucis, 1963.

Schauss, Hayyim, *Guide to Jewish Holy Days*, New York, Schocken Books, 1964.

Scholem, Gershom G., ed. *Zohar, The Book Of Splendor*, New York, Schocken 1949.

Shakespeare, William, *Julius Caesar*, New York, Folger Library, Washington Square Press, 1959.

, *Macbeth*, New York, Folger Library, Washington Square Press, 1959.

Sheba, Lady, *Lady Sheba's Book of Shadows*. St. Paul MN, Llewellyn Publications, 1971.

Smith, Adam, *Powers of Mind*, Ballantine Books, 1975.

Smith, Frank, *Modern Witchcraft*, New York, Harper and Row, 1970.

Spence, Lewis, *The Occult Sciences in Atlantis*, New York and London, S. Weiser Inc. and the Aquarian Press, 1970.

Starkey, Marion L., *The Devil In Massachusetts*, Garden City, New York, Anchor Books, Doubleday & Co., Inc. 1969.

Stone, Merlin, *When God Was A Woman*, New York, The Dial Press, 1976.

, *Ancient Mirrors of Womanhood*, Vols. I & II, New York, New Sybylline Books, 1979.

Summers, Montague, *Geography of Witchcraft*, Secaucus, New Jersey, Citadel Press, 1973.

Tennyson, Alfred, Lord, *The Idylls of The King*.

Trefil James, *"It's All Relative When You Travel Faster Than Light,"* Smithsonian Magazine, vol. 7, No. 8, 1976.

Valiente, Doreen, *An ABC of Witchcraft Past and Present*, New York, Saint Martin's Press, 1973.

Valiente, Doreen, *Where Witchcraft Lives*. Cedar Knolls, New Jersey, Wehman, 1962.

, *Witchcraft For Tomorrow*, N.Y., St. Martin's Press, 1978.

Waite, Arthur Edward, *The Holy Kabbalah*, New Hyde Park, New York, University Books.

, *The Pictorial Key to The Tarot*. New Hyde Park, New York University Books, 1959.

Warner, Samuel J. PhD. *Self-Realization and Self-Defeat*, New York, Grove Press, Inc. 1973.

Watson, Lyall, *Supernature*, New York, Bantam Books, 1973.

Wedeck, Harry E., *Treasury of Witchcraft*, New York, Philosophical Library, 1961.

West, John Antony and Teender, Jan Gerhard, *The Case for Astrology* Baltimore, Md., Penguin Books, 1973.

White, Stuart, Edward, *The Betty Book*, New York, E.P. Dutton, 1937, 1977.

, *The Unobstructed Universe*, New York, Dell Publishing, 1970.

Willhelm, Helmut, *Change, Eight Lectures On The I Ching*, trans. by Cary F. Baynes, Princeton, N.J., Bollingen Series LXII, Princeton University Press, 1960.

Willhelm, Richard, trans. (German) *The I Ching or Book of Changes*, trans. (English) by Cary F. Baynes, Princeton, N.J., Bollingen Series XIX, Princeton University Press, Third Edition 1967, eleventh printing, 1974.

Wilson, Colin, *The Occult*, New York, Random House, Vintage Books, 1973

Woods, William, *A History of The Devil*, New York, G. Putnam/Berkley Windhover, 1975.

"Transits" for 12/6/76, *American Astrology Magazine*, V. 44, no. 10, Clancy Publications, Inc. 1976.

Index

About the Author

Marion Weinstein has worked as a witch on radio since 1969 on WBAI-FM in New York, where her program, "Marion's Cauldron" is heard regularly. Her work includes appearances on national television talk shows, lectures at various institutions of higher education, and stand-up priestess comedy in nightclubs. She holds a degree in English literature from Barnard College and lives on Long Island and in New York City.

Notes

Notes

Notes

Notes

Notes

Notes